Baed

New York

Contents

Contents

Principal Sights of Tourist Interest

Preface

This Pocket Guide to New York is one of the new generation of Baedeker guides.

These pocket-sized city guides, illustrated throughout in colour, are designed to meet the needs of the modern traveller. They are quick and easy to consult, with the principal sights described in alphabetical order and practical details about opening times, how to get there, etc., shown in the margin.

Each guide is divided into three parts. The first part gives a general account of the city, its history, population, culture and so on; in the second part its principal sights are described; and the third part contains a variety of practical information designed to help visitors to find their way about and make the most of their stay. For the reader' convenience this practical information, like the main part of the guide, is arranged in alphabetical order.

The new guides are abundantly illustrated and contain numbers of newly drawn plans. At the back of the book is a large city map, and each entry in the main part of the guide gives the coordinates of the square on the map in which the particular building or feature is situated. Users of this guide, therefore, will have no difficulty in finding what they want to see.

How to use this book

Following the tradition established by Karl Baedeker in 1844, sights of particular interest and hotels and restaurants of particular quality are distinguished by either one ★ or two ★★ stars.

To make it easier to locate the various sights listed in the "A to Z" section of the Guide, their co-ordinates on the large city map are shown in red at the head of each entry, e.g. ★Brooklyn Bridge F 11.

Only a selection of hotels, restaurants and shops can be given; no reflection is implied, therefore, on establishments not included.

The symbol   on a town plan indicates the local tourist office from which further information can be obtained. The post-horn symbol indicates a post office.

In a time of rapid change it is difficult to ensure that all the information given is entirely accurate and up to date, and the possibility of error can never be completely eliminated. Although the publishers can accept no responsibility for inaccuracies and omissions, they are always grateful for corrections and suggestions for improvement.

Facts and Figures

Arms of the
City of New York

General

Although New York is the largest city in the United States and one of the largest cities in the world it is not the national capital, nor even the capital of New York State, more than two-fifths of whose inhabitants live in the city.

Metropolis

The city of New York lies in the NE of the country – the oldest part of the United States – around the mouth of the Hudson River, which here flows into the Atlantic Ocean.

Region

More precisely, it lies in latitude 40° 42′ 26″ N and longitude 74° 0′ 23″ W.

Geographical
situation

New York City reached its present extent in 1898 with the formation of Greater New York, which has an area of 829 sq. km (320 sq. miles). Its present population is over 7 million. A further 10 million live in the economic region around the city, the New York Metropolitan Area, which takes in Westchester, Rockland and Nassau counties in New York State, the southern tip of Connecticut and the northern part of New Jersey.

Area and
population

The city is made up of five boroughs, of which Manhattan is the smallest in area (57 sq.km – 22 sq. miles) and the third largest in population. The other boroughs are Brooklyn (147 sq.km – 57 sq. miles), Bronx (110 sq.km – 42 sq. miles), Queens (313 sq.km – 121 sq. miles) and Staten Island (150 sq.km – 58 sq. miles). Only Bronx is on the mainland: the other four boroughs are on islands, with Brooklyn and Queens occupying the south-western end of Long Island, which extends NE for some 200km (125 miles).

The boroughs

The city's administration is run by the Mayor, who is elected for a four-year term, and the City Council, also elected every four years, the number of its members having been increased to 51 following a referendum in November 1989 to change the city's constitution. This amendment became law on January 1st 1991.

Administration

The levying of new taxes and the passing of new laws in certain fields require the authorisation of the New York State legislature, which meets in the state capital of Albany, some 200km (125 miles) up the Hudson, the seat of the Governor.

Population and Religion

During the 200 years after the first settlement of Manhattan the town developed very slowly, and by the beginning of the 18th c. it had no more than 5000 inhabitants. By 1790 this had risen to 33,000, and in the

Population

◀ *Statue of Liberty*

Manhattan

following ten years this figure almost doubled. Soon New York displaced Philadelphia as the largest town in America, but it was not until the period of mass immigration in the second half of the 19th c. that the population passed the million mark. In the years up to the First World War the immigrants consisted mainly of Irish, Germans (a quarter of a million in the record year of 1882), Italians and Jews from Eastern Europe, with smaller numbers of English and Scottish, Polish and Ukrainian, Czech and Hungarian immigrants. The numbers were much reduced after 1924 when immigration quotas were introduced.

Between 1933 and 1942, and again after the end of the Second World War, New York became a place of refuge for people seeking safety from Nazi persecution or escape from the hardships of the post-war years. During the war there was also a considerable influx of negroes from the southern states, seeking employment and better pay in New York and other north-eastern cities; and this movement continued after the end of the war, when the increasing mechanisation of agriculture in the southern states led to the loss of many jobs. There was also an increasing inflow of Spanish-speaking immigrants, particularly from the American territory of Puerto Rico but also from the Caribbean and Central and South America. There are now more than a million Puerto Ricans in New York – more than in their own capital of San Juan – and Spanish has become the city's second language. The proportion of negroes in the population of New York has risen to 25%; in Brooklyn it is over 32%.

Ethnic variety

This immigration has produced an extraordinary variety of ethnic groups in New York, many of them living in their own quarter of the city – Chinese in Chinatown, Italians in Little Italy, Poles and Ukrainians in East Village, Hungarians, Czechs and Germans in East Side, Latin Americans in the Barrio, negroes in Harlem, Dominicans and Cubans in Washington Heights.

People of New York

In addition to these foreign colonies in Manhattan there are others in Brooklyn – Arabs (mainly Syrians and Lebanese) around Atlantic Avenue, Hassidic Jews in Williamsburg and Boro Park, Norwegians in Bay Ridge. In Queens there is a large Greek colony in the district of Astoria, and many Colombians have settled in Jackson Heights.

All these various groups have their own shops and restaurants, and frequently also churches in which services are held in their own languages.

Well over 100 different religious creeds and denominations are represented in New York, and in Manhattan alone there are something like

Religion

9

650 churches and almost 100 synagogues. Manhattan and Brooklyn are Roman Catholic archiepiscopal dioceses, and Manhattan has a cardinal archbishop. The Episcopalian and the Presbyterian, Methodist and Baptist communities are each of roughly the same size as the Roman Catholics. In addition New York has places of worship belonging to the Quakers, the Mennonites, the Unitarians, the Adventists, the Lutheran and Reformed churches, the Pentecostal movement, the Old Catholics, the Russian and Greek Orthodox churches, the Moravian Brethren, Christian Science and a variety of other sects. There are Buddhist and Hindu temples, mosques and even an (American) Indian church. Some communities, particularly the Roman Catholics and the Jews (ultra-orthodox, reform and conservative), run their own schools. Since there is a complete separation of church and state in the USA, all religious communities depend for finance on contributions from their members.

Transport

The port

Although New York possesses a natural harbour in the Hudson River and New York Bay this is no longer of any great importance. Only a few piers in the 50th–60th Street area are still in use for passenger vessels, almost solely engaged in Caribbean cruises; only one shipping line still plies between Europe and New York and the amount of freight handled has also fallen, since much of the traffic now passes through the container terminal at Port Elizabeth, across the bay in New Jersey.

Airports

New York has three airports – John F. Kennedy (formerly known as Idlewild), with 31.1 million passengers in 1989 and which handles international traffic and services to the western states; LaGuardia (named after the popular Mayor of that name), used only by domestic services (24 million passengers); and Newark (22 million passengers), used by both international and American airlines. The airports are managed by the Port Authority of New York and New Jersey.

The John F. Kennedy International Airport is the largest of the three airports and the farthest from the city centre (26km –16 miles). Newark is 25km (15½ miles) from the city centre, LaGuardia only 13km (8 miles).

Modifications to Kennedy Airport (which are less extensive than originally planned) should be completed by the mid-Nineties.

Rail services

Long-distance trains now run only from Pennsylvania Station and carry a relatively small proportion of the total traffic, most of which goes by air or bus, but Grand Central and Pennsylvania Stations still play an important part in the suburban and commuter traffic to the N and W of the city. Pennsylvania Station is also the terminus of the Long Island Railroad, which carries the heaviest traffic of any suburban line in the United States. There is also the PATH Rapid Transport line (the Hudson Tubes), providing connections with New Jersey.

Bus services

Long-distance and commuter buses leave from the Port Authority Bus Terminal on Eighth Avenue and 42nd Street, where thousands of buses arrive and depart every day.

Subway

The New York Subway, which serves all the boroughs except Staten Island, has a total track length of some 354km (220 miles), with 24 lines and 469 stations. Running 24 hours a day, it carries a daily total of some 3.4 million passengers.

Buses and taxis

Much of the city's internal traffic is carried by its network of bus services, with almost 40 routes in Manhattan alone. New York's trams ceased to run in the 1950s.

New York's public transport systems are supplemented by something like 11,000 taxis.

The main routes out of New York are:

To New Jersey: Holland Tunnel on Canal Street, Lincoln Tunnel on 34th Street, George Washington Bridge on 181st Street.

To upper New York State and the N: Deegan Expressway through the Bronx, then New York Thruway.

To the New England states: Cross-Bronx Expressway, Bruckner Boulevard, Hutchinson River Parkway.

To Queens and Long Island: Queens–Midtown Tunnel (37th Street), Queensboro Bridge (59th Street), Triborough Bridge (125th Street).

To Brooklyn and Queens: Brooklyn Bridge (near City Hall), Manhattan Bridge (Forsyth Street), Williamsburg Bridge (Delancey Street), Brooklyn–Battery Tunnel (at S tip of Manhattan).

Staten Island: ferry from Battery Park, Verrazano–Narrows Bridge from Fort Hamilton Parkway in Brooklyn.

Roads out of New York

Culture

New York is the cultural centre of the United States, with the country's largest concentration of theatres (some 35 on and around Broadway and 200 little theatres), a number of leading museums, two opera-houses, several major orchestras, over a dozen ballet and dance companies and the second largest library in the United States, the New York Public Library.

Here, too, are the headquarters of most US publishing houses and of almost all the leading periodicals. There are large numbers of bookshops and antiquarian booksellers; and the Public Library is backed up

11

by a whole range of smaller libraries catering for special interests. The most respected US newspaper, the "New York Times", is published here, and the country's five main television channels are based in New York. In addition more than 30 cable TV programmes are broadcast 24 hours a day.

Universities and colleges

New York has more than 50 universities and colleges, the great majority of them in Manhattan. The oldest and perhaps the most renowned is Columbia University, founded in 1754 as King's College; the largest New York University, founded in 1831, which has over 40,000 students. Others are the Rockefeller University, which has a mainly scientific orientation, the Roman Catholic Fordham University and the New School of Social Research, which achieved some prominence in the 1930s as the "University in Exile".

New York also has six medical schools, three major academies of music, numerous drama schools and a number of art schools. All these institutions are privately run.

There is also the City University, with 18 colleges in New York City, which was founded in 1849 as the City College, the first higher educational establishment in the United States to charge no fees.

Drama, opera, music

New York holds unchallenged supremacy in the United States as a centre of the performing arts. There are between 300 and 400 premières in New York theatres every year, and during the winter months there are about 100 musical events every week. A special place in the musical world is occupied by the Metropolitan Opera, one of the world's most renowned opera-houses.

All the leading American and many European orchestras perform every year in New York, supplementing the four weekly concerts of the New York Philharmonic Orchestra, which has played a leading part in New York's musical life since 1842.

Bird's-eye view of Columbia University and East Harlem

Statue of Prometheus in front of the Rockefeller Center

With 20 art museums and as many more devoted to science, history and other fields, some 600 galleries and a variety of cultural bodies from many European, Asian and African countries, the New York art scene is rich and varied, covering the whole range from traditional to avant-garde art. — The arts

Art also finds expression in New York in the form of mural paintings on the outsides of buildings and works of modern sculpture set up in the open air (see A to Z, Sculpture).

Commerce and Industry

In spite of the many problems of the past decade – an exodus of population and of large firms, financial crises, shortage of housing, increased crime – New York has retained its economic predominance in the United States and is now the world's largest capital market and its chief financial centre. — New York, centre of world trade

The New York Stock Exchange still sets the pace for the world's markets, even though it did suffer the heaviest losses in its history on October 19th 1987. And in addition to the New York Exchange there are the American Stock Exchange and numerous commodity exchanges.

At the end of the 1960s 140 out of the 500 largest firms in the United States had their headquarters in New York. The figure has now fallen to below 100, since it is in this field that the move out to the suburbs has been most marked.

Five of the country's six largest banks, with total assets of more than 200,000 million dollars (Citicorp, Chase Manhattan Bank, Morgan Guaranty Trust, Chemical Bank and Bankers Trust), are based in New York, as are three of the five largest life insurance corporations (Metropolitan Life, Equitable Life and New York Life); and a third of the country's 50 largest retail firms and almost 17% of wholesalers have their head office in the city.

Regional industries

The industry of greatest importance to New York's economy is textiles, in which around a quarter of a million people are employed. Second and third places are taken by the graphic trades and the foodstuffs industries. All other industries together employ fewer people than the "big three". Of major importance are the construction industries, although these are very sensitive to changing economic conditions and show greater fluctuations in numbers employed than other branches of industry.

Retail trade

New York has a number of large department stores, including Macy's, Bloomingdale's, Abraham and Straus, Lord and Taylor, Saks Fifth Avenue and Bergdorf Goodman which are trend-setters, particularly in the fashion trade. The total number of retail shops is legion, selling every conceivable variety of goods. It is not surprising that New York enjoys the reputation of being the best – and in many fields the cheapest – shopping centre in the world.

Service trades and tourism

New York is without equal in the United States as a centre of the various service industries such as market research, advertising – which has become synonymous with Madison Avenue – public relations, management consultancy, stockbroking and architectural design, which all flourish here.

Some 15,000 restaurants and hundreds of hotels with a total of over 100,000 rooms cater for the needs of the 17 million visitors, including 2 million from outside the United States, who come to New York every year. The number of congresses and conferences is steadily increasing and it is expected that a further boost will be given by the Jacob K. Javits Convention Center (see A–Z) which was opened in April 1986 on the bank of the Hudson between 34th Street and 38th Street.

Finally New York has more lawyers and doctors than any other American city, both proportionately and in absolute terms.

Problems of a metropolis

In 1975 New York was involved in a financial crisis which brought it within sight of bankruptcy. In 1977 the city was 14 billion dollars in debt. The biggest budget item was welfare with payments over 3 billion dollars a year. It was able to meet its obligations only with the assistance of New York State and the federal government and at the price of sacrificing some of its previous budgetary independence and accepting a measure of outside control.

Within a few years the number of municipal employees fell by 20%, whereupon the reduction in police strength was reflected in increased crime and the cutting-down of the cleansing services in dirtier streets. Fares were increased on public transport but the standard of service continued to decline, even though the introduction of new subway trains, built in Japan, France and Canada, gave some hope of an improvement.

At the beginning of the Nineties there are signs of a new financial crisis, with an especially weak property market following a decade of economic stability. Even the banking system is no longer secure, owing to the insolvency of its domestic and foreign debtors. The economic recession in 1991 had an adverse effect on service industries as well, with the result that by the beginning of 1994 the unemployment level was almost 10%, well above the national average.

Famous People

John Jacob Astor, one of the first great American entrepreneurs, came to New York from his native village of Walldorf near Heidelberg in SW Germany at the age of 20. After some time as a dealer in musical instruments he moved into the fur trade, and in 1808 established the American Fur Company. This was followed by two other companies, and he secured almost a monopoly of the American fur trade. Most of his enormous wealth, however, came from speculation in real estate, in the course of which he acquired a great deal of property, particularly in Manhattan. When he died his fortune was estimated at 25 million dollars, making him the richest man in America. Shortly before his death he gave 400,000 dollars for the building of the Astor Library, America's first public library.

John Jacob Astor (1763–1848)

Born in New York – his parents were both musicians – the painter and graphic artist Lyonel Feininger spent 50 years of his life (1887–1937) in Europe, mainly in Germany, where he at first worked as a caricaturist and illustrator and then, in 1907, began to paint. He was friendly with Franz Marc, Kandinsky, Klee and Jawlensky, and from 1919 to 1933 taught at the Bauhaus in Dessau. In 1937 he returned to New York, where he received a number of commissions for the 1939 World's Fair. His work is characterised by interpenetrating planes of prismatic colour and striking light effects. He became best known for his town scapes and seascapes.

Lyonel Feininger (1871–1956)

A native of Pennsylvania, Robert Fulton began his career as a painter but later became an engineer; during the 20 years he spent in London and Paris (1786–1805) he produced a series of inventions, including a submarine and torpedoes, in which he failed to interest either the British or the French. Returning to New York, he built the "Clermont", the first steamship, which in 1807 sailed from New York up the Hudson to Albany and back in 62 hours. Shortly before his death he built the first steam-propelled warship, which was never tried out.

Robert Fulton (1765–1815)

George Gershwin, creator of a distinctively American form of serious music, was a native of Brooklyn who began his musical career as song plugger for a music publishing firm. He published his first song at the age of 18, and gained his first great success three years later with "Swanee". During the twenties he achieved fame with his "Rhapsody in Blue", a symphonic jazz composition, his "Piano Concerto in F Major" and a number of musicals written in collaboration with his brother Ira. His political satire "Of Thee I Sing" won him the Pulitzer Prize in 1931. His most mature work, and his last, was the opera "Porgy and Bess", written in 1935. Two years later he died of a brain tumour. As the first composer to make jazz rhythms acceptable in "serious" music his reputation is secure.

George Gershwin (1898–1937)

Born into a doctor's family in Allenghy, Pennsylvania Martha Graham is regarded as the founder of American dance. She grew up in Santa Barbara, California and was one of the earliest members of Denishawn, the school of Ruth St Denis and Ted Shawn, which was so influential in the development of American dance. She made her debut with her first solo programme in New York at the age of 22. In 1917 she opened her own school, which is still highly regarded internationally. She was a professional dancer, choreographer and teacher. Unlike hardly any

Martha Graham (1894–1991)

Robert Fulton

George Gershwin

Martha Graham

other dancing teacher of the 20th century she succeeded in developing a structured teaching method for non-Classical dance which bases its particular technique upon the contrasts between tension and relaxation on the body. Her film "A Dancer's World" conveys an impressive picture of her dance aesthetics.

Alexander
Hamilton
(1755–1804)

Alexander Hamilton, one of the fathers of the American constitution, came to New York from the West Indian island of Nevis in 1773. At the beginning of the War of American Independence he mustered a troop of artillery and attracted the attention of George Washington, whose confidential secretary he became in 1777. During the war he distinguished himself in a number of engagements.

At the 1787 constitutional convention he favoured a strongly centralised union. As first Secretary of the Treasury (1789–95) he brought order into the country's finances, which had been shattered by the war, on the basis of a new fiscal system. Strongly conservative, he opposed Jefferson's democratic programme and advocated an authoritarian state.

Hamilton died after being wounded in a duel with Aaron Burr, the Democratic presidential candidate.

O. Henry
(1862–1910)

O. Henry (real name William Sidney Porter) was the first great master of the short story. Sentenced to five years in prison for misappropriation of funds in a bank in which he was employed, he wrote his first stories in prison and soon became famous. In 1900 he went to New York, finding an abundance of material for his stories in the people and the life of the great city.

Almost all of his 600 stories are written to the same pattern, with a surprise twist at the end. He did not live long enough to enjoy his fame, dying of tuberculosis in 1910.

Edward Hopper
(1882–1967)

The painter and graphic artist Edward Hopper, who had a studio in Washington Square for many years, was over 50 before the first retrospective exhibition of his work was held in a New York museum. He was unequalled as a portrayer of the life of New York, the activity of its streets and the loneliness of man in the city.

He left more than 2000 oil paintings, watercolours, drawings, sketches and prints to the Whitney Museum of American Art, which organised the first comprehensive exhibition of his work in 1980.

Washington Irving began his working life as a lawyer and spent some time as a diplomat before becoming the first American writer to achieve a reputation outside the United States. His first work was published in 1802, and with the appearance of his burlesque "Diedrich Knickerbocker's History of New York" in 1809 he became the accepted chronicler of his native city. He spent the years 1804–06 and 1815–32 in Europe, and from 1842 to 1845 was American ambassador in Madrid. In addition to his tales and various historical works he wrote a five-volume life of George Washington during the last five years of his own life.

Washington Irving (1783–1859)

Henry James, brother of the philosopher William James, ranks as one of America's leading novelists, though he spent the last 40 years of his life in London and acquired British citizenship in 1915. The themes of his works were supplied by his own experiences in two continents. Written in a very characteristic convoluted style, they depict the encounter between the men and women of the New World and the traditions and conventions of Europe. James wrote more than a dozen novels and over a hundred short stories. In his early work he shows himself to be a skilled portrayer of life in New York. A complete edition of his works published in 1961–64 runs to 26 volumes, plus four volumes of autobiographical writings.

Henry James (1843–1916)

Henry Miller earned more headlines than any other American writer of the 20th c. with works which were decried and banned by some as pornography and celebrated as masterpieces by others. After leaving school early, Miller became a casual worker before beginning to write in the mid twenties. From 1930 to 1940 he lived mainly in Paris, where he wrote his well known novels "Tropic of Cancer" and "Tropic of Capricorn". His novels and stories, containing a strong autobiographical element, were directed against the Puritan taboos of American society. In his trilogy of novels, "Sexus", "Plexus" and "Nexus", he made sexuality his literary theme.

Henry Miller (1891–1980)

After a brief period as a student at Gottingen University, John Pierpont Morgan returned to the United States and arrived in New York at the age of 20. In 1860 he founded the firm of J. P. Morgan and Co., which acted as an agent of his father's banking house in London. Founding his own banking house in 1895, he acquired great influence on railway development in the United States, and in 1901 played a major part in the establishment of the United States Steel Corporation, which developed into the largest steel trust in the United States. In addition he was perhaps the largest private collector of art, manuscripts and books of his day. Most of his pictures are now in the Metropolitan Museum of Art; his other treasures can be seen in the Pierpont Morgan Library which he built in New York.

John Pierpont Morgan (1837–1913)

Together with Giorgia O'Keffee, Louise Nevelson was one of the grand old ladies of American art. Born in Kief, she arrived with her parents at the age of six in New York, where she studied comparative religion and philosophy. After a spell in Munich with the painter Hans Hofmann, she was the assistant of Diego Rivera in Mexico City from 1932 to 1938. She found her own artistic expression in the 1950s with sculptures made from everyday articles – balustrades, table-legs, waste-wood and driftwood, formed into cupboards, shelves and screens and painted in black, white or gold. The mysterious, totem-like and even threatening character of these often larger-than-life shrines and altars soon led to their being found in the major museums of the world. The highlight of Louise Nevelson's career came when she had three rooms devoted to her work in the 1962 Biennial and also exhibits in the 1964 Dokumenta in Kassel. Later experiments with metals and glass were less success-

Louise Nevelson (23.9.1899– 17.4.1988)

Famous People

Theodore Roosevelt

Carl Schurz

Andy Warhol

ful. Her work can be seen in many squares and buildings in New York and indeed throughout the USA.

Adolph S. Ochs
(1858–1935)

The newspaper publisher Adolph S. Ochs, born in Knoxville, Tennessee, the son of a German Jewish immigrant, began his career at the age of 11 as a newspaper-boy in his native town and later became an apprentice printer. In 1875 he went to Chattanooga, Tennessee. Three years later, at the age of 20, he bought the local paper, the "Chattanooga Times", and within four years had made it one of the leading newspapers of the southern states.

Ochs's great coup came in 1896, when he paid 75,000 dollars for the "New York Times", an old-established paper which was in difficulties in the intensely competitive New York newspaper world. By the time of his retirement in 1933 Ochs had built it up into America's leading daily, with the slogan "All the news that's fit to print".

The "New York Times", now a limited company, has grown into a large concern with wide interests in publishing, papermaking, periodicals, radio and television, but it is still directed by Ochs's descendants: the present head of the firm is his grandson, Arthur Ochs Sulzberger.

Eugene O'Neill
(1888–1953)

Eugene O'Neill, the leading US dramatist, spent his early years in New York. Having contracted tuberculosis, he spent some time in a sanatorium, where, at the age of 24, he began to read plays, being particularly influenced by the work of Ibsen and Strindberg. His first one-act play was performed by the Provincetown Players in New York. He received the Pulitzer Prize in 1920 for his first full-length play "Beyond the Horizon", and three further Pulitzers for "Anna Christie" (1922), "Strange Interlude" (1928) and "Long Day's Journey into Night" (1956, posthumously). He was awarded the Nobel Prize in 1936.

Theodore
Roosevelt
(1858–1919)

Theodore Roosevelt, 26th President of the United States (1901–09), is the only President to have been born in New York. He came from a Dutch family which had settled in New York (then called Nieuw (New) Amsterdam) in the middle of the 17th c. After studying law at Harvard and Columbia University he stood for election as Mayor of New York at the age of 28 but was defeated by his Democratic opponent. In 1895 he became president of the New York City Police Commissioners, in 1898 governor of New York State and in 1900 Vice-President of the United States. After President McKinley's murder in September 1901 he became President at the age of 42 – the youngest President ever. He was re-elected in 1904, and in the following year he mediated between

Russia and Japan and brought the Russo-Japanese War to an end, for which he was awarded the Nobel Peace Prize.

In 1908 he secured the election of William H. Taft as his successor, but when Taft proved too conservative for his taste he founded the Progressive party, with himself as presidential candidate at the 1912 election. The result was to split the Republican vote and bring about the election of a Democrat, Woodrow Wilson.

Roosevelt also made a name for himself as a natural scientist and hunter. A river in Brazil which he discovered is named after him.

The politician and publicist Carl Schurz, perhaps the most prominent of the Germans who emigrated to the United States after the suppression of the German revolution of 1848, became a newspaper publisher, general, senator, diplomat and finally Secretary of the Interior under President Grant (1877–91). True to his liberal principles, he sought to achieve better treatment of negroes and Indians and fought against any excesses directed against these population groups. He was also concerned to maintain the interests of German Americans. He is commemorated by the Carl Schurz Park on East River (86th Street) and a monument by the Austrian sculptor, Karl Bitter, in Morningside Park.

Carl Schurz
(1829–1906)

At the early age of twelve, Vanderbilt was helping his father to ferry passengers and luggage from Staten Island to New York. Four years later he owned his own boat, and in a further eight years he was manager of a steamship company, and less than ten years after that he founded his own steamship line, bringing prospectors from Nicaragua to San Francisco during the Californian gold-rush. Finally he started transatlantic services, but as competition from British and German ships became too great he switched to running railway lines. In 1863 he acquired his first railway company, the New York and Harlem Railway, and others followed. When Vanderbilt died the "Commodore", as he was called, left 105 million dollars, an unimaginable fortune for those days. Within eight years his son, William Henry built an empire founded on fifty railway lines with a total network of 25,000km (15,500 miles). The Vanderbilts were the richest family in the USA. For some Cornelius Vanderbilt is the perfect example of the self-made man; for others he is a product of capitalism, who made his fortune by deception, exploitation, bribery and merciless competition – which his competitors were unable to match.

Cornelius
Vanderbilt
(27.5.1794–
4.1.1877)

Probably the best known representative of pop art was actually named Andrew Warhola and was originally a draughtsman for advertisements. At the beginning of the 60s he painted his first pictures, and from then on concentrated on silk-screen printing, by which he mass-produced unusual photographs and series of prints. He usually chose for his subjects everyday articles, such as dollar bills or soup-tins ("200 Campbell's Soup") and pop-idols, including Elvis Presley, Elizabeth Taylor and Marilyn Monroe ("Marilyn Diptych"). The aim of his artistic activity was the integration of art into the mechanical processes of industry. From 1963 he turned to films (including "Sleep", "Blue Movie", "Flesh") and did not return to prints until the 70s ("Willy Brandt").

Andy Warhol
(6.0.1928
22.2.1987)

He produced his works collectively with the members of his living and working community, the "Factory". With his increasing fame Warhol himself became the idol and subject of his own art. In addition to his undoubted artistic gifts Warhol possessed great talent in marketing his own person, and his own artistic sense.

Walt Whitman
(1819–92)

Walt Whitman, the first American lyric poet to achieve world fame, came from a Quaker family. He left school with only a primary education but made up for this by private study. Until the age of 25 he worked as a journeyman printer, journalist and school-teacher; then in 1846 he became editor of the "Brooklyn Daily Eagle", but lost this job after only two years on account of his anti-slavery sentiments.

In 1855 he published the first edition of his most famous work, "Leaves of Grass", of which there were eight further editions during his lifetime. During the 1860s his works both in verse and prose reflected the experience of the Civil War, during which he devoted himself to visiting the wounded.

In 1873 Whitman suffered a stroke which condemned him to relative inactivity for the rest of his life.

The vigorous rhythms of his blank verse, the self-assurance of his manner and the unity of the body and of nature which he proclaimed, influenced the poetry of the 20th c., and the exuberance of his hymns was seen as an expression of the American spirit and of democracy, as the poetry of a new age.

History of New York

The Italian navigator Giovanni da Verrazano sails into New York Bay 1524
and sights Manhattan – the first European to do so. He surveys the E
coast of America on behalf of King Francis I of France and claims the
whole territory for the French crown. But since France is at war with
Spain the new colony attracts no interest.

An Englishman, Henry Hudson, becomes the first European to set foot 1609
on the soil of New York. (He had been commissioned by the Dutch East
India Company to find the North-West Passage to China and Japan, for
the discovery of which the Dutch government had offered a prize of
25,000 guilders.)

Hudson sails W across the Atlantic, reconnoitres the American coast
from Maine to Virginia, then returns N and sails into New York Bay and
up the river which still bears his name, hoping to find a route to the
Pacific.

Recognising his error, he returns down the Hudson, makes several
landings on Manhattan and then sails back to Europe.

The first governor of a number of small Dutch settlements on the banks 1626
of the Hudson and the S end of Manhattan, Peter Minnewitt of Wesel on
the lower Rhine, buys the island from the Manna-hatta Indians for only
60 guilders and names the settlement Nieuw Amsterdam (New
Amsterdam).

The establishment of the Dutch East India Company promotes the
development of trade, including trade with the Indians.

Foundation of Breuckelen (Brooklyn). 1646

Peter Stuyvesant is appointed governor. He soon develops into a 1647
dictator, suppresses political opposition, abolishes freedom of worship and attempts to prevent the immigration of Jews and Protestants.

New Amsterdam has a population of barely 1000. 1650

Stuyvesant has a wall built from the Hudson to East River, along the 1653
line of present-day Wall Street, as a protection against British attacks.

During the second Anglo-Dutch war (1664/65–67) New Amsterdam is 1664
taken by a British fleet without a shot being fired. The settlement is
renamed New York and becomes the property of the Duke of York,
Charles II's brother.

The Dutch retake New York and change its name to Nieuw Orange 1673
(New Orange).

The Dutch are driven out by British forces. 1674

The result of a legal suit by the colonial governor against the publisher 1735
of the first opposition newspaper, the "New York Weekly Journal", is to
establish the freedom of the press in America.

Outbreak of the War of American Independence. New York has a 1776
population of 25,000. Its port handles a bigger trade than Boston or
Philadelphia.

George Washington, leader of the rebellious colonies, moves his head- April 1776
quarters from Boston to New York, but loses the battle of Long Island
and is compelled to leave the British in occupation until the end of the
war.

The Continental Congress carries a motion for the independence of the 2 July 1776
13 states on the E coast of America. Two days later the Declaration of
Independence is adopted.

1626: Peter Minnewitt buys Manhattan from the Indians

19 October 1781	British troops surrender at Yorktown.
1783	Treaty of Paris: Britain recognises the independence of its former American colonies. During the long period of British occupation New York has been plundered and partly destroyed by fire and the population has been decimated.
1784	The first meeting of New York State legislature is held in the city (which remains capital of the state until superseded by Albany in 1797).
1789	New York briefly becomes capital of the young nation and seat of the Union government (a role it loses to Philadelphia in the following year). George Washington is sworn in as first President of the United States in Federal Hall. The population of New York is now over 30,000.
1820	With a population of over 150,000, New York displaces Pennsylvania as the largest city in the country, in spite of epidemics of cholera and yellow fever, a series of fires and civil disturbances.
1825	After the opening of the Erie Canal the first ship from Buffalo sails down the Hudson to New York. The city's predominance is enhanced by this new route to the W.
1848 onwards	After the repression of the 1848 revolutions in Europe there is an influx of political refugees and other immigrants, bringing the population over the half-million mark.
1853	First New York International Exposition in the newly built Crystal Palace.

Eleven southern states secede from the Union over the slavery question and form a separate Confederation. The Civil War ends, after much loss of life, in the victory of the northern states. After the war many negroes come to New York from the southern states.   1861–65

Central Park (at this time lying on the northern outskirts of the city) is opened.   1869

The population passes the million mark. The revelation of large-scale corruption in the city administration, involving the misappropriation of 75 million dollars, does not destroy the city's creditworthiness.   1870

Continuing influx of immigrants. The number of Germans coming in reaches the record figure of a quarter of a million, some 200,000 of whom remain in New York.   1882

Opening of Metropolitan Opera House and Brooklyn Bridge.   1883

Erection of the Statue of Liberty.   1886

Establishment of Greater New York by the amalgamation of New York (Manhattan) with the counties of Kings (Brooklyn), Bronx, Queens and Staten Island. With a population of almost 3·5 million, New York is second largest city in the world.   1898

First Automobile Show held in Madison Square Garden.   1900

First subway line opened (City Hall to Times Square). Times Square becomes the first square lit by electricity.   1904

The population of Greater New York passes the 5 million mark. Manhattan, with almost 2·4 million inhabitants, reaches its highest population. (By 1980 it has fallen by over a million.)   1913
   Completion of the Woolworth Building, the highest building in the world until 1931.

The Wall Street crash on "Black Friday" marks the beginning of a world economic crisis which lasts almost ten years.   October 1929

William F. Lamb builds the Empire State Building, for 40 years the highest in the world (381m – 1250ft). Also constructed at this time are the Chrysler Building, the RCA Building and the George Washington Bridge over the Hudson.   1931

Opening of Radio City Music Hall.   1932

New York's second World's Fair, held in Flushing (Queens). Opening of the LaGuardia Airport, named after Fiorello LaGuardia, Mayor of New York.   1939–40

The United Nations move into their new headquarters on East River from their temporary home in a converted factory on the outskirts of the city.   1952

Two aircraft collide over New York, with 134 deaths.   1960

An aircraft crashes soon after take-off from Idlewild (now J. F. Kennedy) Airport, with 95 deaths.   1962

History of New York

8–9 November 1965
In the year of the third New York World's Fair the city is paralysed for 16 hours by the failure of the power supply. Soon afterwards life in New York is brought to a standstill again by a ten-day strike of subway and bus staffs.

1970
The completion of its N tower (420m – 1380ft) makes the World Trade Center briefly the world's highest building (soon to be superseded by the Sears Tower in Chicago).

1975
New York City faces bankruptcy, but is saved from total collapse by a bridging loan from the federal government, accompanied by the establishment of a control agency to watch over municipal finances and a reduction in the number of municipal employees.

July 1977
New York suffers a further breakdown in the power supply, this time lasting 27 hours.

April 1980
A further strike by subway and bus staffs, lasting 14 days.

1981
The building of new luxury hotels and large skyscrapers points to the city's gradual recovery from economic stagnation. There is a fall in the number of unemployed; a recovery is in progress. On the other hand crime increases; public transport is worse than ever and the rehabilitation of slum areas makes only slow progress.

1982
In spite of the poor state of the economy, the continued erection of skyscraper office blocks is seen as a sign of confidence in the future by the business world.

1983
The financial crisis of the city appears to have been finally overcome. Building activity, primarily in the field of commercial property but also of luxury homes, quickly increases; tax income shows a tendency to rise and unemployment decreases.

1984
More new skyscrapers are completed than ever before in the history of the city, including the Trump Tower at Fifth Avenue (56th Street), the IBM Tower and the A. T. & T. skyscraper, both on Madison Avenue, between 56th and 57th Streets and 54th and 55th Streets respectively.

1985
Mayor Edward Koch is elected for his third four-year term with an overwhelming majority. Sociologists maintain that the gulf between rich and poor, especially in Manhattan, is becoming wider. The first buildings of Battery Park City are inaugurated.

1986
One of the greatest scandals of corruption in the city administration breaks out, brought to light by the suicide of a senior official, and the consequences can not as yet be foreseen. The Jacob K. Javits Convention Center, a new congress building on the Hudson, between 34th and 38th Streets, is opened. Plans for the erection of a 150-storey-high building, the tallest in the world, on the west side of Manhattan, are published.

1987
"Black Monday" on Wall Street with a drop of 30% in the total value of all trading shares and the resulting dismissals by the large financial companies spells catastrophe for the city. The city administration announces new economy measures.

1988
Owing to the continued strength of the economy in the construction industry and service industries, the unemployment figure for New York falls below 4% for the first time in decades.

The main part of the World Financial Centre in the south of Manhattan is completed, as is Battery Park City to the south. Controversial reforms in public transport are introduced. Newer and improved buses and trains are introduced on nearly all lines. 1989

On January 1st David Dinkins becomes the first Black mayor following his narrow victory in November 1989 over a white candidate. The reduced income from taxes forces staff reductions in public services. 1990

As a result of the Gulf War the number of tourists falls for the first time for many years, in spite of the favourable rate of the dollar. 1991

After extensive rebuilding work the Guggenheim Museum and the Jewish Museum are re-opened. 1993

The Republican Rudolph Giuliani is elected Mayor of New York. 1994

Quotations

Anonymous

"Fifth Avenue is a street where a lot of people spend money on buying things they don't need in order to impress people they don't like."

Simone de Beauvoir (1908–86)

"I shall never encompass New York in words. I no longer seek to encompass this city: I become dissolved in it. Words, pictures, knowledge, expectations are of no service: it is pointless to establish whether they are true or false. There is no confrontation possible with the things to be encountered in New York. They exist in a fashion all their own: they are *there*. And I gaze and gaze, astonished as a blind man must be who has recovered his sight."
("L'Amerique au jour le jour")

Horst Bienek (b. 1930)

"New York is a myth, and much more than that – a demon, a sphinx, a crater, a Moloch, an idol, a hell, a snakepit, an excrement, a volcano and much else besides. Writers and journalists, painters and photographers have repeatedly tried to uncover this myth and reveal the reality behind it; but this can never be more than partially achieved, for everything that is said about this city is right and at the same time wrong. For every theory there is a proof, there is a proof for every assertion . . . New York is myth and reality at the same time, and you are continually tempted to compare the images that emerge from the subconscious with what you see in front of you: to compare and sometimes to confuse . . .

"A city of stone and of human faces, a city that lives in the permanent and in the transient . . . When the theatres come out and people stream to the taxi-ranks and the subway each face has its individual stamp, each face tells a different story, contains a different secret . . .

"In these faces I have tried to understand this country – its history and its present, and sometimes too its future."

Charles Dickens (1812–70)

"The tone of the best society in this city is like that of Boston; here and there, it may be, with a greater infusion of the mercantile spirit, but generally polished and refined, and always most hospitable. The houses and tables are elegant; the hours later and more rakish; and there is, perhaps, a greater spirit of contention in reference to appearances, and the display of wealth and costly living. The ladies are singularly beautiful."
("American Notes")

Gustav Frenssen (1863–1945)

"I am staying in the largest hotel in the world. I take the express lift up to my room on the 17th floor, from which I have a wide view over the Hudson; far below me are houses and churches. They want to hear that it all makes a powerful impression on me; but it does not. It does not strike me with astonishment, and I feel not the slightest inclination to admire what I see. I am not a man who measures greatness with a yardstick: my scale of measurement is beauty. And so the greatest things I have seen have been the clouds which lowered over the Hudson yesterday and a pretty girl who walked across the lobby with a splendidly lively gait. They know how to walk here, I can tell you: here every limb, every muscle is in play. It is strange that in an old country like Europe we should have to re-learn the art of walking; but you will see, we shall learn it . . . from these American girls."
("Letters from America")

"Bagdad-on-the-Subway."

O. Henry
(1862–1910)

"New York is a vertical city which bears the mark of the new age. It is a catastrophe which an unkind fate has brought down on a courageous and confident people, but a grandiose and magnificent catastrophe." ("Quand les cathédrales étaient blanches")

Le Corbusier
(1887–1965)

"I love New York on weekdays in autumn and on working days.

"At six in the morning storm and rain. And cloud – cloud that will last until midday.

"We are overwhelmed with electric light. The huge bulk of the buildings and the movement of the traffic seem multiplied tenfold in the mirror into which rain has converted the asphalt. In the narrow spaces between the buildings the wind, now a hurricane, howls like a trumpet blast. It tears the placards off the walls and tries to blow the passers-by off their feet. It rages with impunity along the streets which stretch for miles from end to end of Manhattan and, far away, hurls itself into the ocean . . .

"Out there, in the hours before dawn, there passes the dark purple mass of the negroes who are given all the hardest and dirtiest work. Later, around 7 o'clock, the human flood is entirely white. Hundreds of thousands of men and women are hurrying to their work. At this hour there are still no automobiles or even taxis to be seen . . .

"New York feels at its best in the morning and during a thunderstorm, when no idlers or superfluous people are to be seen on the streets – only members of the great army of workers who live in this city of ten million people."
("My Journey to America")

Vladimir
Mayakovsky
(1893–1930)

"New York is not America, but it is easy to see that the whole of America would like to be New York."

Paul Morand
(1888–1976)

"On the summit of the Empire State Building is an observation platform. When you stand up there, with the wind blowing round you, and look down on this giant of a city, this octopus of a city – call it what you will – you cannot but feel excitement. Huddled together far below are the skyscrapers, and between them are what appear to be swarms of ants and a thousand tiny toy cars. There are East River and Brooklyn Bridge . . . and there the Hudson with its piers and its shipping . . . The only place where I have had a similar feeling was on the summit of Mount Elbruz. The Caucasus at your feet and the whole world below you! There you are overwhelmed by the grandeur and beauty of nature, here by the grandeur and beauty of man; for all this he has made – made it with his brain and his hands."

Viktor Nekrasov
(1911–87)

"New York appears to me as infinitely more American than Boston, Chicago, or Washington. It has no peculiar attribute of its own, as have those three cities, Boston in its literature and accomplished intelligence, Chicago in its internal trade, and Washington in its congressional and State politics. New York has its literary aspirations, its commercial grandeur, and – heaven knows – it has its politics also. But these do not strike the visitor as being specially characteristic of the city. That it is pre-eminently American is its glory or its disgrace, as men of different ways of thinking may decide upon it. Free institutions, general education, and the ascendancy of dollars are the words written on every paving-stone along Fifth Avenue, down Broadway, and up Wall Street."
("North America", 1862)

Anthony Trollope
(1815–82)

"To tell the story of New York would be to write a social history of the world."

H. G. Wells
(1866–1946)

27

New York from A to Z

Alexander Hamilton Custom House

See Museum of the American Indian

American Craft Museum   D 6

The American Craft Museum, founded in 1956, is situated on the ground floor of one of the office blocks opposite the Museum of Modern Art, designed by the well-known firm of architects Kevin Koche and John Dinkeloo. It contains everyday objects such as baskets, chairs, teapots, etc. and craftwork made from every conceivable material – clay, glass, metal, wood, wool and cotton.

Address
40 West 53rd Street

Subway stations
Fifth Avenue (lines E, F)
50th Street (lines B, D, Q)

The main collection is of 20th c. American craftwork, of which there are special exhibitions, including items on loan, reflecting the latest developments in this field.

Tours take place on Tuesday evenings and Saturday mornings. Group visits by prior arrangement (tel. 956–6047).

Buses
2, 3, 5, 7

It is open Tues. 10am–8pm, Wed.–Sun. 10am–5pm Closed Monday and public holidays.

Admission fee

American Museum of the Moving Image

Although it is situated in Queens the film museum is well worth a visit. It can be reached by subway from Manhattan and is not far from 36th Street station. Opened in 1988, it stands alongside a studio belonging to Paramount Pictures dating from 1920, when interior filming took place in New York with such actors as Gary Cooper, the Marx Brothers and W. C. Fields. The museum building (designed by Gwathmey and Siegel) houses a cinema with seating for almost 200 (Riklis Theater) and a small demonstration room with 60 seats where there are daily performances (Mon.–Fri. 2.30pm, Fri. also 7.30pm, Sat. and Sun. 1 and 4pm).

Address
35th Avenue at 36th Street (Astoria)

Subway station
36th Street (Queens) (line R)

On the second floor there is a permanent exhibition "Behind the Screen" showing how a film is made and visitors can even take part by writing the script, cutting the film and assisting with make-up. A booklet lists 150 job descriptions involved in film production. There are short films of different genres and headphones provide a commentary by actors, directors and agents.

Opening times
Wed.–Sat. noon–4pm, Sun. 1–5pm

Apart from the practical exhibition there are hundreds of historical film artefacts on view and a photographic display of the development of the cinema from the 5 cent Nickolodeon to the Multiplex Theatre.

★★American Museum of Natural History and Hayden Planetarium   C/D 4

The American Museum of Natural History, founded in 1869, is New York's oldest museum. With considerable extensions to the original buildings, it is now one of the largest museums of its kind in the world.

Situation
Central Park West and 79th St

◀ *World Financial Center in Battery Park City*

American Museum of Natural History

Subway station
81st Street (line C)

Buses 10, 79

Opening times
Sun.–Thur.
10am–5.45pm,
Fri., Sat.
10am–8.45pm

It is housed in one of the monumental Roman-style triumphal buildings which were built between 1874 and 1899 with the façade by John Russel facing Central Park. Considerably extended, its exhibits on the natural history of man and animals covering 50,000sq.m (59,800sq.yd), are of exceptional interest. The vast size of the collection makes it impossible to describe it all in this guide. The visitor is advised to use the short descriptions and plans to select certain exhibits. There is no admission fee after 5pm on Fridays and Saturdays.

First floor

The first floor (in British terms the ground floor) is mainly devoted to the natural history of the North American continent. Together with the flora and fauna the lives of the north-west coast Indians and Eskimos are documented. Life-size models are to be found in most departments with the model of the whale in the "Hall of Ocean Life" being especially impressive. The collection of precious stones and minerals contains replicas of famous jewels and the 463 carat "Star of India", the largest cut sapphire and a 100 carat ruby. The museum has had in its possession since 1985 the largest cut jewel in the world, the "Brazilian Princess", a light blue topaz weighing 21,327 carats (4.3kg), which was donated by an unknown benefactor. A special attraction for children is the "Discovery Room" where they can carry out, under guidance, experiments on the sense of touch (free admission tickets available from the information desk in the entrance hall).

Second Floor

On this floor are major exhibits illustrating the cultural and natural history of black Africa and Central America together with the world of birds. Special exhibitions and lectures regularly take place in the "People Center".

Third floor

Exhibits on the history and life of the North American Indians in the forests of the east coast and on the Prairies. Other rooms contain the birds of North America, primates, reptiles, amphibians and African mammals.

Fourth floor

There are exhibitions on the history of the Earth, early and late mammals, numerous dinosaurs of the earlier and later periods with skeletons and reconstructions (closed until 1994 for refurbishment) and a collection of fossil fishes. The Library and Library Gallery are also housed on this floor.

Naturmax Theater

Films and multi-media shows on various aspects of natural history are shown on a giant screen.

Other activities

The Museum has its own research laboratories and sends out expeditions to all parts of the world. It also publishes a monthly journal, "Natural History" and it puts on many special exhibitions every year.

Hayden Planetarium

Opening times
Mon.–Fri.
12.30–4.45pm
Sat. and Sun.
noon–4.45pm
(from Oct.–June
Sat.
10am–5.45pm,
Sun.
noon–5.45pm)

Admission fee

Within the Museum is the Hayden Planetarium, which can be visited separately (entrance 81st Street). It has excellent explanatory displays illustrating phenomena in the atmosphere and space. Of particular interest are the "Williamette" meteorite, the largest ever found in the USA, the "Hall of Sun", one of the most comprehensive exhibitions about the sun, and the "Sky Theatre" which has a Zeiss VI projector that makes visits into space possible. At the weekends a laser show with rock music takes place here.

There are special presentations on astronomy using 22 space projectors in the "Guggenheim Space Theatre". Below the roof a model of the solar system imitates its movements and in the middle of the room is an Aztec solar calendar.

Sky Show: Mon.–Fri. 1.30 and 3.30pm; Sat. 11am and then hourly 1–5pm; Sun. hourly 1–5pm. Laser Rock Show. Fri. and Sat. 7pm, 8.30pm, 10pm.

THIRD FLOOR

FOURTH FLOOR

THIRD FLOOR
1 North American birds
2 Primates
3 Gallery 3
4 Indians of the eastern woodlands and plains

9 Reptiles and amphibians
13 African mammals
FOURTH FLOOR
1 Library
2 History of the Earth
2B Library Gallery

3 Late mammals
5 Early mammals
9 Late dinosaurs
13 Early dinosaurs
F Fossil fishes
T Toilets

American Museum of Natural History

FIRST FLOOR
1 Indians of the NW coast
1A Gallery 77
2 77th Street Foyer
2A Molluscs and man
2B Museum shop
3 Man and nature
4 Biology of man
5 North American forests
7 Auditorium
7A Eskimos
7B Small mammals
8 Minerals and precious stones

9 Biology of the invertebrates
10 Life in the ocean; biology of fishes
11 Education Hall
11A Education Gallery
12 Theodore Roosevelt Memorial
13 North American mammals
18 Planetarium
19 Biology of birds
D Discovery Room
P Car park
T Toilets

SECOND FLOOR
A People Center
B Calder Laboratory
C Center Gallery
D Natural Science Center
1 Man in Africa
2 Birds of the world
4 Mexico and Central America
7 Akeley Gallery
12 Theodore Roosevelt Memorial
13 African mammals
19 Oceanic birds
T Toilets

FIRST FLOOR

SECOND FLOOR

American Museum of Natural History

Asia Society Gallery   E 5

Situation
725 Park Avenue
and 70th Street

Subway station
68th Street (line 6)

Buses
1, 2, 3, 4, 101, 102

In April 1981 the new home of the Asia Society, founded in 1956 by John D. Rockefeller III, was opened after a building period of two years. It contains galleries for Rockefeller's extensive collection of sculptures, ceramics and paintings from China, Japan, India and South-East Asia. There are also rooms for temporary exhibitions, an auditorium with a capacity of 250, a comprehensive library and space for offices of the Society which was lacking in the old building (112 East 64th Street, a fine building designed by Philip Johnson, now occupied by the Russell Sage Foundation). There are branches of the Society in Washington and Houston. As well as art its interests also extend into the fields of music, cinema and other aspects of Asian culture (open: Tues.–Sat. 11am–6pm, Fri. until 8.30pm, Sun. noon–5pm).

Former AT & T Building · Sony Building   E 6

Address
550 Madison
Avenue and 56th
Street

Subway stations
53rd Street
(lines E, F)

Buses
1, 2, 3, 4

The building was the headquarters of the AT & T telephone company from 1983 to 1991 before it was leased for 20 years to the Japanese company SONY in 1992.

Philip Johnson, once the enthusiastic champion in America of Mies van der Rohes, created a skyscraper about 195m (640ft) high built in the style of classical skyscraper architecture in 1983. This pinkish-grey granite building has a gabled roof and a six-storey-high entrance, its interior was decorated with modern wall paintings until 1993.

Until 1991 the statue of the "Golden Boy" stood in the lobby, a symbol of modern news technology created by Beatrice Longman. It is again in place in the old AT & T building.

Sony Building

El Barrio

El Barrio is the name given to an area in East Harlem occupied mainly by Puerto Ricans and other Spanish-speaking population groups who have come to New York in recent years from the Caribbean area and from Central and South America. The boundaries of the area, which is steadily expanding, are not exactly defined; but broadly it lies to the E of Fifth Avenue between 103rd Street and 125th Street (which is one of the main streets of Harlem). This part of the town is estimated to have more burnt-out, vandalised and unoccupied houses than any other area in New York except the southern Bronx, but nevertheless has a population of something like 200,000.

Location
North-east of Manhattan

Subway station
116th Street (line 6)

Bus
102

This is a district which most visitors will fight shy of, for it is one of New York's worst slum areas, and its rehabilitation is likely to be a lengthy process. One feature of potential interest is the Marqueta, a market held under the railway viaduct (Park Avenue, 110th–115th Streets), where good bargains can sometimes be obtained.

★Battery Park City

Of all the building projects which were begun in the 80's and which are now approaching completion, the most important is Battery Park City in the south of New York between West Street and the Hudson, and in its extent it can only be compared to the Rockefeller Center (see entry).

The development on built-up terrain excavated from the World Trade Center (see entry) comprises a commercial and residential quarter with

Location
South-west tip of Manhattan on the Hudson River

Battery Park City: Flats and Esplanade

Subway stations
Cortlandt or
Rector Street
(lines 1, R)
Chambers Street
(lines 1, 2, 3, A)
World Trade
Center
(line E)

more than 30 buildings designed by Alexander Cooper and Stanton Eckstut, which extends from Chambers Street to the southern tip of Manhattan.

The central section, the World Financial Center, is the most flourishing; here in a building designed by the Argentinian architect Cesar Pelli are situated the headquarters of American Express, Dow Jones and Merril Lynch.

A winter garden 38m (124ft) high and 61m (200ft) long with palm trees provides a welcome relief to the high architecture on the Downtown Manhattan side of the Plaza. Performances often take place here and in the square. This part of the World Financial Center houses several elegant shops and restaurants. Information and plans relating to the project are on display.

Gateway Plaza is an already completed gigantic residential block; on the south dwellings surround Rector Place. There will eventually be living space for 25,000 people. There is a 2km (1 mile) long esplanade where the new quarter meets the Hudson River which will extend to the southern edge of Manhattan.

North towards Chambers Street a park with playgrounds has been laid out. North Park is a favourite spot for families, for joggers to take an early morning run and for roller skaters and skateboarders to meet.

The high-rise blocks, some of which are finished, some still under construction and some at the planning stage contain private and rented apartments. The Regatta, between the Esplanade and South End Avenue, is the most luxurious to date.

Two smaller buildings opposite are approaching completion, one of which will house three cinemas.

Winter Gardens: World Finance Center

At the south end stands the tallest residential block at a height of 110m (361ft) with 40 floors. To the north, at the top of Chambers Street, stands the new building of the Stuyvesant High School, one of the most prestigious public technical colleges. Another half dozen apartment blocks are planned to form the northern perimeter of this giant project.

When it is all completed there will be living space for 35,000 to 40,000 people and several thousand will be employed here. Battery Park City has altered the skyline of New York and in particular the World Trade Center has lost its isolated situation.

Bowery   E 9/F 10

The Bowery, New York's second oldest street (after Broadway), is one of the widest streets in the city. Once renowned as being the main haunt of alcoholic dropouts Bowery's reputation of being one of the worst streets in the city is nowadays not strictly true, as the large numbers of alcoholics and homeless are also to be found in other parts of the city and no longer only restricted to the Bowery.

Originally laid out by Peter Stuyvesant as an approach avenue to his estate "Bouwerie" it is exactly one mile (1.6km) long and runs from Chatham Square in Chinatown to Cooper Square but it is by no means as bad as its reputation. It is perfectly safe to visit the Bowery provided you do not take photographs or otherwise draw attention to yourself: the worst that is likely to happen to you is to be pestered for money. In addition to the hostels for alcoholics ("flop houses") run by the Salvation Army and other charitable organisations, there are numerous shops, theatres, rock clubs, etc., and artists and writers live in the apartment blocks, many of them very much down at heel – the kind of mixture that can perhaps be found only in New York.

Location
From Chatham Square
(Chinatown) north to Cooper Square

Subway station
Astor Place (line 6)

35

Bowne House

Address
37–01 Bowne
Street, Flushing
(Queens)

This house, built in 1661 by John Bowne, a Quaker, is the oldest building within the city limits. The furniture and furnishings date mostly from the 17th and 18th c. The kitchen with its huge chimney has been preserved almost exactly as it was more than 300 years ago.

Subway station
Main Street
(line 7)

Bowne House is open to the public on Tues., Sat. and Sun. from 2.30 to 4.30pm. (Admission fee.)

Bridges

New York is a city of bridges due to its geographical situation on the East and Hudson rivers. No fewer than 65 span the waterways, 18 of which connect Manhattan with the other Boros and New Jersey.

Brooklyn Bridge   See entry

**George
Washington
Bridge**
West 179th Street

Completed in 1931 as the Hudson River Bridge it is a 2650m (8697 ft) long suspension bridge between two 194m (636ft) high pylons. It consists of a pedestrian level and two road levels (14 lanes), the lower was added from 1959 to 1962. It connects Manhattan with Fort Lee in New Jersey.

Hell Gate Bridge
Queens

This iron arched bridge from 1917 runs from Queens to Ward's Island in East River.

High Bridge
West 174th/175th
Street

Built between 1837 and 1848 to carry the Croton aquaduct this 13-arched construction is the oldest pedestrian bridge in Manhattan which crosses the Harlem River.

Manhattan Bridge
Bowery/Confucius
Plaza

This road bridge from Manhattan to Bronx was designed by Gustav Lindenthal in 1909.

**Queensboro
Bridge**
Second Avenue/
East 60th St

Also completed in 1909 this bridge (length 2271m (7450ft)) forms a wide arch over Roosevelt Island, where the construction of a residential suburb began in the Seventies.
From the west side of Second Avenue (corner East 60th Street) it is possible to travel to the island by an aerial tramway 965m (3167ft) long, 43m (141ft) above East River.

Triborough Bridge
Franklin D.
Roosevelt
Drive/East 125th
Street

This bridge connects Manhattan with the Boros of Queens and Bronx, via Randall's Island or Ward's Island (built 1936; total length 5km (3 miles), including access and ramps 23km (14 miles). From Carl Schurz Park (East End Avenue; see Practical Information, Parks) there is a marvellous view of the bridge.

**Verrazano
Narrows Bridge**
Brooklyn,
Gowanus
Expressway

Named after Giovanni da Verrazano, who discovered New York harbour bay, this bridge connects Brooklyn with Staten Island across the Narrows. With a total length of 4176m (13,705ft) (longest span 1298m (4260ft)) it is one of the longest suspension bridges in the world. At the head of the bridge is a stone monument of Castle Verrazona in Tuscany.

Manhattan Bridge

Built in 1903 this suspension bridge, with a span of 488m (1601ft), joins Manhattan Lower East Side with the Brooklyn suburb of Williamsburg.

Williamsburg Bridge
Delancey Street

★Bronx Zoo (New York Zoological Park)

Officially the New York Zoological Park but known to New Yorkers only as the Bronx Zoo, this is the largest of New York's five zoos, with an area of 300ha (750 acres), the other four are in Central Park (see entry), Manhattan; Prospect Park, Brooklyn; Flushing Meadows, Queens; and Barrett Park, Staten Island), and is one of the most important zoos in the world.

Situation
Southern Boulevard & 185th Street (Bronx)

Subway stations
Pelham Parkway (line 2; or line 5 to East 180th Street, change to line 2)

The Bronx Zoo – which, like the New York Botanical Garden (see entry), is part of Bronx Park – was originally laid out in 1899, but a programme of reconstruction carried out in recent years and not yet complete has largely transformed it. The old cages have been almost all replaced by open enclosures, in which the animals live in surroundings as similar as possible to their natural habitat. There are also many modern houses for birds, monkeys, beasts of prey, waterfowl, reptiles, penguins and gorillas (open: daily 10am–5pm, Sun. and public holidays to 5.30pm, Nov.–Mar. until 4.30pm; Tues.–Thur. admission fee discretionary, applicable at other times; Senior Citizens free).

Of particular interest are "Jungle World", a newly built enclosure for animals from tropical Asia, the "World of Birds", which is architecturally unusual, and the "World of Darkness" enclosure for nocturnal animals. There is a 25 minute safari tour by train, the "Bengali Express", through the

Jungle World
World of Birds
World of Darkness

37

Asian countryside with some 350 species of free-roaming animals including elephants and tigers. The "Children's Zoo" is a must for families with children.

★Brooklyn Botanic Garden

Address
1000 Washington
Avenue (Brooklyn)

Subway stations
Eastern Parkway/
Brooklyn Museum
(lines 2, 3, 4)

Opening times
Tues.–Fri.
8am–4.30/6pm;
at weekends
and holidays
from 10am

This botanic garden, easily reached from Manhattan, has steadily grown more attractive over the 70 years of its existence. Within its 21ha (52 acres) it contains more than 12,000 different species of plants, including 900 kinds of roses alone, presenting a glorious spectacle during their summer flowering period. There is also a beautiful avenue of Japanese cherry-trees, seen at their best at the end of April and beginning of May. A garden has been created for the blind, where plants are arranged according to their scent. A new glasshouse was opened in spring 1988.

A visit to the Botanic Garden can conveniently be combined with a visit to the Brooklyn Museum (see entry).

There is no charge for admission, except at weekends for the Japanese Gardens.

★Brooklyn Bridge   F 11

Location
From southern
Manhattan over
the East River to
Brooklyn

Subway station
Brooklyn Bridge
(lines 4, 5, 6)

The huge ramp of Brooklyn Bridge, the oldest bridge over the East River linking Manhattan with Brooklyn, begins south-east of city hall. This massive suspension bridge supported on two pylons 40m (131ft) above the water was the first bridge made of steel cables. It was designed in 1867 by the German-American engineer John A. Roebling and completed in 1883 by his son Washington A. Roebling, 1052m (3453ft) long, between the two pylons, it has impressive views (especially at night) of the Manhattan skyscrapers, South Street Seaport and the Statue of Liberty. On both sides of the bridge's approach are high-rise buildings; to the south Southbridge Towers and to the north Governor A. E. Smith Houses and the striking Chatham Green Houses and Towers.

Brooklyn Children's Museum

Brooklyn: 145
Brooklyn Avenue
(Brooklyn)

Subway stations
Kingston Avenue
(lines 3, 4),
Kingston/Throop
(line A)

Brooklyn Children's Museum, founded in 1899, aims to give children an understanding of the various aspects of technology, ethnology and natural history in the most vivid and interesting way. Altogether it has more than 50,000 exhibits, including working models which enable children to have experience of many fields of knowledge in a practical way.

The museum also has a large collection of dolls, rocks and fossils, shells, costumes and African artefacts (open: Mon., Wed.–Fri. 2–5pm, Sat., Sun., public holidays 10am–5pm; admission fee).

★Brooklyn Museum

Address
200 Eastern
Parkway

Were it not that the Brooklyn Museum lies rather off the usual tourist track, it would be one of the most visited museums in New York. Its departments of Egyptian, Near Eastern and Oriental art rank among the finest collections

Brooklyn Bridge

of the kind to be seen in the city. It can be reached by subway from Manhattan in half an hour.

The building was originally erected in 1897 but has undergone much subsequent alteration, not always to its advantage. Thus the flight of steps leading up to the second floor (in British terms first floor) has been removed, leaving the museum with a very unimpressive ground-floor entrance. In 1994 the refurbished new west wing was opened with additional rooms for the Egyptian Collections (open: Wed.–Sun. 10am–5pm; admission fee).

Subway station
Eastern Parkway/
Brooklyn Museum
(lines 2, 4, 5)

The Sculpture Garden in the courtyard contains some historically interesting items saved from demolished old buildings, especially from Manhattan.

Frieda Schiff
Warburg
Sculpture Garden

Primitive arts (from Africa, the South Seas, American Indians and pre-Columbian peoples); special exhibitions. Museum shop.

First floor
(ground floor)

Mainly devoted to the art of China, Japan, Thailand, India and Persia.

Second floor

Coptic, Egyptian, Greek, Roman and Near Eastern cultures; Wilbour Library of Egyptology.

Third floor

European and American costume; 25 completely furnished American rooms (1715–1880); a Brooklyn house of the Dutch colonial period (1675), transported here from its original site; silver and pewter, china, glass and furniture from the early days of America.

Fourth floor

European and American painting and sculpture. The collection of American art is particularly extensive. Throughout the year there are interesting temporary exhibitions on this subject.

Fifth floor

Brooklyn Museum

A visit to the Museum can conveniently be combined with a visit to the adjoining Brooklyn Botanic Gardens (see entry).

Castle Clinton National Monument   E 12

Situation
Battery Park

Subway stations
Bowling Green
(lines 4, 5),
South Ferry
(line 1),
Whitehall Street
(lines N, R)

Buses 1, 6

Castle Clinton has had many vicissitudes in the course of its history.

It was built before the 1812 war with Britain, but had only a short military career: after serving for some years as the headquarters of the 3rd Military District it was converted in 1824 into a place of entertainment (fireworks, brass band concerts, etc.).

Twenty years later it was roofed over and became a concert hall, in which the famous "Swedish nightingale", Jenny Lind, sang before an audience of 6000 in 1850.

From 1855 Castle Clinton was used as a depot for immigrants, and from 1896 to 1941 it housed a popular aquarium. Thereafter it was unoccupied for 34 years and lost its roof and upper floor; then in 1975 after extensive restoration work it was reopened as a national monument (open: Apr.–Dec.: Mon.–Fri. 9am–5pm; in summer also Sat., Sun. 9am–5pm).

★Cathedral Church of St John the Divine   C 2

Situation
Amsterdam
Avenue and
112th Street

If it is ever completed, this church – the building of which began in 1891 – will be the largest in the world.

The first part of the church (apse, choir and crossing), designed by Heins and LaFarge, was in Byzantine-Romanesque style. After their death (1911) it was continued by Ralph Adams Cram on a new design for a Gothic cathedral for the following 30 years.

40

Cathedral Church of St. John the Divine

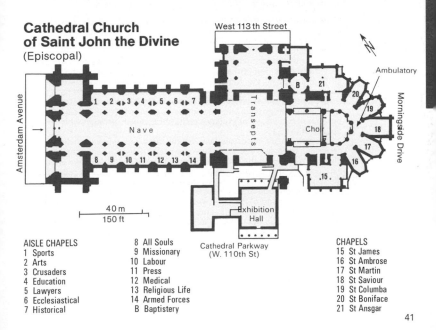

Cathedral Church of Saint John the Divine
(Episcopal)

West 113th Street

Ambulatory

Amsterdam Avenue

Nave

Transepts

Choir

Morningside Drive

20
19
18
17
16
.15.
B 21

40 m
150 ft

Exhibition Hall

Cathedral Parkway
(W. 110th St)

AISLE CHAPELS
1 Sports
2 Arts
3 Crusaders
4 Education
5 Lawyers
6 Ecclesiastical
7 Historical

8 All Souls
9 Missionary
10 Labour
11 Press
12 Medical
13 Religious Life
14 Armed Forces
B Baptistery

CHAPELS
15 St James
16 St Ambrose
17 St Martin
18 St Saviour
19 St Columba
20 St Boniface
21 St Ansgar

Central Park

Subway station
116th Street
(line 1)

Opening times
Daily 7am–5pm

Conducted tours
Mon.–Sat. 11am
Sun. 12.45pm

Information
Tel. 316 7540

The church is 183m (600ft) long and will be 101m (332ft) wide across the transepts, making it currently the second largest after St Peter's in Rome. In a building of this size the mixture of styles is hardly noticeable, the Gothic element being predominant.

It contains a wealth of decorative material from a variety of sources: 16th c. Italian paintings, 17th c. tapestries, icons, a Bohemian candelabra (present from Czechoslovakia) and various sculptures.

The Romanesque apse has seven chapels (stained glass by J. Powell, London; beautiful vaulted arch in St Martin's chapel). Behind the marble main altar is the tomb of Bishop Horatio Potter (died 1887), the founder of the church. The octagonal baptistery contains eight figures from New York history. The chancel is worked in Tennessee marble.

Above the square tower, above which a 137m (450ft) high spire will eventually tower, is a temporary dome. There are good views of the portal rose from here. A model of the cathedral, which will have 76m (249ft) high towers, is on display in the exhibition area.

★★ Central Park   D/E 2–5

Subway stations
Fifth Avenue
(lines N and R),
59th Street
(lines A, C, D, 1),
72nd Street, 81st
Street, 86th Street
and 96th Street
(line C)

Buses
1, 2, 3, 4, 9
(59th Street),
79 (79th Street),
186 (86th Street),
19 (96th Street),
66 (66th Street),
30 (72nd Street)

Guided tours
at weekends from
"The Dairy"
Tel. 397 3156

Events
Tel. 360 1333

Central Park is the principal "lung" of New York City, with an area of 340ha (840 acres), 5% of the total area of Manhattan. It extends for 4km (2½ miles) from 59th to 110th Street, with a breadth of 500m (550yd) between Fifth Avenue and Central Park West, the continuation of Eighth Avenue.

The idea of a park for the rapidly growing city of New York was first put forward in the 1840s, and Central Park was laid out between 1859 and 1870 on a site which was then on the northern outskirts of the city. The layout was designed by Frederick Law Olmsted and Calvert Vaux, whose "Greensward Project" was selected following an open competition.

The construction of Central Park involved the removal of much stone and rock and the bringing in of 10 million wagon-loads of soil and humus. The park is now a natural monument, and no alteration of its layout is permitted.

The numerous bridges and the four sunken carriageways for through E–W traffic were part of the original plan. These roads were asphalted in 1912, and most of the footpaths were also asphalted soon afterwards. There are altogether some 30 miles of roads and footpaths in the park.

At weekends and at certain times on weekdays the whole of Central Park is closed to motor traffic, and the wide carriageways become the exclusive preserve of cyclists, roller skaters and the horse-drawn carriages which still operate in the park.

The park, which in consequence of the New York financial crisis was neglected for several years, has been renovated since the beginning of the Eighties, partly with the help of private organisations which were set up expressly for this purpose. The architecture of buildings was repaired, many trees, shrubs and flowers planted, the wide expanses of grass resown and immoderate use consequent on summertime events reduced.

The southern part of the park, which is much the most frequented, is an area of quieter and gentler beauty than the northern part (beyond 86th Street), which has been left in its natural state and is scenically more attractive. It is inadvisable to venture into this unfrequented northern area, even during the day, except in groups.

After dark the park should be avoided, except for theatrical and other events in summer.

Pond, Wollman
Rink,
The Mall

Just at the south-east entrance (60th Street) is the Pond (bird sanctuary), and immediately north of this is the Wollman Memorial Rink (ice skating, roller-skating). Farther north is a small zoo (reopened after reconstruction),

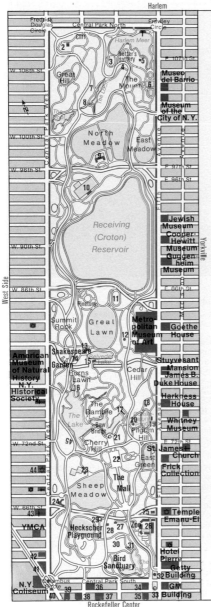

Central Park

1 110th Street Boathouse
2 Blockhouse
3 Lasker Pool Rink
4 Fort Fish
5 Fort Clinton
6 Conservatory Garden
7 Huddlestone Arch
8 Glen Span
9 Handball Courts
10 Tennis Courts
11 Basketball Courts
12 Cleopatra's Needle
13 Delacorte Theater
14 Swedish Cottage
15 Belvedere Castle
16 Bank Rock Bridge
17 Loeb Boathouse
18 Alice in Wonderland Statue
19 Kerbs Memorial Model Boathouse
20 Hans Christian Andersen Statue
21 Bethesda Fountain
22 Bandshell
23 Mineral Spring
24 Tavern-on-the-Green
25 Children's Zoo
26 Arsenal
27 Dairy
28 Chess and Checkers
29 Friedsam Memorial Carousel
30 Wollman Memorial Rink
31 Gapstow Bridge
32 Sherman Statue
33 Pulitzer Fountain
34 Plaza Hotel
35 Solow Building
36 N.Y. Athletic Club
37 Cami Hall
38 American Fine Arts Building
39 Lincoln Art Theater
40 N.Y. Convention and Visitors Bureau
41 Gulf & Western Building
42 Hotel Mayflower
43 Holy Trinity Lutheran Church
44 Spanish & Portuguese Synagogue
45 Strawberry Fields

500m
0,3 mi

Central Park

Central Park, New York's "Green Lung" . . .

and to the north-west of this runs the Mall, a straight avenue of elms lined with busts of writers and composers, including Shakespeare, Burns, Scott, Beethoven and Schiller.

Central Park Zoo
Opened in 1989 the zoo consists of three main enclosures; a "tropical zone" with a recreated rain forest (monkeys, crocodiles, snakes, bats and other tropical animals); a "moderate zone" (Asian and North American animals); and the "polar zone" with animals from the Arctic and Antarctic (polar bears, sea lions, penguins, polar foxes, etc.). Access to this small but modern zoo is from Fifth Ave and 64th Street. Opening times: Apr.–Oct.: Mon.–Fri. 10am–5pm, also Tues. (May–Sept.) open until 8pm, Sat., Sun. until 5.30pm; Nov.–Mar. 10am–4.30pm (admission fee).

The Dairy
To the west of the zoo is "The Dairy", a reconstruction of an old park building from Olmsted and Vaux, containing an exhibition of the park's history.

Sheep Meadow, Bethesda Fountain, Lake
To the west of the Mall extends Sheep Meadow, the finest expanse of grass in the park. From the end of the Mall a flight of steps leads down to the Bethesda Fountain and the Lake (hire of boats in summer).

Strawberry Fields
The "John Lennon Peace Gardens", named after a Beatles song, was established in 1985 by the west entrance to the park on 72nd Street. It has plants donated by 123 countries and commemorates the musician who was murdered in front of the Dakota Building in 1980 on the pavement opposite.

Conservatory Pond
To the east of the Lake is the Conservatory Pond, the preserve of model yachts and motorboats. On its west side is a statue of Hans Christian Andersen, and to the north of this is a bronze group (by José de Creeft) of "Alice in Wonderland".

44

. . . and "The Pond" a bird conservation area

Continuing north-west, we come to Belvedere Castle (now a weather station), on the highest point in the park. Beyond this are the Belvedere Lake, surrounded by blossoming Japanese cherry-trees in mid April, and the Delacorte Theater, in which dramatic performances (admission free) are given in summer.

Belvedere Castle

The adjoining Great Lawn is used by young people for various ball games (baseball, football). In summer the Metropolitan perform operas here and the New York Philharmonic put on concerts.

Great Lawn

Behind the Metropolitan Museum of Art (see entry) is an Egyptian obelisk known as Cleopatra's Needle, sister to the obelisk of the same name in London, which was presented to New York by Khedive Ismail Pasha in the latter part of the 19th c. The obelisk is now badly weathered.

Cleopatra's Needle

Beyond the Great Lawn is the Reservoir, which occupies a quarter of the area of the park, extending from 86th Street to 96th Street. There is a pleasant walk around the Reservoir at any time of year.

Reservoir

To the north of the Reservoir there is much less in the way of man-made landscape: here nature has been left largely to itself. One attractively laid-out area, however, is the Conservatory Gardens (entrance at 105th Street and Fifth Avenue).

Conservatory Gardens

At the extreme north-east end of the park is the Harlem Meer, a pond on which rowing-boats can be hired. Beyond 110th Street (Central Park North) is the beginning of Harlem (see entry).

Harlem Meer

There are a variety of facilities for eating and drinking in Central Park; the Ice Cream Café and Deli on the east side of the Conservatory Pond (open:

Catering facilities

45

In Central Park – a green oasis between skyscrapers

7.30am–8pm); a small cafeteria on the Lake (open: 9am–sunset); and the Tavern-on-the-Green, near the park entrance on Central Park West and 67th Street (open: 11am–10pm, Sat. 11am–1am on Sun. morning, Sun. 10am–midnight; chamber music 11am–3pm). It is advisable to book a table at the Tavern-on-the-Green, particularly at weekends (tel. 873 3200).

During the warmer months of the year, and particularly at weekends, there are at least 50 frankfurter and hot-dog stalls in and around Central Park.

There are a number of ways of getting about in Central Park: Bicycle and boat rental: Loeb Boathouse; Rental of roller skates: Central Park West (72nd St); Pony and trap: 59th St/Fifth Ave. (south entrance); Horses to ride: Claremont Riding Academy, 179 West 89th St.

China House Gallery

E 5

Address
125 East 65th
Street

Every year from mid March to the end of May and from October to January this gallery puts on outstanding exhibitions of classical Chinese art which are notable for their unity of theme.

Subway station
68th Street (line 6)

The gallery is open on weekdays 10am–5pm, on Sat. 11am–5pm and on Sun. 2–5pm (admission fee).

★Chinatown

E/F 10

Location
South of
Manhattan

This exotic area, steadily expanding eastward and northward, is the largest Chinese town outside China, occupied by tens of thousands of Chinese, most of them living in apartment blocks a hundred or more years old and

Chinatown: Fishmarket . . .   *. . . and Bakery*

making a living by running their several hundred restaurants, foodshops and gift shops, and giving the district an exotic flavour.

Chinatown proper is bounded on the east by the Bowery (see entry), on the west by Baxter Street, on the north by Canal Street and on the south by Worth Street and Chatham Square.

The first Chinese settlers were seamen who came to New York in the junk "Kee Ying" in 1847 and decided to stay. They were followed some 20–25 years later by unemployed Chinese coolies who had been working on the construction of the transcontinental railway to California and settled here on land belonging to John Mott and Joshua Pell.

Thereafter Chinese immigration was prevented by legislation, and it was only after the amendment of the immigration laws in favour of Asians in 1965 that a further great influx of Chinese immigrants began.

Thousands of the new arrivals found in this restricted area not only accommodation but employment – the men mainly in restaurants and shops, the women in some 300 small clothing factories.

Of the estimated 300,000 Chinese living in New York 70,000–125,000 live in the narrow streets of Chinatown (the exact number has never been recorded), Hong Kong Chinese live chiefly in the Brooklyn district, Sunset Park and the Taiwanese predominantly in Elmhurst (Queens) and Willowbrook (Staten Island).

In Chinatown there are some eight Chinese-language daily newspapers, all set by hand (compared with only five English papers), reflecting the political and regional differences and conflicts among the Chinese population. On East Broadway (Nos. 11 and 75) are two Chinese cinemas, mainly showing films from Hong Kong and Taiwan in the original (sometimes with English subtitles). There is much of interest to be seen in a stroll through the narrow streets of Chinatown, even the telephone boxes are in pagoda-style.

Subway stations
Canal Street
(lines 6, N, R),
Brooklyn Bridge/
City Hall
(lines 4, 5, 6)

Chrysler Building

Chinese Museum (Chinatown Museum)

There are, for example, the Chinese Museum at 8 Mott Street (open: daily 10am–6pm) and a number of Buddhist temples, in particular one at 64 Mott Street. The Chinatown History Museum (70 Mulberry Street) has photographs illustrating the history of Chinatown.

Information

Information can be obtained from the Chinese Community Center, 62 Mott Street (tel. 226 6280), or the Chinese Community Cultural Center, 10 Confucius Plaza (tel. 925 2245). Information about cultural events is supplied by the Chinese American Arts Council, 456 Broadway (tel. 431 9740).

★Chrysler Building   E 6

Address
425 Lexington Avenue

Subway station
Grand Central (lines 4, 5, 6, 7)

Buses
104, 106

Opening times
During office hours

The Chrysler Building, with which the automobile manufacturer Walter P. Chrysler sought to immortalise his name, was built in 1930, and for a year, until the completion of the Empire State Building in 1931, was New York's tallest skyscraper (319m/1045ft high).

The Chrysler Building's most striking feature, visible from all over the city, is the sharply pointed spire with its arches and triangular windows of stainless steel. The Art Deco style which inspired the architect, William Van Alen, to create this unusual building, which when first constructed was decried as eccentric and bizarre, is seen also in the entrance hall and the 18 lifts (with different patterns of intarsia decoration), which have been restored to their original condition.

★City Hall   E 11

Situation
City Hall Park, Broadway

Subway stations
Brooklyn Bridge (lines 4, 5, 6), Park Place (lines 2, 3), City Hall (lines N, R)

Buses 1, 6

Opening times
Mon.–Fri. 10am–3.30pm Parties by arrangement

City Hall standing in the heart of Lower Manhattan houses the official rooms of the Mayor and the City Council (51 members).
The south façade was originally finished in marble but today it is sandstone. Built between 1803 and 1812 by J.-F. Mangin and J. McComb in "Federal Style" it has elements of French Renaissance with a colonnaded portico, projecting side wings and a domed bell tower (crowned with Justitia). The designers were awarded the competition prize of 350 dollars!

City Hall is the finishing point of the "Tickertape Parades", now a rarity, whereby particularly popular personalities such as the first astronauts on the moon, are honoured by having confetti and strips of paper thrown at them. This custom is now frowned upon for environmental reasons.

Inside the building a double staircase leads up to the second floor (first floor in British parlance). The Governor's Room is now a museum containing furniture made for the original City Hall, including chairs used at the first US Congress, the chair on which George Washington sat when he was made President and the desk at which he wrote his first message to Congress. On the walls of this and other rooms are portraits of military heroes and important state guests, such as that of Lafayette in the Council Chambers (painted by the inventor S. F. B. Morse in 1824) and those of Washington and Hamilton, both by J. Trumbull.

City Hall Park

South-west is City Hall Park with a statue of the patriot Nathan Hale (by F. McMonnies), hanged as a spy by the British. The same year one of the first public readings of the declaration of independence took place here.

Chrysler Building ▶

Civic Center

This complex of Municipal, State and Federal offices, shows a mix of many architectural styles. The most notable buildings are the following.

Subway stations
Brooklyn Bridge
(lines 4, 5, 6)
Municipal
Building

The Municipal Building, at the corner of Chambers and Centre Streets above the subway station of Brooklyn Bridge, was built in 1914 by the New York firm of architects McKim, Mead and White. This 36-storey skyscraper is topped by a copper statue of "Civic Virtue" (by Adolph Weinman).

This building, at 52 Chambers Street, is named after one of New York's most notorious political bosses. Designed by John Kellum in the style of an Anglo-Italian palazzo, it was completed in 1872. The building (entrance in basement) is now rather the worse for wear.

Tweed
Courthouse

The Surrogate's Court Building (31 Chambers Street) was erected in 1911 and is one of many public buildings in New York in the "Beaux Arts" style.

Surrogate's Court

Opposite the Municipal Building and linked by a plaza, the Police Headquarters, built in 1973, is the most recent structure in the Civic Center.

Police
Headquarters

The United States Courthouse, seat of the Federal District Court, occupies a central position in the Civic Center. Built in 1936, it was designed by Cass Gilbert, architect of the Woolworth Building (see Skyscrapers), and his son.

United States
Courthouse

Opposite the United States Courthouse is the New York County Courthouse (by Guy Lowell, 1912), with a façade in the style of a Roman temple.

New York County
Courthouse

On the opposite side of the square stands the Federal Office Building, erected in 1967 by Alfred Easton Poor, Kahn and Eggers. With its many small windows it has something of the appearance of a chessboard.

Federal Office
Building

The Criminal Courts Building, at 100 Centre Street, designed by Harley Wiley Corbett, was erected in 1939. A new prison has been built on the site of the notorious "Tomb Prison".

Criminal Courts
Building and
Tombs Prison

★★The Cloisters

The Cloisters, built in 1938 to the design of the architect Charles Collens, combine fragments of European buildings of the 12th–15th c. with modern architecture. The tower is modelled on that of the 12th c. French monastery of St Michel-de-Cuxa, a cloister from which is incorporated in the building.

Situation
Fort Tryon Park at
the northern tip of
Manhattan

The Cloisters are a branch of the Metropolitan Museum of Art (see entry), housing its collection of medieval art. Most of the works of art were presented by John D. Rockefeller Jr (1874–1960), who also financed the construction of the Cloisters in Fort Tryon Park, which he had presented to the city. From the Cloisters there is a magnificent view, in clear weather, of the Hudson river. Admission fee is discretionary. This includes admission to the Metropolitan Museum of Art on the same day.

Subway station
190th Street
(line A)

Bus 4

Opening times
Mar.–Oct.
Tues.–Sun.
9.30am–5.15pm;
Nov.–Feb.
9.30am–4.45pm
Guided tours

Tues. and Thur. 3pm; Tues.–Fri. and Sat., Sun. mornings for groups by appointment; tel. 923 3700.

Tour

In the Romanesque Hall doorways from French churches and monasteries have been rebuilt: an entrance doorway from Poitou (mid. 12th c.), a doorway from Reugny in the Loire Valley (end 14th c.) and one from the Monastery of St Jean in Burgundy (13th c.).

Main Floor
Romanesque

◀ *City Hall*

MAIN FLOOR

GROUND FLOOR

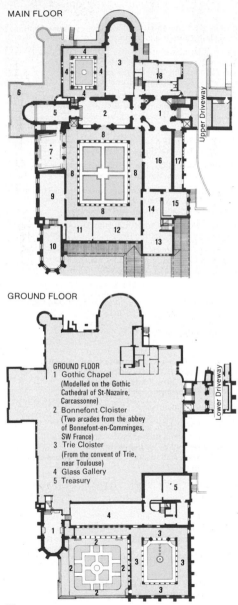

The Cloisters

Museum of Medieval Religious Art and Architecture

MAIN FLOOR

1 Entrance Hall
2 Romanesque Hall
   (Doorways from France)
3 Fuentidueña Chapel
   (Apse from the church of San Martin de Fuentidueña, near Segovia)
4 St-Guilhem Cloister
   (Cloister from the Benedictine abbey of St Guilhem-le-Désert in southern France)
5 Langon Chapel
   (Parts of the church of Notre-Dame du Bourg, Langon, SW France)
6 West Terrace
7 Pontaut Chapter House
   (Chapter house of the abbey of Notre-Dame de Pontaut, SW France)
8 Cuxa Cloister
   (Cloister, partly reconstructed, from the monastery of St Michel-de-Cuxa in the French Pyrenees)
9 Early Gothic Hall
   (Figures of saints)
10 Gothic Chapel
    See Ground Floor
11 Nine Heroes Tapestry Room
12 Hall of Unicorn Tapestries
13 Boppard Room
    Stained glass from the Carmelite convent of St Severin, Boppard am Rhein)
14 Burgos Room
    (Flemish tapestry from Burgos Cathedral)
15 Spanish Room (Campin Room)
    (Merode altarpiece, an "Annunciation" by Robert Campin; Gothic ceiling paintings from Castile)
16 Late-Gothic Hall
    (In the style of a medieval refectory)
17 Froville Arcade
    (Gothic arcade from Froville priory, Lorraine)
18 Books and reproductions

GROUND FLOOR

1 Gothic Chapel
   (Modelled on the Gothic Cathedral of St-Nazaire, Carcassonne)
2 Bonnefont Cloister
   (Two arcades from the abbey of Bonnefont-en-Comminges, SW France)
3 Trie Cloister
   (From the convent of Trie, near Toulouse)
4 Glass Gallery
5 Treasury

In the Cloisters

The apse of this chapel comes from the Spanish church of San Martin de Fuentidueña near Segovia (*c.* 1160). Notable exhibits include a fresco from San Juan de Tredòs, a secco from San Baudelio de Berlanga in Catalonia and a carved ivory cross (12th c.) from the abbey at Bury St Edmunds in Suffolk, England.

Fuentidueña Chapel

Founded in 806 the Benedictine abbey at St Guilhem-le-Désert near Montpelier was dissolved during the French Revolution. The 13th c. cloisters and capitals with ornate acanthus leafwork are on show.

St Guilhem Cloisters

This is named after parts of the church of Notre Dame-du-Bourg in Langon (Southern France; 12th c.). Also stained glass thought to be from Troyes/Seine; 13th c.), a Madonna with Child (*c.* 1200) and a 12th c. Italian ziborium.

Langon Chapel

This late-Romanesque chapterhouse of the former Cistercian and later Benedictine monastery of Notre Dame-de-Pontaut in Gascony (France) was the morning meeting place for the monks.

Pontaut Chapter House

A cloister (partly original, partly reconstructed) from a Benedictine abbey in the Pyrenees which was dissolved during the French Revolution.

Saint Michel-de-Cuxa Cloisters

The Early Gothic Hall contains sculptures and paintings from the 13th to the 16th c. Noteworthy are the Holy Virgin of Strasbourg, a Madonna with Child (France) and the St Catherine (Rhineland).

Early Gothic Hall

Five of the nine French tapestries depicting the Nine Heroes of medieval legend (three Jewish, three heathen and three Christian survive). They are David, Joshua, Alexander the Great, Julius Caesar and King Arthur (Judas Maccabaeus, Hector, Charlemagne and Godfrey of Bouillon are missing). These 14th c. tapestries are thought to be by Nicolas de Bataille.

Nine Heroes Tapestry Room

Cooper-Hewitt Museum

Unicorn Tapestries Hall	The 15th c. set of tapestries depicting scenes from a hunt for the mystical unicorn are one of the museum's outstanding treasures. They were woven for the marriage of Louis XII to Anne of Britanny and were once owned by the De La Rochefoucauld family.
Boppard Room	The Boppard Romm is named after the six stained glass panels from the Carmelite monastery of St Severin at Boppard on the Rhine.
Burgos Tapestry Room	In this room is the only surviving tapestry out of a set of eight, woven for the Emperor Maximilian in 1495, which formerly belonged to Burgos Cathedral.
Spanish Room (Campin Room)	It contains a Gothic painted ceiling from Castille and a Mérode winged altar from Flanders (c. 1425).
Late Gothic Hall	This late-Gothic hall has been preserved in the style of a medieval refectory. Particularly noteworthy are the stained glass from the Dominican monastery at Sens (France; 15th c), altars and parts of altars (Spain; 14th c.) and the "Worship of the Three Kings" (Ulm; end 15th c.).
Froville Arcade	A Gothic arcade from the Lothringian monastery at Froville.
Ground Floor Gothic Chapel	This chapel is modelled on the Cathedral of St Nazaire in Carcassone and contains 13th and 14th c. tombstones.
Bonnefont Cloisters	The 13/14th c. cloister of the French Cistercian monastery at Bonnefont-en-Comminges has been rebuilt here. The herb garden has over 250 different herbs selected and grown according to the medieval study of herbs.
Trie Cloisters	The Trie Cloister was built in the 15th c. near Tarbes (Southern France) and destroyed by the Huguenots 100 years later. The reproduced cloister garden contains original capitals. It has been planted with the flowers and herbs depicted on the Unicorn tapestry.
Glass Gallery	Together with 15th c. sculpture and stained glass the altar paintings "Birth of Christ" and "Dream of the Three Wise Men from the East" from the Roger van der Weyden School and the courtyard of a house from Abbéville are of interest.
Treasury	The main attractions of the Treasury are an early-Christian silver chalice from Antiochia, a 13th c. golden Bertinus chalice and a Eucharist dove of Limosin enamel, also 13th c.

Cooper-Hewitt Museum   E 3

Situation
Fifth Avenue and
91st Street

Subway station
86th Street
(lines 4, 5, 6)

Buses 1, 2, 3, 4

Opening times
Tues. 10am–9pm,
Wed.–Sat.
10am–5pm
Sun. and public
holidays
noon–5pm

The only museum of design in New York, the Cooper-Hewitt Museum belongs to the group of museums run by the Smithsonian Institution, whose other major museums are in Washington.

Although the Cooper-Hewitt collection was established in 1897, it was housed until 1963 in the Cooper Union in southern Manhattan and was not open to the public. It is now located in the former Carnegie Mansion, one of the few detached private houses in Manhattan, which was built by the Scottish-born steel king Andrew Carnegie in 1901 and was occupied by the Carnegie family until 1949. Thereafter the house was used by Columbia University, and finally was presented by the Carnegie Foundation to the Smithsonian.

A sumptuous mansion in a version of Renaissance style, originally containing 64 rooms, the house was renovated and reconstructed for the purposes of the Museum in 1977.

The collection includes wallpaper, textiles, furniture, glass, china, jewellery, clothing, drawings and prints, and there is also a large picture reference archive. The Museum puts on periodic special exhibitions.

Admission charge
Free Tues. after 5pm

Dyckman House Museum and Park

The only farmhouse which still survives in Manhattan is the Dyckman House, built in 1783 on the site of an earlier house destroyed during the War of American Independence.

Situation
Broadway and 204th Street

Built by William Dyckman, grandson of a Westphalian named Jan Dyckman who had emigrated to New Amsterdam, the house remained until 1915 in the hands of the Dyckman family, who then presented it to the city.

Subway stations
207th Street (line A),
Dyckman Street (line 1)

In the basement of the house is the winter kitchen, on the ground floor living rooms, on the upper floor five bedrooms, and above this an attic. The house contains the original 18th c. furniture.

Opening times
Tues.–Sun.
11am–5pm

The garden behind the house, restored to its original form, still has one of the cherry-trees for which the Dyckman farm was famed (admission free).

★ Ellis Island and Immigration Museum

Ellis Island, one of the 40 islands in the waters round New York, was famous between 1890 and 1917 as the point of entry for immigrants to the United States. Originally a fortification and munitions depot it assumed its new function in 1892 when the federal government assumed responsibility for immigration control.

Dykman House, Manhattan's last surviving farmhouse

Great Hall in the Immigration Museum on Ellis Island

Immigrants had to undergo health examinations before being granted permission to continue their journey to Manhattan or New Jersey. Those denied entry were sent back or interned until the outcome of their appeal was decided. The years between the 1890s and the First World War saw the largest influx with *c.* 17 million people being processed here.

At times the influx was so great that each customs officer interviewed 400 to 500 people a day. The fate of entire families was often decided in a few minutes which led to Ellis Island being called the "island of tears", as it was known to immigrants detained here.

After 1917 Ellis Island served as a reception camp where deportees and political refugees awaited immigration clearance (see Quotations, Egon Erwin Kisch), during the Second World War it was an internment camp for foreigners.

Immigration Museum

Opening times
Daily 9.30am–5pm

Following several years refurbishment the main building on Ellis Island was reopened in 1990 as a museum. There is an impressive exhibition of photographs, artefacts and films depicting the arduous conditions under which more than 17 million immigrants into the USA were held. The visitor is made aware how the various ethnic groups with their different cultures and languages have enriched the country. The dates of entry of the immigrants to Ellis Island are held on computer and can be consulted.

★★Empire State Building   D 7

Situation
Fifth Avenue and
34th Street

Although now exceeded in height by the World Trade Center (see entry), the Empire State Building, erected in 1931, is still the principal emblem and landmark of New York. From its two observatories (viewing terraces) on the 86th and 102nd floors there are incomparable views over Manhattan,

Empire State Building ◀

Subway stations
34th Street
(lines B, D, F, N, Q
and R)

Buses
2, 3, 4, 5, 16

Opening times
Daily 9.30am–
midnight

Admission fee

extending in clear weather to other parts of the city and the neighbouring state of New Jersey.

Built of sandstone and granite, the Empire State Building is in some ways a vertical city in itself, with a total height of 448m (1472ft) to the tip of the television aerial on its summit. 60,000 tonnes of steel were used in its construction, together with 100km (62 miles) of water pipes and 5630km (3500 miles) of telephone cable; 72 lifts travel in 11km (7 miles) of lift-shafts. Originally the aerial mast was intended to provide anchorage for airships. In the film "King Kong" the top of the Empire State Building was where the giant gorilla finally fled before crashing to his death.

The stainless-steel window framing gives it a characteristic glitter both by day and by night. The upper 30 floors are illuminated from 9pm to midnight by powerful coloured floodlights.

The ascent of the Empire State Building is equally rewarding either during the day or in the evening. In hazy weather, such as New York frequently experiences during the summer, it is best to go early in the day.

Federal Hall National Memorial   E 11

Address
25 Wall Street

Subway stations
Wall Street
(lines 4, 5),
Rector Street
(line R)

Buses
1 (Mon.–Fri.), 6

Opening times
Mon.–Fri.
9 a.m.–5 p.m.

This building at the junction of Wall Street and Nassau Street, originally the City Custom House, was completed in 1842 after a building period of eight years. It marks the high point of Greek Revival architecture in New York. The Wall Street façade of the building, conceived in the style of a Doric temple, is like a simplified version of the Parthenon, without a frieze. The interior is in the form of a rotunda, more Roman than Greek in inspiration.

From 1862 to 1920 Federal Hall was occupied by a department of the US Treasury. In 1955 it became a National Memorial, commemorating the fact that George Washington was inaugurated as first President of the United States on this spot in 1789. The site was then occupied by New York's old City Hall, built in 1701 and modernised by Pierre L'Enfant, famous as the planner of the new federal capital in Washington. It was the seat of US Congress in 1789/90.

★★Fifth Avenue   E 1–9

Subway stations
Fifth Avenue/60th
Street (lines N, R),
Fifth Avenue/53rd
Street (lines E, F),
Fifth Avenue/42nd
Street (line 7)

Buses: 1, 2, 3, 4, 5,
103 (59th Street),
28 (57th Street),
32 (60th Street),
104 (42nd Street),
16, 34 (34th Street)

Side streets

Fifth Avenue, in particular the section between 59th and 34th Street (roughly 2km (1¼ miles) in length), is New York's best known thoroughfare, a magnificent avenue which has an endless fascination for visitors, as well as for New Yorkers. Among its attractions are numerous luxury shops, banks, airline offices, churches, the Rockefeller Center, the New York Public Library, the Empire State Building (see entries) and much else besides. Fifth Avenue divides Manhattan into an eastern and a western part, and since New York lacks any large central squares it is the real centre of the city.

The numerous ethnic parades start from here and the avenue is also closed to traffic on other festivals. A stroll along Fifth Avenue is an essential element in the process of getting to know New York.

While walking along Fifth Avenue do not forget to look along some of the side streets, such as 47th Street West, home of the diamond trade, in which Hassidic Jews have a virtual monopoly, or 46th Street West, which has become a kind of Little Brazil. From the corner of 43rd Street there is a particularly fine view of the Chrysler Building (see entry).

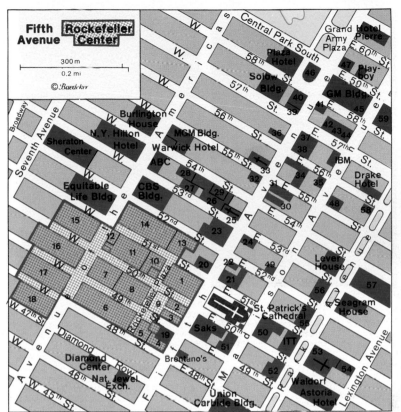

ROCKEFELLER CENTER

1 International Building
2 British Empire Building
3 Maison Française
4 Sinclair Oil Building
5 One Rockefeller Center
6 U.S. Rubber Company
7 General Electric Bldg. West
8 General Electric Bldg.
9 Sunken Plaza / Prometheus
10 Associated Press Building
11 Radio City Music Hall
12 Amer. Metal Climax Building
13 15 W. 51st St. Building
14 Sperry Rand Building
15 Time & Life Building
16 Exxon Building
17 McGraw Hill Building
18 Celanese Building
19 Swiss Center

20 640 Fifth Avenue Building
21 Olympic Tower
22 Cartier (jewelers)
23 Tishman (666 5th Ave.) Building
24 Rolex Building
25 St. Thomas Episcopal Church
26 Museum of Modern Art
27 Museum of Contemporary Crafts
28 Hotel Dorset
29 A.A. Rockefeller Garden
30 Elizabeth Arden (beauty)
31 St. Regis Sheraton Hotel
32 Hotel Gotham
33 Fifth Ave. Presbyterian Church
34 Corning Glass Building
35 AT & T Building
36 Doubleday (books)
37 Tiffany's (jewelers)
38 Trump Tower
39 Van Cleef (jewelers)

40 Bergdorf Goodman (fashion)
41 Bergdorf Goodman (fashion)
42 Galeries Lafayette
43 Escada (fashion)
44 Hermès (fashion)
45 F.A.O. Schwarz (toys)
46 Pulitzer Memorial Fountain
47 Hotel Sherry - Netherland
48 Hotel Winslow
49 Hotel Inter-Continental
50 Palace Hotel
51 Newsweek Building
52 Colgate Palmolive Building
53 St. Bartholomew's Church
54 General Electric Building
55 Manuf. Hanover Bank Bldg.
56 Racquet & Tennis Club
57 Citibank Building
58 Mercedes - Benz
59 Standard Brands Building

Window displays . . .   *. . . on Fifth Avenue*

The view of the Empire State Building, however, which could be seen from the Metropolitan Museum (see entry) on Fifth Avenue is today blocked by the building 712 Fifth Ave, completed in 1990. Only the aerial tower is visible until crossing 55th Street.

Notable buildings

Apart from the buildings which have an entry to themselves in this guide, Fifth Avenue has few other individual buildings of particular interest.

Worth a look in passing, however, are the Plaza Hotel (59th Street: see Practical Information, Hotels), in the style of a French château (by Henry J. Hardenbergh, 1907); Trump Tower, corner of 56th Street (see entry); the Corning Glass Building (No. 717, corner of 56th Street), designed by Harrison and Abramowitz, architects of the Rockefeller Center (see entry) and the Metropolitan Opera in the Lincoln Center – see entry (see Practical Information, Music); the new Japanese department store Jakashimaya (no. 693); the Metropolitan Club at the corner of 60th Street, in the style of a Florentine palazzo (by Stanford White, 1893); and the University Club at the corner of 54th Street (by Charles F. McKim, 1899).

At the corner of 52nd Street is the last survivor of the mansions built below 59th Street in this area at the beginning of the 20th c. by wealthy families such as the Astors, Vanderbilts and Goulds; the building is now occupied by Cartier, the internationally known jewellers.

Fraunces' Tavern   E 12

Address
54 Pearl Street

The block on which Fraunces' Tavern is situated is the only one in the financial district where there are no skyscrapers. The Fraunces' Tavern is the oldest house in Manhattan (built in 1719, burnt down in 1837 and 1852, rebuilt in 1907 in late-Colonial style). It is not a copy of the inn which became famous during the American Revolution but a faithful restoration of the original 18th c. building by the architect William Mersereau in 1928.

Georgo Washington spent his last days as general of the American forces here in the winter of 1783. On December 4th he took leave of his officers before retiring to his estate at Mount Vernon, near the future capital of the Union which was to bear his name. Today it is a very popular restaurant. On the upper floors are a museum containing mementoes of the American Revolution and a library of 4000 volumes and manuscripts relating to the revolution and history of New York (temporary exhibitions).

The admission fee is discretionary; on Thursdays admission is free.

Subway stations
Bowling Green
(Lines 4, 5),
South Ferry
(lines 1, 9),
Wall Street
(lines 2, 3)

Bus 15 (to Broad
Street)

Opening times
Mon. and Fri.
10am–4pm
Sun. noon–5pm

★★Frick Collection   E 5

The private collection of the Pittsburgh steel magnate Henry Clay Frick (1849–1919) was opened to the public in 1935 on the ground floor of the former mansion, designed by Thomas Hastings in 1913/14 in French Classical style, on the site of the old Lennox Library. The house is typical of the numerous palatial mansions built by millionaires on Fifth Avenue. By erecting this mansion Frick wanted to outdo his former partner Andrew Carnegie's house (now the Cooper-Hewitt Museum (see entry)). Further extensions and alterations to the garden took place in 1977.

Much of the character of a private residence has been preserved in the museum. The outstanding works of art, in particular the paintings from the 14th to the 18th c., bronzes from the Italian Renaissance and enamel work (Limoges), are exhibited in the intimate setting of rooms decorated in Empire style. Over the past 45 years relatively few works have been added but all are of the highest quality. The Frick Collection is very different, therefore, from the normal art gallery. There is no attempt at chronological order: the main consideration has been the aesthetic effect of the arrangement.

Address
Fifth Avenue &
70th Street

Subway station
68th Street (line 6)

Buses
1, 2, 3, 4

Opening times
Tues.–Sat.
10am–6pm,
Sun. 1–6pm,
closed on public
holidays

Admission fee

**Photographs not
allowed**

Tour

The room, in the style of a French boudoir, contains eight allegorical pictures "The Arts and the Sciences" by François Boucher painted for Madame de Pompadour's boudoir in the château of Crécy. Also Sèvres porcelain and French furniture. — Boucher Room

Temporary exhibitions, mostly engravings and drawings from the collection. — Anteroom

The dining room has been left as it was in Henry Frick's lifetime with 18th c. English paintings including Hogarth's "Miss Mary Edwards" (1724), "Walk in St James's Park" by Gainsborough and the portrait "General John Burgoyne" by Reynolds. — Dining Room

Boucher also painted the "The Four Seasons" for Madame de Pompadour which is on display here. The writing table is by André-Charles Boulle. — West Vestibule

The main attraction of this room is the fourteen-part set of paintings "Les Progrès de l'Amour" by Fragonard. Also noteworthy are a marble bust of the Comtesse de Cayla (1773) by Houdon and fine examples of French 18th c. furniture including pieces by Riesener, Lacroix and Martin-Carlin. — Fragonard Room

Some of the paintings in the richly decorated former living room are Giovanni Bellini's "The Ecstasy of St Francis" (about 1480), two portraits by — Living Hall

East 71st Street

| West Gallery | East Gallery |

14 · West Gallery · 15 · East Gallery · 13 · 16 · Lecture Hall · 11 · 12 · Living Hall · 17 · 9 · 3 · 10 · 2 · 18 · 7 · 8 · 1 · 6 · 5 · 4

Fifth Avenue

East 70th Street

Frick Collection

The Frick Collection is displayed on the ground floor of the mansion built for Henry Clay Frick (1849–1919) in 1913–14, on a site previously occupied by the Lenox Library. The house was designed by Thomas Hastings in a style reminiscent of 18th c. European domestic architecture.

1	Entrance Hall	10	South Hall
2	Reception Hall	11	Library
3	Sales Room	12	North Hall
4	Boucher Room	13	Portico
5	Anteroom	14	Enamel Room
6	Dining Room	15	Oval Room
7	West Vestibule	16	Garden Court
8	East Vestibule	17	Green Room
9	Fragonard Room	18	Terrace

Titian "The Man in a Red Cap" and "Pietro Aretino", El Greco's "St Jerome", "Sir Thomas More" and "Thomas Cromwell" by Holbein the Younger; also Italian Renaissance bronze sculpture, including "Hercules" by Pollaiols and furniture by Boulle.

South Hall   Vermeer's "Officer and Laughing Girl" (about 1656) and the "Music Lesson" (1660; disputed), "Mother and Two Children" by Renoir, Paolo Veneziano's "Coronation of Maria", a year clock by Berthoud, Caffieri and Lieutaud, and drawers and writing desk belonging to Marie Antoinette.

Library   The library chiefly contains portraits including "Henry Clay Frick" by Johansen, "George Washington" by Stuart and others by Gainsborough, Lawrence and Romney. Landscapes by Constable and Turner.

North Hall   The focal point of the North Hall is the portrait of the "Comtesse d'Haussonville" by Ingres; also Houdon's bust of the "Marquis de Miromesnil", "Bust of a Young Woman" by Andrea del Verrochio, "Beatrice of Aragón" by Francesco Laurana and a table by Belanger and Gouthière.

West Gallery   In the West Gallery is a self-portrait by Rembrandt from 1654 and "Polish Rider" also by him, "Wisdom and Strength" and "Hercules's Choice" by Veronese, "The Forge" by Goya (1818), portraits by El Greco, van Dyck, Hals, Bronzino and Velásquez ("Phillip IV of Spain"; 1664), landscapes by Ruisdael, Constable and Turner, one of the few works by de la Tours to be found in America and Italian Renaissance furniture.

Enamel Room   The adjoining Enamel Room contains Jan van Eyck's "Madonna with Saints and Creator", "St Simon" by Pierro della Francesca and a four-part altarpiece by the same painter from the church of St Agostino in Borgo San Sepolcro (Italy), "The Temptation of Christ" by Duccio da Buoninsegna (14th c.), a French Pietà from the 15th c. and Limosin 16th and 17th c. enamel painting.

Oval Room   Two portraits by van Dyck and Gainsborough hang opposite each other in this room so that the influence van Dyck had on Gainsborough can be observed.

East Gallery   In the East Gallery are "The Sermon on the Mount" by Lorrain, portraits by Goya and Whistler's "Robert, Comte de Montesquiou-Fenzenac".

Garden Court   This courtyard, with a vaulted glass roof and a beautiful fountain, contains a bronze angel by Jean Barbet and other busts. Occasional exhibitions consisting of works of art from the store room are mounted here. There is a splendid show of magnolias in spring.

In the Lecture Hall illustrated lectures on particular themes and an in- **Lecture Hall** troduction to the collection are given.

Under the new director Charles Ryskamp temporary exhibitions of the collection take place.

Lectures are held Oct.–May: Tues.–Fri. 11am (introduction) and Thur. and Sat. afternoons (general).

Goethe House, New York   E 6

The New York branch of the Goethe Institute of Munich has now returned to this handsome mansion opposite the Metropolitan Museum (see entry) following refurbishment. It offers a wide programme of German cultural events, and a monthly programme is available.

Address
1014 Fifth Avenue
and 83rd Street

Subway station
86th Street
(lines 4, 5, 6)

German newspapers and magazines are forwarded by airmail and are available in the library which is open to the public.

Opening times: Tues., Thur. noon–7pm; Fri., Sat. noon–5pm.

Buses
1, 2, 3, 4

★Gracie Mansion   F 3

The Gracie Mansion, since 1942 the residence of the Mayor of New York City, was originally built in 1799 for a Scottish importer named Archibald Gracie but was much altered and enlarged in subsequent years, most recently in 1966. It has been open to the public since the autumn of 1980.

Situation
Carl Schurz Park,
at end of East 88th
Street and East
End Avenue

The house had many owners before being acquired by the city in 1891. From 1925 to 1935 it was occupied by the Museum of the City of New York (see entry).

Bus 19

Opening times
Mar.–Nov., Wed.
10am–4pm

The Carl Schurz Park, named after New York's best-known 19th c. German immigrant (1829–1906; see Famous People), is one of the city's most pleasant little green oases (see Practical Information, Parks).

Information
Tel. 570 4751

★Greenwich Village   D/E 9

Greenwich Village, known to its inhabitants simply as "the Village", has preserved nothing of the village-like character it must have had when it first grew up in the 18th c.

Originally this was the site of the Indian settlement Sapa Kanik. These people were driven out by the Dutch settlers who established tobacco plantations on the fertile ground. During the British period (when it acquired the present name of the London suburb) the area developed into an elegant residential district from which some of the older brick buildings remain.

Subway stations
4th Street (lines A,
B, C, D, E, F),
Sheridan Square
(line 1), 8th Street
(lines N, R)

Buses
2, 3, 6

This area on the W side of Broadway, between 14th Street in the N and Houston Street in the S, became known in the first 30 years or so of this century as the centre of New York's *vie de Bohême* and was inhabited by intellectuals, writers and artists, who found cheap lodgings here and frequented its little theatres and numerous cafés. In those days there were no buildings higher than three or four storeys, rents were low, and the residents felt that they had little to do with the rest of New York.

Greenwich Village

The number of writers and artists who have lived in the Village is legion. Among the writers have been James Fenimore Cooper, Theodore Dreiser, Willa Cather, Edgar Allan Poe, Richard Wright, Henry James, Edith Wharton, John Dos Passos, Marianne Moore, Mark Twain, Sinclair Lewis, Dorothy Thompson, Thomas Wolfe, Hart Crane, Mary McCarthy, E. E. Cummings, William Styron and Edward Albee; among the artists Edward Hopper, William Glackens and Rockwell Kent. Only a few houses, however, have plaques commemorating former famous residents.

Greenwich Village has now become a respectable residential area: although many of the old low houses still survive there are now numerous modern apartment blocks and the rents are among the highest in New York (second only to Upper East Side), while the little restaurants (mainly French and Italian) are just as dear as those in other parts of the city. In other words the Village has now been fully integrated into New York.

Washington Square

Once a place of execution, a paupers' cemetery and a drill ground, Washington Square is now the principal square of the Village, the scene of constant bustle and activity, particularly at weekends when it becomes a kind of microcosm of the whole city, with people of all races, nations and ages playing, making music, roller skating or merely sitting quietly in the sun.

On the square stands the massive Washington Centennial Memorial, a triumphal arch 26m (85ft) high built by Stanford White in 1889–92 to commemorate the centenary of the election of George Washington as the first US president. On the south side is the Garibaldi Monument. Lining the square are buildings of the New York University, founded by Albert Gallatin in 1831.

Main Street

Main Street, 8th Street, leads E from the Avenue of the Americas to Broadway; between Fifth Avenue and the Avenue of the Americas it is particularly interesting because of its lively atmosphere.

Washington Square in Greenwich Village

This is another interesting street, with numerous antique shops, restaurants, night spots, cinemas, theatres and the Bayard Building (No. 65, east of Broadway), the only building in New York by the Chicago architect Louis Sullivan (1898).

Bleecker Street

After Bleecker Street the most interesting streets are MacDougal Street, with MacDougal Alley, which branches off near 8th Street; Minetta Lane; Bedford Street, at No. 75 of which is the oldest house still preserved in the Village (1799); Commerce Street, Grove Street and Sheridan Square; Christopher Street, the haunt of homosexuals; St Luke's Place (between Leroy and Hudson Streets), with a group of houses dating from 1855, still in their original form; and Hudson Street, with the church of St Luke in the Fields (No. 485). The church, built in 1822, still has something of the air of a village church in spite of later alterations; it was badly damaged by fire in 1981. In this part of Hudson Street there are many antique shops, selling mainly Americana.

Other streets

This striking building at the corner of the Avenue of the Americas and 10th Street, in a splendidly exuberant Venetian Gothic, was erected in 1876 and until 1945 served as a courthouse. In 1967 it was reopened as a branch of the New York Public Library (see entry).

Jefferson Market Library

This square, on the northern edge of the Village, was the entertainment quarter of New York around the turn of the 19th–20th c., with numerous theatres and hotels and some of the city's best shops. After years of neglect the square has been renovated to something like its original condition, and on the east side there is arising new building with shops, offices and four residential tower blocks.

Union Square

As Greenwich Village became increasingly fashionable its less prosperous residents moved east. During the 1960s St Mark's Place, the continuation of

East Village

Street scene in East Village

8th Street, became the great centre of activity of the "flower people", and this area was christened East Village; but little is now to be seen of this short-lived phenomenon.

In more recent years, however, art galleries and fashionable restaurants have opened in this run-down area. This led to an influx of prosperous residents moving into East Village making the area a fashionable address. Property developers bought up houses charging exorbitant rents, driving out the occupants who had always lived there by criminal methods, so that they could convert them into luxury flats and shops. The juxtaposition of poverty and ostentatious wealth is regarded as "chic" by some, but it merely increases the conflicts.

Towards the end of the last century East Village was a German district. Some buildings still provide evidence of that, for example, the house at 12 St Mark's Place (1885) which was acquired by the German-American Protection Society, the Ottendorf branch of the Public Library (135 Second Ave; 1884) and the Stuyvesant Polyclinic, until 1918 the German Polyclinic (137 Second Ave; 1884). The English poet W. H. Auden spent his last years at 60 St Mark's Place.

The Ukrainians own shops, restaurants and meeting-places in this area, including, since 1977, a church in 7th St between 2nd and 3rd Avenue. On the north-east side of Cooper Square stand the buildings of the Cooper-Union (Art and Technical College), founded in 1859, in the middle of the square a bronze seated figure of the inventor Peter Cooper (1791–1883). At 428–434 Lafayette Street, Colonnade Row, an entire house front from 1836 has been preserved.

Greenwood Cemetery

Location
Brooklyn, about
1.5km (1 mile)
south-west of
Prospect Park

Subway station
25th St
(lines N, R)

Interesting
graves

Situated on Gowanus Heights in Brooklyn the main cemetery of New York was romantically laid out in 1840 with hundreds of Victorian mausoleums, monuments and statues.

The main entrance to the cemetery is on 5th Ave and 25th St (in Brooklyn!) through a brownstone gateway in "Gothic Revival" style decorated with reliefs and a 30m (98ft) high tower. Alongside earlier graves moved here from Manhattan, numerous prominent personalities of the 19th c. have found their lasting resting place, including:

Peter Cooper (1791–1883, businessman and inventor), Samuel Finley Breese Morse (1792–1872, inventor of the telegraphic code named after him; on his grave: "S.F.B.M."), Elias P. Howe (1819–67, inventor of the first sewing machine), James Gordon Bennett (1795–1872, founder of the "New York Herald"), Lola Montez (1818–61, dancer famous for her influence on King Ludwig I of Bavaria; on her grave: "Mrs Eliza Gilbert"). The largest plots are the "Niblo Tomb" (on Crescent Water) for the theatre and restaurant owner William Niblo, and the pompous "Whitney Tomb" (on Ocean Hill) for the cotton magnate Stephen Whitney.

It is particulary beautiful at the end of May/early June when the cherry trees, rhododendrons and azaleas are in bloom.

Grey Art Gallery and Study Center   E 9

Address
33 Washington
Place

This gallery, opened in the autumn of 1977, belongs to New York University and houses the University's permanent art collection, made up solely of works presented or bequeathed to it.

It consists mainly of American art from 1940 to the present day, but there are also collections of contemporary art from Turkey, Iran, India and Japan. The gallery also puts on interesting special exhibitions.

The Grey Gallery is open from September to the end of May on Tues. and Thur. 10am–6.30pm and Wed. 10am–8.30pm; in June, July and August it is open Mon.–Fri. 11am–7pm Admission free.

Subway stations
West 4th Street
(lines A, B, C,
D, E, F),
8th Street
(lines N, R),
Astor Place (line 6)

Buses
1, 2, 3, 5, 6

Guggenheim Museum

See Solomon R. Guggenheim Museum

Harlem   D/E 1

In spite of its reputation as being a black ghetto and the rather run down appearance of many parts of this area Harlem is still worth visiting.

Peter Stuyveant founded the settlement of Nieuw Haarlem (New Harlem, named after the Dutch town) in 1658 in the area where 1st Ave and East 125 St meet today. It retained its rural character until 1832 when the first rail link was established with urban south Manhattan and Harlem grew into a respectable suburb with solid brownstone houses.

Bounded on the south by 110th Street (called Central Park North in the section running along the north end of Central Park), on the east by Madison Avenue, on the north by 150th Street and on the west by Eighth Avenue, Harlem consists mainly – apart from a number of contemporary skyscrapers – of houses built about the turn of the 19th and 20th c. for the prosperous middle classes. The houses are better built than in other parts of Manhattan, and the streets (such as Lenox Avenue, which with 125th Street forms the real centre of Harlem) are wider than any others in New York. As a result of overbuilding, however, the houses could not be let, and a black estate agent persuaded the owners to accept as tenants the blacks who were being driven out of their slum dwellings in the 30th and 40th streets by the steady commercial development of that area. By about 1910 the population of Harlem was almost entirely black.

Nowadays little is left to bear witness to the splendours of Harlem's early days. Numbers of empty houses, some of them burned out and boarded up, give many Harlem streets the appearance of an area which has recently suffered an air raid. The effect of the high unemployment rate – traditionally higher among blacks than among whites, and here particularly affecting the young – also makes itself felt here: nowhere else are to be seen so many men with nothing to do as in Harlem, particularly during the warmer months of the year.

The question is often asked: is it safe to go about Harlem on foot? The answer must be that it is safe, provided that you bear one or two rules in mind. Do not go in large parties, and do not take photographs of the people of Harlem or stare at them, since this might reasonably cause offence. You should visit Harlem in the evening only if you have a particular destination in mind, such as a jazz club, a dance hall or a theatre.

If you wish to visit Harlem on your own the best plan is to go on one of the three-hour bus tours of Harlem run by the (black) Penny Sightseeing Co. or

Location
North of Central Park

Subway stations
125th Street
(lines A, D, 4, 6),
125th Street and
Lenox Avenue
(lines 2, 3)

Buses
2, 5, 10

Note

Tours

Harlem: the cheerful face of a black ghetto

one of the Harlem Renaissance Tours (see Practical Information, Sight-seeing tours). On these tours experienced guides will point out the positive as well as the negative aspects of Harlem, and you will be told where you can take photographs and where you should not. After a trip of this kind you may even be tempted to come back and have another look on your own: once you know the area you may be less hampered by the inhibitions and apprehensions which can be aroused by sensational reports in the press and on television.

Literature

The best place to go for literature by and about blacks is the Liberation Bookstore (Lenox Avenue and 131st Street).

Sights in Harlem
New buildings

Among recently erected buildings in Harlem are the two high-rise apartment blocks, built in 1975, on the Arthur A. Schomburg Plaza (110th and 111th Streets, between Fifth and Madison Avenues); the New York State Office Building (163 West 125th Street); Lenox Terrace (between Fifth and Lenox Avenues and 132nd and 135th Streets), the largest housing estate in Harlem (1957); the Schomburg Center for Research in Black Culture (see entry), corner of Lenox Avenue and 135th Street, completed in 1980; Riverbend, one of the finest modern housing estates in New York (on Fifth Avenue, between 138th and 142nd Streets: 1967); and the Harlem School of the Arts (645 St Nicholas Avenue, on 141st Street: 1977).

Churches

The most interesting of Harlem's older buildings are the numerous churches, including the Church of St Thomas the Apostle (1907), at 260 West 118th Street; St Martin's Episcopal Church (1888), at the corner of 122nd Street and Lenox Avenue; the Bethel Gospel Pentecostal Assembly (1889), at 36 West 123rd Street, a fine neo-Romanesque church which was formerly occupied by the Harlem Club; and the Ephesus Seventh Day

Adventist Church (1887), at 267 Lenox Avenue, originally a Dutch Reformed church.

One church particularly worth seeing is All Saints (1894), at the corner of Madison Avenue and 129th Street, which was designed by James Renwick, architect of the Grace Church and St Patrick's Cathedral. Perhaps the best known of all Harlem's churches, however, is the Abyssinian Baptist Church, at 132 West 138th Street, in which Adam Clayton Powell and his son of the same name (who was also a member of Congress) preached their fiery sermons.

The Williams Christian Methodist Episcopal Church (2225 Seventh Avenue, between 131st and 132nd Streets) is of interest only because it has taken over the Lafayette Theater, which was the best known black theatre between 1910 and 1940.

A black Jewish congregation, the Ethiopian Hebrew Congregation, meets in a 90-year-old neo-Renaissance mansion at 1 West 123rd Street.

Synagogue

The Dance Theater of Harlem, directed by Arthur Mitchell, occupies a former garage at 466 West 152nd Street, converted for the purpose in 1971.

Dance Theater of Harlem

The old Lenox Casino at 102 West 116th Street became in 1965 Muhammad's Temple of Islam. Following a split in this black sect it is now the Malcolm Shabazz Mosque No. 7.

Malcolm Shabazz Mosque No. 7

Harlem possesses two apartment blocks which are among the finest in the whole of New York. They lie on 138th and 139th Streets, between Adam C. Powell Jr Boulevard and Seventh Avenue, and are known as Strivers' Row. These well-preserved and partly restored blocks were built in 1891 by four firms of architects for a contractor who set out to show that good and roomy houses could be built at a reasonable price.

Strivers' Row

The famous Apollo Theater at 253 West 125th Street, one of New York's great temples of jazz in which many black musicians performed, was converted into a cinema in the early 1970s and in 1976 was finally closed. This marked the end of an era in Harlem show business, which had begun to flourish so remarkably in the twenties and thirties. In 1984 it was rebuilt and is now open again on some weekday evenings for "live" shows. The Apollo was opened in 1913, but no blacks were admitted until 1934. Among the galaxy of stars who performed here in the next 40 years were Bessie Smith, Billie Holiday, Huddie Ledbetter, Duke Ellington, Count Basie, Dizzie Gillespie, Thelonius Monk and Aretha Franklin.

Apollo Theater

Hayden Planetarium

See American Museum of Natural History

Hispanic Society of America Museum

The museum and its library are devoted to the cultures of the Spanish-speaking peoples from prehistoric times to the present day. The pictures include works by El Greco, Velázquez and Goya, and there is a rich collection of applied art and crafts, including pottery, tiles, ironwork and silver.

Situation
Broadway and
155th Street

A statue of Don Quixote stands in front of the entrance.

Opening times: Tues.–Sat. 10am–4.30pm; Sun. 1–4pm; admission fee.

Subway stations
157th Street (lines
1, 9), 155th Street
(line C)

69

IBM Gallery of Science and Art   E 6

Location
Madison Avenue
and 56th Street

Subway Station
53rd Street
(lines E, F)

This gallery, opened in 1984 in the IBM skyscraper, has in the short time that it has been in existence acquired a good reputation through excellent temporary exhibitions of old, modern and popular art and photography. The exhibition rooms, situated in the basement of the building, are among the best organised in New York.

Opening times: Tues.–Fri. 11am–6pm; Sat. 10am–5pm

International Center of Photography   E 3

Address: 1130
Fifth Avenue,
(94th Street)

Subway station
96th Street (line 6)

Buses
1, 2, 3, 4, 19

Opening times
Tues. noon–8pm,
Wed.–Sun.
11am–6pm

The only museum which is exclusively dedicated to photography, has from its inception had exceptionally interesting exhibitions, of which several are running at any one time, and gradually its own stock has been built up.

Aesthetic photography is displayed alongside photographs making a statement; the main accent is on the work of living photographers. Associated with the ICP is a school of photography offering courses and events. There is no charge for admission after 5pm on Tuesdays.

In 1989 the ICP opened a gallery in 1133th Avenue of the Americas, known as "ICP Midtown" because of its location, with four times the exhibition area of the "ICP Uptown". Several exhibitions are always being held simultaneously here making an effective contribution to the photographic departments of the major New York museums and galleries (open: Tues., Wed., Fri.–Sun. 11am–6pm, Thur. 11am–8pm).

Jacob K. Javits Convention Center

70

Jacob K. Javits Convention Center   B/C 7

This congress centre, opened in 1986, is the third largest in the USA (after Chicago and Las Vegas). With an area of almost 80,000 sq.m (95,680 sq.yd), it has replaced the Coliseum at Columbia Circle.

Location
11th Avenue,
between 34th and
38th Streets

The centre was designed by the architects I. W. Pei and James Ingo Freed, and is unlike other buildings of its type with its gigantic glass walls in which the New York skyline is reflected by day and which make the illuminated building appear transparent by night.

Bus
34, 42

The centre with building costs of 486 million dollars has a total surface area of about 80,000sq.m (95,680sq.yd), the largest exhibition hall measuring about 38,000sq.m (45,448sq.yd) with an average height of 11 metres (36ft). Six conventions and 100 meetings can take place at the same time. The entrance, the "Crystal Palace Lobby", 50m (164ft) high is particularly impressive. The building, which is named after the late New York senator Jacob K. Javits, is situated in an area at present undeveloped between 11th and 12th Avenues and 34th and 18th Streets; other buildings will probably be erected here, including a residential block.

Subway stations
34th or 42nd
Street
(lines A, E)
then bus

Jacques Marchais Center of Tibetan Art

This collection of Tibetan art, the largest in the West, is difficult to get to but is well worth the trouble for anyone with interests in this field. Assembled by a woman art dealer of New York, it is housed in a building modelled on a Tibetan monastery.

Address
338 Lighthouse
Avenue, Staten
Island

In addition to Tibetan art, which constitutes the main part of the collection, there are also examples of Chinese, Japanese, Korean, South-East Asian, Indian and Persian art.

Boat
Staten Island ferry
from Battery Park
and bus

Opening times are: Apr.–Nov.: Wed.–Sun. 1–5pm. Admission fee.

Japan Society Gallery   G 6

The Japan Society was founded in 1907 to promote better relations between the two countries.

Address
333 East 47th
Street

This gallery puts on special exhibitions periodically of Japanese art of high quality.

Subway station
51st Street (line 6)

The building, designed in Japanese style, also contains a theatre in which there are frequent showings of Japanese films and occasional lectures.

Buses
15, 27, 101, 102

The gallery is open daily except Mon. from 11am–5pm, Fri. until 6.30pm (admission fee).

Jewish Museum   E 3

This museum, run by the Jewish Theological Seminary of America, was founded in 1904 and has been housed since the end of the Forties in the former mansion which belonged to the banker Felix M. Warburg. The modern annexe, opened in 1962, was demolished in 1993 and the museum extended in the neo-Gothic style of the mansion. At the end of 1993 the newly refurbished museum was opened and with a collection of about 27,000 Judaic exhibits is the largest and most important Jewish museum in the United States.

Address
1109 Fifth Avenue
(92nd Street)

Subway station
96th Street (line 6)

Buses
1, 2, 3, 4

The museum has the world's largest collection of Jewish material, in particular cult objects from synagogues and Jewish establishments in many countries, including Torah scrolls with their gold and silver plates,

Sabbath candlesticks, Kiddush cups and jewellery, etc., belonging to the Harry G. Friedman Collection.

The museum also contains the Benguiat Collection, which includes material ranging in date from medieval to modern times. There are regular special exhibitions of Jewish art and displays on various Jewish themes.

★Lincoln Center for the Performing Arts   C 5

Situation
Broadway,
between 61st and
66th Streets

Subway stations
66th Street
(lines 1, 9)

Buses
5, 7, 11, 66, 104

Conducted tours
Daily 10am–5pm
Information: tel.
811 1800 ext. 512

New York's vast cultural centre for the performing arts with events including theatre, opera, ballet and concerts developed mainly in the Sixties under the direction of W. K. Harrison.

The construction of the Lincoln Center has not only transformed a whole district of New York but has also provided a model and a stimulus for many other American cities which have developed similar projects.

Building began in the 1950s, the cost (165 million dollars) being met from private sources; the only financial contribution by public authorities was towards the purchase of the site. The individual buildings were designed by different architects, but their neo-Classical exterior elevations give them a considerable degree of unity. The material used in all the buildings was Italian travertine, which is resistant to the effects of dust and pollution and does not become discoloured.

The artistic decor of the the cultural centre was of great importance to the builders and architects so that it merits a visit not only for the cultural events and architecture but also to see the works of famous artists.

Information
Center

Details about all the activities in the Lincoln Center are available from the information centre on the lower floor of the entrance to the Metropolitan Opera.

Lincoln Center
Plaza

The central point of the complex is the Plaza, which opens out onto Columbus Avenue (in the middle is a dark marble fountain by Philip Johnson), around which the three main buildings and several smaller ones are grouped. During the month of August performances of street theatre and other displays take place for which there is usually no charge.

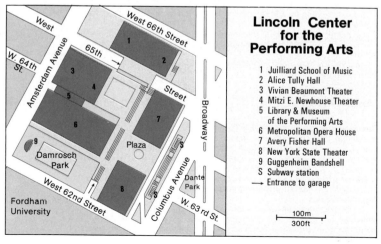

Lincoln Center for the Performing Arts

1 Juilliard School of Music
2 Alice Tully Hall
3 Vivian Beaumont Theater
4 Mitzi E. Newhouse Theater
5 Library & Museum
  of the Performing Arts
6 Metropolitan Opera House
7 Avery Fisher Hall
8 New York State Theater
9 Guggenheim Bandshell
S Subway station
→ Entrance to garage

100m
300ft

Lincoln Center: Metropolitan Opera

The Avery Fisher Hall, formerly known as the Philharmonic Hall, was the first of the buildings to be finished in 1962. It stands on the north side of the Plaza and was designed by M. Abramovitz in the style of an ancient Greek temple as the home of the New York Philharmonic Orchestra. The concert hall, which has seating for 2800 and an organ with 5500 pipes, has undergone alterations over the years to improve the acoustics and was completely refitted in 1976, since when it has been named after its patron who donated vast amounts of money for the renovations. In the lobby is a metal sculpture entitled "Orpheus and Apollo" by Richard Lippold weighing five tons.

Avery Fisher Hall

As well as the New York Philharmonic Orchestra, who play from mid-May to mid-September, famous national and international orchestras and soloists perform in the concert hall. The Philharmonic Orchestra also perform concerts in the parks during the summer (see Practical Information, Music).

Opposite the Avery Fisher Hall is the New York State Theatre (by P. Johnson and R. Foster, 1964), home of the New York City Opera Company and the New York Ballet. The foyer of the theatre contains a bust of Mahler by Rodin, a Beethoven mask by Bourdelle and two large statues of females by Elie Nadelmann (see Practical Information, Music).

New York State Theater

On the west side of the Plaza is the main building of the Lincoln Center, the "Met", one of the world's leading opera houses. Built in 1966 by W. K. Harrison the building is impressive with its high arcaded portico and the two large murals "Les Sources de la Musique" and "Le Triomphe de la Musique" by Marc Chagall in the foyer. The auditorium seats 3800 spectators; Germany contributed to the stage technology and the large crystal chandeliers are Austrian. In the covered walks hang portraits of famous singers who have appeared at the "Met" (see Practical Information, Music).

Metropolitan Opera House

Tours
Mon.–Fri. 3.45pm,
Sat. 10.30am
(booking
recommended)
tel. 582 3512
(admission fee)

73

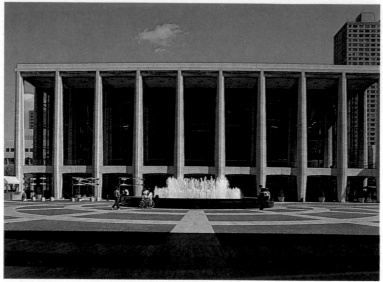

Lincoln Center: The New York State Theater

Damrosch Park

Behind the Metropolitan Opera House is Damrosch Park with the Guggen-heim bandstand where concerts are held during the summer.

Vivian Beaumont Theater

On the west side of the Avery Fisher Hall another courtyard opens out with a large square pond in the middle of which is Henry Moore's six ton bronze sculpture "Reclining Figure".

On the opposite side of the square is the Vivian Beaumont Theater, designed by Eero Saarinen, probably the finest theatre in New York. Nowadays very popular (1140 seats) but after its opening in 1968 it had an unhappy history and was even closed for eight years until it reopened in 1986 under new management. The adjoining Mitzi E. Newhouse stage with 300 seats (see Practical Information, Theatres) is also very successful.

Library & Museum of the Performing Arts

This narrow building by Skidmore, Owings and Merill from 1965 stands between the Metropolitan Opera House and the Vivian Beaumont Theater. The museum has archives on the history of theatre, film, dance and music, including a recordings collection. Also part of the lending and media library, a branch of the New York Public Library (see entry), is the Bruno Walter Auditorium, named after the German conductor, where free concerts, exhibitions, lectures, poetry readings and film shows are held. Guided tours take place on Thursdays at 11am.

Juiliard School of Music and Alice Tully Hall

To the north of West 65th St. New York's leading conservatory is housed in a building designed by P. Belluschi in 1968, which together with a modern opera theatre, lecture halls and practice rooms also houses the Alice Tully Hall for chamber music and solo concerts. The New York Film Festival takes place here annually in early autumn.

Street café in Little Italy

Little Italy   E/F 10

Immediately north-west of Chinatown (see entry) is another of New York's
smaller ethnic enclaves, Little Italy, now increasingly losing its identity as a
result of the northward movement of the Chinese population.

Little Italy, bounded on the south by Canal Street, on the north by Houston
Street, on the west by Lafayette Street and on the east by the Bowery, is
now mainly occupied by the older Italian American population, since the
younger generation has followed the general outward movement to the
suburbs. The main N–S streets in Little Italy are Mulberry and Mott Streets,
the main E–W streets Grand and Broome Streets.

In Mulberry Street are many Italian restaurants (one of the best known
being Paolucci, No. 149, in a building dating from 1816) and Italian-style
cafés (the best known of which is Ferrara, established 1892, at 195 Grand
Street, around the corner from Mulberry Street). There are also numerous
Italian shops and men's clubs in Little Italy. The former police headquarters
at 240 Centre Street, a building in the style of a French town hall erected in
1909, has been turned into a luxury residence which in time could possibly
change the area.

The most interesting time to visit Little Italy is during the second week in
September, when there are celebrations for the feast of St Januarius, who
is regarded as the patron saint of the quarter (see Practical Information,
Events). During this week more than 300 stalls selling a variety of goods
and refreshments are set up along both sides of Mulberry Street and the
other streets of Little Italy.

Location
North-west of
Chinatown
("downtown")

Subway stations
Spring Street
(line 6)
or Prince Street
(line N, R)

Lower East Side   F/G 9

Location
Between First
Avenue and East
River
("downtown")

Subway station
Delancey Street
(line F)

Bus 9

One of the more cosmopolitan of Manhattan's ethnic enclaves is Lower East Side, an immense huddle of the apartment blocks in which the great waves of immigrants between 1880 and 1914 found some kind of living accommodation.

In contrast to Harlem (see entry), which was originally a good residential district, Lower East Side was built to house the poorer classes of the population, and apart from one or two modern apartment blocks has retained its original character. At the beginning of the 20th c. this was a purely Jewish area, as witness its 500 or so synagogues and schools, only a few of which still serve their original purpose.

Later the Chinese moved into Lower East Side as they did into Little Italy (see entry), coming from Chatham Square by way of East Broadway; and a new wave of Spanish-speaking immigrants from Puerto Rico and Central and South America moved in from the east. As a result the area has lost the clear identity which it formerly possessed.

The Jewish element is still strongest in Hester, Essex and Rivington Streets and above all in Orchard Street, where there are large numbers of fashion, shoe, fur and other shops, many of them displaying and selling their wares on the street.

The area is at its busiest on Sundays (the Jewish shops being closed on Saturdays), with something of the atmosphere of a North African or Near Eastern bazaar. Since prices are low and quality is remarkably high, the Orchard Street shops are patronised by many people from "uptown".

Lower East Side
Tenement
Museum

The museum at 97 Orchard Street documents the history of the immigrants from the end of the 19th c. to the beginning of the 20th c. (open: Tues.–Fri. 11am–4pm, Sun. 10am–4pm).

East Village

See Greenwich Village.

★★Metropolitan Museum of Art   D/E 4

Situation
Fifth Avenue and
82nd Street

Subway station
86th Street
(lines 4, 5, 6)

Buses
1, 2, 3, 4, 18, 79

Opening times
Sun., Tues.–Thur.
9.30am–5.15pm,
Fri., Sat.
9.30am–8.45pm

Admission fee
Discretionary

Note
Some galleries
may be closed
owing to staff
shortages

The Metropolitan Museum of Art – America's largest museum of art and the third largest in the world, only the British Museum and the Hermitage in Leningrad being larger – was founded in 1870 on the private initiative of a group of New York citizens who believed that their city, with a population then approaching a million, ought to have an art museum of its own. The museum's first home was on West 14th Street, in those days the city centre; soon afterwards it moved to a mansion on Lower Fifth Avenue; and finally the city set aside a site on the E side of the newly created Central Park (see entry) for the building of a new museum. In 1880 Calvert Vaux, who was closely involved in the planning of Central Park, erected a red-brick building which is now visible only from Central Park. The present main building on Fifth Avenue was opened in 1902, the central range being designed by Richard Morris Hunt and Richard Howland Hunt (father and son), the two side wings by McKim, Mead and White. Apart from a number of minor alterations there was no further extension of the building until 1965, when the Thomas J. Watson Library was opened, followed by the Robert Lehman Pavilion (1975), the Sackler Wing, housing the Temple of Dendur (1978), the American Wing (1980), the Michael C. Rockefeller Wing (1982) and the Lila Acheson Wallace Wing (1987).

Although the Museum will have more than 300 galleries when the present building programme is complete, it will still be unable to display more than a quarter of its holdings, which increase more rapidly (mainly by gifts) than the space available to show them. Moreover the increasing number of special exhibitions mounted by the "Met" make ever greater demands on

Metropolitan Museum of Art

display space at the expense of the permanent collection. The Museum's total stock amounts to 3,300,000 items, and even the 100,000 items that are normally on display are far more than any visitor can take in even on repeated visits. The best plan, therefore, is to be selective: make sure that you see what really interests you, and be content with a general impression of the rest.

The museum has many services to offer the visitor: **Museum services**

Parties by prior arrangement (tel. 570 3711); individual visitors should enquire at the "Walking Tour Kiosk" in the entrance hall (tel. 879 5500) where cassette recorders are available for hire.
  Brochures in different languages are on the information stand in the entrance hall.
  For the disabled there is a wheelchair hire service from the cloakrooms; the upper floor can be reached by escalators and lifts. There are also special tours for the visually handicapped (tel. 879 5500) and for the deaf (tel. 879 0421).
  Photography is allowed without tripods and flash lights; permission is necessary for special exhibitions. Video cameras are not allowed.

Main Floor

Going up the broad flight of steps in front of the Museum (on which hundreds of people are glad to rest and enjoy the sunshine during the summer months), we enter the large entrance hall, in which are an information desk, a large museum shop selling reproductions, gifts and books (perhaps the largest selection of art books in New York), cloakrooms (coat check), the ticket office (suggested voluntary admission fee) and a desk at which recorded "Autoguides" can be hired.

Main entrance of the Metropolitan Museum of Art

Together with the main art collections there are a cafeteria and a restaurant on the ground floor. The Thomas J. Watson Library is the largest art library in the USA.

There are frequent concerts and recitals in the Grace Rainey Rogers Auditorium, which is also on the Main Floor (for information tel. 570 3949).

Egyptian Art

The Egyptian collection, one of the largest of its kind in the world, has been substantially enriched by expeditions organised by the Museum in 1930–36 and by the purchase of important private collections. The Temple of Dendur, which was removed from its original site during the construction of the Aswan Dam, was presented by Egypt to the United States and assigned by the US government to the Metropolitan Museum where it has been rebuilt in its original form in a specially constructed glass extension.

From the period of the Old Kingdom (3rd–6th dynasty, 2600–2160 B.C. the mastaba of the chamberlain Pernebi and the tomb chapel of Prince Rauemkai (5th dynasty) are on show. The Middle Kingdom (11th and 12th dynasty, 2040–1785 B.C.) is represented by material from tombs and painted stelae from excavations at Thebes. The showpiece of the New Kingdom (18th–20th dynasties, 1552–1070 B.C.) is a helmeted head of Rameses II together with 14 statues of King Hatschepsut from the temple at Dêr el-Bahri/Thebes, a bust of the eldest Echnaton daughter Meryetaten, a head of Tutenkhamun as a boy and a seated figure of General Haremhab. The figure of the falcon god Horus and the Metternich stele date from the period of the last dynasties. Also of interest in this department are the portraits of the mummies (painted wooden panels from the oasis at Fayyum, 2nd c. B.C.), a facsimile document on tomb and temple painting and art from the period of Greek and Roman rule.

Gold Room

The main attraction of this small room is the treasure of Illâhun, gold jewellery and cosmetic utensils decorated in precious stones belonging to

Temple of Dendur

Princess Sit-Hathor-Junut (about 1900 B.C.) and gold head jewellery belonging to three ladies of Thuthomis III's harem. There is also ivory, scarabs and glass.

The collection of Greek and Roman art dates back to the 3rd millennium B.C. with a series of Cycladic idols. The oldest part of the museum collection are Cypriot vases, terracottas, reliefs and jewellery, brought back by the first director of the museum, Count Luigi Palma de Cesnola. The Minoan culture of Crete is represented by finds from the palace of Knossos. Also from Ancient Greece are a jug with a spout from Mycenae (c. 1200–1125 B.C.), kuroi and tomb stelae ("Boys and Girls", 6th c. B.C.). **Greek and Roman Art**

Classical Greece is mainly represented by Roman copies of Hellenistic sculpture including "Wounded Man" and an "Amazon" based on originals by Kresila and a statue of Aphrodite by Praxiteles. A grave relief "Girl with Two Doves" is probably from the island of Paros. Along with late-Roman portrait sculpture and sarcophagi ("Badminton Sarcophagi", c. 220–230 A.D.) there are wall paintings from a villa in Boscoreale which was buried by the eruption of Vesuvius in 79 A.D. which show the complete decoration of a bedroom.

The exhibition is continued on the second floor with ancient bronze mirrors (6th c. B.C.), a Corinthian bust of a woman's head, possibly a sphinx (about 500 B.C.), Attic ceramics from the 5th and 8th c. including painted amphorae and the Euphronius crater, Corinthian and Hellenistic ceramics, a bronze figure of Eros sleeping and a golden sacrificial bowl. From the Etruscan-Roman period there are interesting bronze relief panels from an Etruscan hearse from the 6th c. B.C. and a bronze Roman boy's head from the 1st c. A.D.

The museum's collection of medieval art occupies five galleries and is supplemented by the material displayed in the associated museum at the Cloisters (see entry) at the northern tip of Manhattan. **Medieval Art**

79

Metropolitan Museum of Art

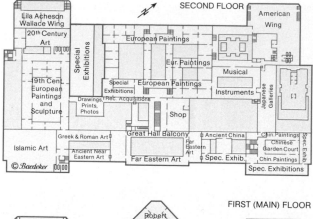

SECOND FLOOR

Lila Acheson Wallace Wing
20th Century Art
Special Exhibitions
European Paintings
Eur. Paintings
American Wing
Musical Instruments
Japanese Galleries
19th Cent. European Paintings and Sculpture
Special Exhibitions
European Paintings
Drawings, Prints, Photos
Rec. Acquisitions
Shop
Islamic Art
Greek & Roman Art
Ancient Near Eastern Art
Great Hall Balcony
Far Eastern Art
Ancient China
Chin. Paintings
Chinese Garden Court
Spec. Exhib.
Far Eastern Art
Spec. Exhib.
Chin. Paintings
Spec. Exhibitions
© Baedeker

FIRST (MAIN) FLOOR

Robert Lehman Collection
American Wing
Lila Acheson Wallace Wing 20th Century Art
Europ. Sculpture Court and Decor. Arts
French Period Rooms
English Period Rooms
American Wing Garden Court
Michael C. Rockefeller Wing Art of Africa, the Americas and Pacific Islands
Europ. Sculpture and Decor. Arts
Medieval Art
Europ. Sculpture and Decor. Arts
Audio
16th Cent. Span. Patio
Library
Shop
Member-ship
G.R. Rogers Audit.
Sackler Wing: Temple of Dendur
Restaurant
Greek and Roman Art
Shop
Great (i) Hall
Audio
Egyptian Art
Egyptian Art
Main Entrance: Fifth Avenue & 82nd Street
© Baedeker

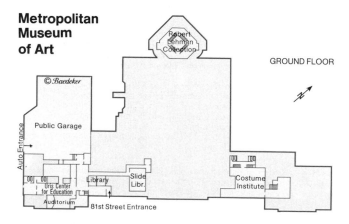

Metropolitan Museum of Art

Robert Lehman Collection

GROUND FLOOR

© Baedeker

Public Garage

Auto Entrance

Uris Center for Education
Library
Slide Libr.
Costume Institute
Auditorium
81st Street Entrance

Dating from the early-Christian period are marble reliefs, bronze lamps, pyxides, "Barbarian" gold clasps and belt buckles from the 4th c. The collection of Byzantine art contains the marble bust of a woman, a marble head of Emperor Constantine (4th c.), enamel and ivory work and gold necklaces. Also Cypriot silver plates (6th c.) and the "Albanian Treasure" (gold, siver).

The entrance to the sculpture gallery is formed by rood screens from the cathedral at Valladolid (Spain). Interesting exhibits are statues and reliefs from the altar of the cathedral at Pisa, the head of King David (12th c.) from the St Anne's doorway of Notre-Dame in Paris, "Pietà" and "The Mourning of Christ" (early 16th c.) from Biron château (France). `Sculpture Gallery`

The tour continues past a Romanesque marble doorway from the abbey church at Sangemini (Umbria), a 12th c. processional cross from northern Spain, Gothic church windows with stained glass from the Paris abbey of St Germain-des-Prés, sacral ivory, metal and enamel work from France (14/15th c.) to the large tapestry gallery which contains valuable pieces from Germany, France and Flanders ("Annunciation", "Rose", "Trojan Wars", "Baptism", all 15th c.) and English embroidery. `Tapestry Gallery`

The main attraction of this department is the Blumenthal Patio, a marble patio from a Spanish castle Vélez Blanco (early 16th c.) with a fountain from the Donatello school, which stood in the garden of the Palazzo Pazzi in Florence. There are more than 20 rooms from European palaces and mansions: the study from the ducal palace of Gubbio (Umbria, about 1480), Elizabethan room from Yarmouth (17th c.), Swiss room from Films (17th c.), bedroom from the Venetian palace of Sagredo (early 18th c.), carved wooden staircase from Cassiobury Park in Hertfordshire (1677–80), salon from Kirlington Park in Oxfordshire (1748), wallpapered room from Croome Court in Worcestershire (about 1760), dining room from Landsdowne House (1768), carved wooden shop front with Sèvres porcelain from the Ile Saint Louis in Paris (about 1775), Rococo salon from the Hôtel de Varengeville 1735), salon from the Viennese Baroque palace at Paar with a Savonnerie carpet from Louis XIV's Louvre gallery. The exhibition is continued on the lower floor with 17th and 18th c. sculpture, stucco reliefs by Clodion, sculptures, majolica from Spain and Italy, including the "Mourning of Christ", one of the oldest majolica sculptures from Faenza (1487), a porcelain collection with pieces from Meissen, French faïences, silver, clocks and ornaments. `European Sculpture and Decorative Arts, English Rooms, French Rooms`

The museum owns the largest collection of this kind in the United States. Highlight of the newly (1991) refurbished rooms is the Equestrian Court where knights on horseback and weapons (14th to 18th c.) can be seen from Germany (Nürnberg, Augsburg), Italy, Spain, France and England. The adjoining rooms contain helmets, among them a 6th c. Frankish helmet and an Italian lionhead helmet (c. 1460), and other weapons from the most famous European armourers, in particular those in Toledo; all kinds of weapons including 10th c. Viking swords, a show dagger from 1606 and the crossbow belonging to the Hungarian king Mathias I Corvinus from 1489. `Arms and Armour`

As a condition of acquiring the private art collection assembled by the banker Robert Lehman (the value of which was estimated at 100 million dollars when it was presented to the Museum some ten years ago) the Met undertook to erect a special building to house it; and an excellently contrived annexe was built for this purpose by Kevin Roche and John Dinkeloo, the architects responsible for the other recent extensions to the Museum. `Robert Lehman Collection`

The collection is displayed in seven rooms modelled on those in the former Lehman mansion on West 54th Street and in a number of other galleries laid out round a glass-roofed courtyard. It includes 300 pictures, over 1000 drawings and numerous other items, and enjoys a virtual independent existence within the Museum, with its own keeper, who is solely responsible for the special exhibitions put on here.

Of particular interest are: almost 1000 drawings (on the ground floor), by artists such as Leonardo da Vinci, Pollaiulo, Pisanello, Tintoretto, Dürer, Ingres, Cézanne, Signac, Matisse, Degas and Modigliani. Early Italian painting is particularly well represented with Buoninsegna ("Crucifixion"), Ugolino da Siena, Lippo Vanni, Sassetta ("St Anthony in the Wilderness"), Giovanni di Paolo ("Expulsion from Paradise"), Bartolo di Fredi, Botticelli ("Annunciation"), Francesco del Cossa, Crivelli and Ucello. Also Hans Meming ("Young Man", "Annunciation"), Lucas Cranach the Elder, Hans Holbein the Younger ("Erasmus"), Simon Marmion, Gerard David, Petrus Christus ("St Eligius the Goldsmith"), Elgreco ("St Jerome"), Rembrandt ("Gerard de Lairesse"), Goya ("Countess Altamira"), Utrillo, Ingres ("Princesse de Brogilie"), van Gogh, Gauguin, Matisse, Dérain, Vlaminck, Braque, Seurat, Vuillat, Corot, Dupré. Finally an illuminated page by J. Fouquet from the book of hours by Etienne Chevalier deserves special mention.

American Wing

The American Wing (opened 1980), which covers all aspects of American fine art and applied art, can be reached by way of the Arms and Armour hall of the Temple of Dendur. Of its 63 galleries 40 are on the Main Floor and the rest are on the Second Floor.

In the centre of this wing is the glass-roofed Engelhard Court, around which have been re-erected the façade (1822–24) of the old United States Bank in Wall Street, a loggia from the villa of Louis Comfort Tiffany with its famous Art Nouveau stained glass, and a staircase (designed by the well-known architect Louis Sullivan) from the old Stock Exhange in Chicago.

Other features of particular interest are furnished rooms from different parts of the USA (from top to bottom) in almost chronological order including the living room from Thomas Hart House in Ipswich (Massachusetts, about 1700), rooms from John Wentworth House in Portsmouth (New Hampshire, about 1700), Powel Room from the mayor of Philadelphia's house (end of colonial period), meeting room from Gadsby's Tavern in Alexandria (Virginia, 1793) and the entrance hall from Van Rensselaer House in Albany (New York, 1765–68). The department is completed by the Phyfe Gallery with furniture and decorative art and everyday objects from the 17th to the 19th c.

American Paintings and Sculpture

Of the 1000 or more paintings and sculptures by American artists in the American Wing only a few have been singled out: J. S. Copley "Midshipman August Brine" (1782), B. West "The Battle of La Hogue", J. Peale "Still Life: Balsam Apple and Vegetables" (about 1820), R. Peale "Still Life with Cake" (1818), E. Hicks "The Falls of Niagara", S. F. B. Morse "The Muse" (his daughter), "Washington Crossing the Delaware" by E. G. Leutze; from the Hudson River School, T. Cole "The Oxbow" (1836), A. B. Durand "The Beeches", J. F. Kensett "Lake George", A. Bierstadt "The Rocky Mountains", F. E. Church "Heart of the Andes" (1859), G. Inness "Peace and Plenty" (1865); T. Eakins "Max Schmitt in a Single Scull", A. P. Ryder "Moonlight Marine", J. A. McNeill Whistler "Arrangement in Flesh, Colour and Black" (portrait of Theodore Duret), J. S. Sargent "Madame X" (portrait of Madame Pierre Gautreau), Mary Cassatt "The Cup of Tea" (1879) Winslow Homer-Saal.

Michael C. Rockefeller ("Primitive art")

This newly furnished imposing addition commemorates the son of Nelson Rockefeller, Michael, who was lost in the Pacific some 30 years ago. There are several thousand exhibits from Oceania (Asmat ancestral pillars, New Guinea; Melanesia, Polynesia), Africa (Benin bronzes, Nigeria; wooden figures from Dogon, Bambara, Senufo and Fang) and from pre-Columbian America (stone sculptures from Veracruz, clay figures from Mexico, goldwork from Panama, Costa Rica and Columbia; silverwork, featherwork and textiles from Peru) and craftwork by US American Indians.

This latest addition to the museum dedicated to the art of the 20th c.
extends over three floors and is named after the late Lila Acheson, co-
founder of the "Reader's Digest" and a generous patron of the arts. With
some notable exceptions the collection is confined to works by American
painters – the competition in this period from other museums is great (see
Museum of Modern Art, Whitney Museum of American Art).

Lila Acheson
Wallace Wing
(20th c. art)

Of particular architectural interest is the 9m (29ft) high Gerald Cantor
sculpture garden on the roof with works by Louise Bourgeois, Reuben
Nakian and a huge wooden sculpture by the late Louise Nevelson (d. 1988),
from here there is a unique view of the Manhattan skyline. On permanent
display on the interim floor, which is used to mount photographic exhibi-
tions, is the Paul Klee collection, bequeathed by the Paris art dealer, Heinz
Berggruen, in 1984. Among the famous European artists represented are:
Bonnard "Terrasse à Vernon", Vuillard, Picasso "Portrait of Gertrude Stein"
(1906), Kupka "Plans par verticales" (1912/13), Kandinsky "Improvisation
No. 27" (1912), Klimt; American artists: Weber, Stella "Coney Island",
Hartley "Portrait of a German Officer" (1914), Georgia O'Keeffe "Cow's
Skull: Red, White and Blue", Demuth "I saw the Figure 5 in Gold", Gorky
"Water of the Flowery Mill" (1944), Hopper "The Lighthouse at two Lights"
(1929), Marsh, Bishop, Shahn, Wyeth "A Crow Flew By", Pollock "Autumn
Rhythm" (1950), De Kooning "Easter Monday", Rothko, Gottlieb, Kline,
Kelly, Newman, M. Louis "Alpha-Pi", Noland, Motherwell among others.
German immigrant painters include George Grosz, Joseph Albers and
Hans Hofmann.

As well as paintings and sculpture (David Smith, Marisol) there are vases
by Gallé, glass and jewellery by Lalique, Tiffany lamps; furniture by
Bugatti.

Second Floor

On the second floor the collections of Greek and Roman art, the American
Wing and Lila Acheson Wallace Wing are continued. The largest area is
devoted to the central feature of the museum, the collection of European
paintings.

The collection of European painting from the 14th to the 18th c. is housed in
34 galleries, arranged in approximate chronological order. The list that
follows contains some of the most important artists and their works.

European Painting

Raphael "Coronation of Madonna with Child and Saints" (1504/05), Titian
"Venus and the Lute Player" (c. 1560) and "Venus and Adonis", Del Sarto
"Holy Family" (1525), Tintoretto "Finding of Moses" (c. 1550), Veronese
"Mars and Venus United by Love" (1576), Bronzino "Young Man", Giotto
"Epiphany", Bonaventura, Gaddi, Giovanni di Paolo "Paradise" (c. 1450)
and "Scenes from the Life of St Catherine of Siena", Botticelli "Last Rights
of St Jerome", Fra Angelico, Carpaccio "Meditation of the Passion" (c.
1450), Bellini, Reni, Caravaggio "Musicians" (1504), Tiepolo "Triumph of
Marius".

Italian Masters

Terbrugghen "Crucifixion" (c. 1620), Frans Hals "Jonker Ramp and his
Sweetheart" (1623) and portraits, Rembrandt "Aristotle Comtemplating a
Bust of Homer", "Self-portrait" (1660) and numerous others, Vermeer van
Delft "Young Woman with a Water Jug" (1664) and "Female Lute Player",
de Hooch, Steen, ter Borch, Van Goyen, De Moljiln, Salomon and Jacob van
Ruysdael.

Dutch Painting

The most important works of 19th c. French painting have been transferred
to the André Meyer Galleries (see below) so that the main remaining works
are: Clouet "Guillaume Budé", Poussin "Rape of the Sabines", de la Tour

French Painting

"Soothsayer", Duplessis "Benjamin Franklin" (1778), Nattier, Boucher "Toilette de Venus", Chardin "Blowing Bubbles", Fragonard and Greuze.

Flemish and German Painting

Jan van Eyck "Crucifixion", "Last Judgment" and two panels of a triptych, van der Weyden, "Christ Appears to his Mother" (c. 1450), Dirk Bouts, Hugo van der Goes, Hans Memling "Tommaso", "Maria Portinari" (1472), "Portrait of an Old Man" and others, Breughel the Elder "Corn Harvest" (1665), Rubens "Venus and Adonis" (1635), van Dyck, Jordaens, Lucas Cranach the Elder "Judgement of Paris" (1528) and "Duke John of Saxony", Dürer "The Virgin and Child with St Anne" (1519), Holbein the Younger "Portrait of a Member of the Wedigh Family".

Spanish Painting

Many of the Flemish and German pictures came from the collection of the New York businessman Benjamin Altman, as did many of the museum's Spanish paintings. These include: El Greco "Grand Inquisitor Cardinal Don Fernando Nino de Guevara" (1598), "View of Toledo" (1604–14) and others, Zurbarán "Battle of Jerez", de Ribera "Holy Family with St Catherine" (1648), Velásquez "Philipp IV", "Duke of Olivares", "Juan de Pareja" and "Christ and the Disciples of Emmaus" (c. 1620), Murillo "Virgin and Child", Goya.

British Painting

Hogarth "The Wedding of Stephen Beckingham and Mary Cox" (1729), Reynolds "Colonel George K. H. Coussmaker" (1782) and "The Honourable Henry Fane", Gainsborough "Mrs Grace Dalrymple Elliott", Lawrence "Elizabeth Farren", Raeburn, Constable "Salisbury Cathedral" (1823), Turner "Canale Grande in Venice" (1835).

André Meyer Galleries
(19th c. European Painting and Sculpture)

These galleries, opened in 1980, display the Museum's collection of 19th c. French art (the boundaries of the period being sufficiently widely drawn to include Jacques-Louis David on the one hand and Henri Rousseau and Bonnard on the other). There are also a number of works by Goya and pictures by Turner, Constable and various minor Italian, German and Russian masters.

The first gallery is devoted to neo-Classical and Romantic art, including David's "Death of Socrates" and several portraits by Ingres. The next gallery ("Origins of the 19th Century") contains ten pictures by Goya (the best known perhaps being "The Two Majas on the Balcony"), major works by Delacroix, Constable and Turner, and a picture by the Swiss woman artist Angelica Kauffmann ("Telenachus and Calypso's Nymphs").

The third gallery is devoted to Courbet; its 22 pictures constitute one of the largest assemblages of his work in the world. Then follows a collection of Salon paintings (i.e. mostly pictures exhibited at the annual Salons of the French Royal Academy).

Three small rooms are occupied by works of the Barbizon school (Millet, Daubigny, Théodore Rousseau, Corot, Daumier). Beyond this is a room containing works by the Symbolists (Puvis de Chavanne, Gustave Moreau, Edward Burne-Jones) and – a little out of place in this company – two portraits by Gustav Klimt.

A long sculpture gallery contains 40 works by Rodin (in bronze, marble, terracotta and plaster) and others by Bourdelle, Maillol and Jules Dalou.

Not surprisingly, the most prominent place is occupied by the Impressionists and Post-Impressionists. Manet is represented by "Femme au perroquet" (1868), "George Moore" (1879) and "En Bateau" (1879) among others, Claude Monet by "Renoulière" (1869), "Cathédrale de Rouen" and "Terrasse à Saint-Adresse" (though they include none of his greatest works). A "Still Life with Flowers and Fruit" by Henri Fantin-Latour. Van Gogh is represented by "Irises" and "L'Arlesienne" while "Le Golfe de Marseille vu de l'Estaque" (1883/85) and "La Montagne Sainte-Victoire" among others illustrate the work of the dominant post-Impressionist Paul Cézanne. There are also pictures by Renoir, Seurat, Signac, Bonnard and two Gauguins ("La Orana Maria", 1891; "Tahitiennes aux Mangos").

Marisol: "The Last Supper"

Returning towards the Rodin gallery, we come to three galleries containing about 100 works by Edgar Degas – one of the largest collections of this artist's work in any museum. They include paintings "Femmes aux Chrysanthèmes", "Repétition" (1878), pastels and sculpture.

In ten galleries adjoining the André Meyer Galleries Islamic art from the 8th to the 19th c. is documented. The exhibits come from Iran, Iraq, Egypt, Turkey, Spain and India. Early Islam is represented by a pair of doors from Samara (8/9th c.), a 9th c. Persian glass container, Abbasidic ceramics including a 10th c. bowl with Kufic ornamental script and Fatimidic carving from the 10th and 11th c. There are ceramics and metalwork from the Seljuk period, a Koran stand from west Turkestan (1360) and a metal bowl inlaid with gold and silver (14th c.). From Persia a tiled prayer niche from Isfahan (1354) and an ornately illuminated manuscript of the Persian national epic "Shah-Nameh" (14th c.), from Egypt a pair of doors from the Mameluk period (13/14th c.) and a glass flask (1320). Numerous carpets from Egypt, the Safavid period in Iran (16th–18th c.), the Osman period in Turkey and from India during the Moghul period (16th–19th c.). In another room the completley furnished living room of an early 18th c. house in Damascus. **Islamic Art**

Although the museum's collection of ancient Near Eastern art is not large it contains a number of choice items from the 6th millennium B.C. to the 7th c. A.D. These include a decorated clay pot from Persia (c. 3100 B.C.), the statuette from Tell Asmar (3rd millennium B.C.), Sumerian scroll seals from the 3rd to the 1st millennia B.C., a stone seated figure of the Gudea of Ur (2100–2000 B.C.), a gold jug (3rd/2nd millennia B.C.) and ivory carving (1900–1800 B.C.) from Anotalia, a copper head from north-west Persia (2nd millennium B.C.), a bronze helmet and gold container from north Persia (c. 1000 B.C.), ivory figures and plates (9th–7th c. B.C.) and bas-reliefs from the palace of Assurbanipal II (9th c. B.C.) in Nimrud, fragments from **Ancient Near Eastern Art** the processional wall in Babylon (6th c. B.C.), gold and silverwork and stucco relief from Ktesiphon (3rd/4th c. A.D.).

Far Eastern Art

The museum has a considerable collection of Far Eastern art amounting to more than 30,000 items. Art from China takes up much of the space with ceramics, porcelain, bronze, jade and enamelwork, sculptures (including a 4m (13ft) high Bodhisattva) and paintings (giant Buddhist wall paintings) from Shansi province.

The Japanese material from the Harry C. Packard Collection includes picture scrolls, sculptures, ceramics and lacquer-work from Neolithic times to the 20th c. In addition there are Indian sculptures and Buddhist objects from Tibet, Nepal, Kashmir, Korea, Cambodia and Central Asia.

Drawings, Prints and Photographs

These include drawings and works by Carpaccio, Leonardo da Vinci, Raphael, Titian, Veronese, Michelangelo, Dürer, Rubens, Rembrandt, Tiepolo, Canaletto, Watteau, Boucher, Fragonard, Gainsborough, Hogarth, Rowlandson, Turner, Goya, Ingres, Daumier, Seurat, Degas, Matisse, and American artists such as Homer, Eakins, Sargent and Demuth.

Mention should also be made of wood-cuts by Cranach and Goya, copper engravings by Pollaiulo and Rembrandt, and other works by Toulouse-Lautrec, Bonnard, Picasso, Vuillard, T. A. Steinlen and Will Bradley, graphics by Picasso and advertising graphics.

Art photography by Alfred Stieglitz, Margaret Cameron, Adolphe Braun and Thomas Eakins among others.

Musical Instruments

The greater part of the Museum's collection of musical instruments was the result of a bequest of 3000 instruments from all parts of the world which were left to it by a New York banker's widow at the beginning of the 20th c. This has been supplemented by another 1000 items acquired since then.

From time to time the museum puts on recitals of early music played on instruments of the period.

It is worth hiring "telesonic" headphones which reproduce the sound of the instruments and provide an explanation on understanding them. Among the wind instruments are a French ivory hunting horn (c. 1700), a south German porcelain flute (c. 1760) and a sarrusophone, a kind of oboe. Among the keyboard instruments are a Venetian spinet (1540), a double virginal from Antwerp (1581), a golden cembalo from Italy (mid-17th c.), the first pianoforte (by B. Crisofori, Florence 1720) and an English Erard grand piano from 1840. The collection of stringed instrument consists of three Stradivarius violins, among them "Francesca" (1694) and "Antonio" (1721). Exotic instruments: Arabic kettle drums, Far Eastern gongs, African horns and sitars from India.

Costume Institute

In the basement is the Costume Institute which possesses a large collection of clothes from which there are temporary exhibitions, ladies and men's clothing and accessories from the 17th to the 20th c., theatrical and film costumes (Hollywood) and folk costumes from all over the world.

Uris Center for Education and Slide Library

Also housed in the basement this institution is intended to introduce visitors, especially young people, to the treasures of the museum and to art in general.

The information kiosk in the entrance hall has details on the use of the Slide Library.

Morris Jumel Mansion

Situation
160th Street and
Edgecombe
Avenue

This historic mansion on the northern outskirts of Harlem (see entry) is one of the oldest buildings still standing in Manhattan. It was built by Roger Morris in 1765 and was used by Washington as his headquarters after the American forces withdrew to New York in face of the British advance.

In 1883 Aaron Burr, vice-president from 1801 to 1804, was married here. After shooting his opponent Hamilton in a duel in 1804 he was despised in politics (see Trinity Church).

The house contains interesting 18th and 19th c. American furniture and pictures, drawings, silver, china and glass dating from the early days of the United States.

Subway stations
163rd Street
(line C),
157th Street
(line 1)

Opening times
Tues.–Sun.
10am–4pm

El Museo del Barrio   E 2

This museum, founded in 1969, is the only one in the United States exclusively devoted to Puerto Rican and Latin American art. The collection, which is steadily growing, is supplemented by exhibitions of pictures, sculpture and photographs.

The Museum is open Wed.–Sun. 11am–5pm.

Address
1230 Fifth Avenue

Subway station
103rd Street
(line 6)

Museum of African Art   E 7

The Center for African Art which has existed for several years became a small museum in 1992. Each year it puts on numerous exhibitions on African art and publishes a catalogue of outstanding quality.

The adjoining shop sells African crafts and literature on the art history of African artists and styles (open: Wed., Thur., Sun. 11am–6pm; Fri., Sat. 11am–8pm).

Address
593 Broadway

Subway station
Prince St.
(line N, R)

Buses
1 (Mon.–Fri.), 6

Museum of American Financial History   E 11

The Museum of American Financial History in Wall Street (see entry) is for the visitor interested in the history of the Stock Exchange. For over 30 years John E. Herzog collected exhibits on the financial history of the United States and in 1994 they finally received their own museum.

Since then the collection has been enriched by numerous donations and loans from various Wall Street companies as well as from the New York and American Stock Exchange.

Address
24 Wall Street

Subway station
Wall Street
(line 4, 5)

Buses
1 (Mon.–Fri.), 6

Museum of American Folk Art   C 5

The Museum's collection of predominantly American Folk Art – including textiles, patchwork quilts and figures of Indians used as tobacconists' signs as well as pictures and sculpture from colonial times to the present day – is displayed in a series of special exhibitions devoted to particular subjects or themes which have attracted considerable interest by their originality.
   Since moving to new premises it has increased its exhibition space and an interesting museum shop with American craftwork has been added. The final move to 53rd Street West is planned for 1992, the same block upon which the Museum of Modern Art (see entry) and the American Craft Museum (see entry) are located.
   Opening times: Tues.–Sun. 11.30am–7.30pm.

Address
61 West 62nd
Street

Subway station
66th Street
(lines 1, 9)

Buses
5, 7, 11, 104

Museum of the American Indian (in Alexander Hamilton House) E 11

Location
1 Bowling Green

Subway stations
Bowling Green
(lines 4, 5)
South Ferry
(line 1, 9)

Buses
1, (Mon.–Fri.), 6

Named after the first American Finance Minister Alexander Hamilton (1755–1804) this neo-Classical building, situated in the southern tip of Manhattan, was built by Cass Gilbert, the architect of the Woolworth Building (see entry). Chester French created the sculpture group at the entrance with its figures representing America, Asia, Africa and Europe.

After standing empty for more than 20 years the building took on a new function housing the Museum of the American Indian which until July 1994 was located in the complex of the Washington Heights Museum Group at Aubudon Terrace. The largest part of the Museum of the American Indian is to be transfered in the next few years to the Smithsonian Institute – named after the British patron of the arts James Smithson (1765–1829) – in Washington where a new Museum of the American Indian is to be built in 1996.

Originally this museum, founded by one of Rockefeller's associates, George C. Heye in 1916, was designed to house only its own collection of artefacts from the American South-West but was later extended to cover the native cultures of the whole American continent from the Arctic to Tierra del Fuego. It is dedicated to preservation and research of all forms of culture relating to America's original inhabitants over a period of 10,000 years. The collections are internationally recognised as the largest and most important of their kind and contain unique exhibits.

Among the exhibits are objects which belonged to the North American Indians from the forests of the east, across the Prairies of the Mid-west to the North American plateau. These include silver jewellery and pearl of the Iroquis, Huron embroidery in elk hair, tomahawks and headdresses of the Sioux together with craftwork by the original inhabitants of Alaska, Canada, the north-west Pacific coast, California and the south-west of the USA. Of particular interset are old decoy ducks from Nevada, Kachina dolls of the Hopi, Apache playing cards and ancient and modern pottery of the Pueblo Indians.

Also on display is archaeological material from the West Indies, Central and Southern America, including ancient textiles from Peru, drinking vessels of the Incas, tropical featherwork and blowpipes and shrunken heads from the Amazon.

Museum of the City of New York E 2

Situation
Fifth Avenue and
103rd Street

Subway station
103rd Street
(line 6)

Buses
1, 2, 3, 4

In spite of its name this museum, like all the other New York museums, is privately run. Founded in 1923, it is concerned with the history of the city, stretching back for more than 300 years.

The Museum was originally housed in the Gracie Mansion (see entry): the present neo-Classical building was erected in 1932. It now contains a total of some 500,000 objects and documents, including an extensive archive of material on the history of the theatre and concerts in the city (open: Tues.–Sat. 10am–5pm, Sun. and public holidays 1–5pm).

Layout

First Floor

Dioramas and other exhibits illustrating the early development of New York, from the colonial period to the American Revolution.

Second Floor

Of particular interest are the interiors of New York houses of the 17th–19th c., with life-size figures in contemporary dress.

On this floor is a very large collection of dolls' houses, toy theatres and toys of earlier days. There is also a series of shop-fronts from old New York shops.

Third Floor

Reproductions, accurate to the smallest detail, of two rooms from the Rockefeller mansion on West 54th Street, pulled down 30 years ago.

Fifth Floor

History of the New York fire brigade and of the national sport of baseball

Ground Floor

Between October and April the Museum organises on Sun. at 11am conducted walks through different parts of Manhattan (see Practical Information, Sightseeing Tours). From October to May there are concerts in the Museum, and regular special exhibitions on particular aspects of the city's history. Puppet festivals in winter and spring are a particular attraction for children.

Note

★★Museum of Modern Art

E 6

The Museum of Modern Art, founded in 1929, was one of the first museums devoted exclusively to modern art. It defines this term to include artists born after about 1880 (with the exception of Matisse, Monet, Rodin, Rouault and Vuillard) and, with some reservations, young contemporary painters and sculptors.

Address
11 West 53rd
Street

Subway station
Fifth Avenue
(lines E, F)

The Museum was originally housed in an office block at 730 Fifth Avenue (corner of 57th Street), where its first exhibition of 100 pictures by French Impressionists (all loans to the Museum) was held in November 1929. In January 1930 its entire stock consisted of one painting, one piece of sculpture and seven prints; but in the following year it received its first sizeable gift of pictures following the death of Lillian P. Bliss, one of the Museum's founders. Another of its founders, Mrs John D. Rockefeller, donated in the course of her life no fewer than 190 pictures, 137 drawings, 44 works of sculpture and more than 1600 prints by modern artists.

Buses
1, 2, 3, 4, 5

Opening times
Sat.–Tues.
11am–6pm,
Thurs., Fri.
noon–8.30pm,

Thurs. only
5.30–8.30pm
admission with
voluntary
contribution

After being accommodated for seven years in a mansion belonging to the Rockefeller family on West 53rd Street, the Museum moved into the first section of a new building on the same site (architects Philip Goodwin and Edward Durell Stone) in May 1939. In 1951 an annexe designed by Philip Johnson was opened; in 1963 the Museum acquired an adjoining building vacated by the Whitney Museum (see entry) on its move to Madison Avenue; and in 1964 and 1968 further extensions were built. In consequence the complex of buildings occupied by the Museum has a rather heterogeneous aspect.

In the middle of 1983 a 58-storey high skyscraper with 260 private apartments was erected over the museum. After reconstruction the museum has doubled its exhibition space. Even now, however – without taking account of its periodic special exhibitions – it is able to show barely a quarter of its total collection, which in the course of its 50-odd years of existence has risen to 100,000 pictures and pieces of sculpture, more than 3,000,000 drawings, prints, photographs, etc., and 8000 films. The annual number of visitors has for several years exceeded a million.

The new building of the Museum was opened in June 1984 and as a consequence there was a complete reorganisation of the contents of the various rooms. The new building, designed by the Argentinian architect Cesare Pelli, is about 100m (110yd) in length and is situated on the north side of 53rd Street. The new façade formed of glass sheets of varying sizes in grey, blue and white now dominates the whole block, particularly the tower of private flats.

89

Museum of Modern Art

Museum services The museum offers the following sevices:
Guided tours for parties by prior arrangement only (tel. 708 9685) begin from the entrance on 16 West 54th Street.
Wheelchairs can be hired from the entrance hall; individual floors can be reached by lifts and escalators.
Film performances take place daily (for programme information tel. 708 9490).
For information on special exhibtions tel. 708 9480.
Photography without tripods and flash is allowed.

Basement

Two cinemas of the "Roy and Niuta Titus Theatre" are located in the basement where the established Film Department shows all types of old and new films (mostly in series) and video films in the "Video Gallery". The admission fee includes entry to the Film Theatre.

The adjoining "René d'Harnoncourt Galleries" house the important special exhibitions which take place five to six times a year.

First (Ground) Floor

The entrance hall on the ground floor has been enlarged considerably in comparison with the old building and has an information kiosk, cloakrooms and museum shops.

Pop Art by Roy Lichtenstein in the Museum of Modern Art

Garden Hall with escalators in the Museum of Modern Art

The Garden Hall, where escalators carry the visitor to the upper floors, leads through to the most attractively laid out Abby Aldrich Sculpture Garden with numerous works of modern sculpture by Max Ernst, Alexander Calder, Henry Moore, Maillol, Matisse, Nadelman and Nevelson. Picasso's "The Goat" and an example of Auguste Rodin's "The Burghers of Calais" are set among trees, flowers and benches.

Abby Aldrich Rockefeller Sculpture Garden

Also on the ground floor are another gallery for temporary exhibitions, the "Edward John Noble Education Center", where talks on the MOMA's collections are held, and the Garden Café (Fri.–Tues. 11am–4.30pm, Thur. to 8pm).

Second Floor

This floor, like the first floor, is essentially devoted to painting and sculpture. The various intentionally small rooms reserved for particular styles or individual artists are in general arranged in chronological order.

Following the major exhibition of Matisse's work the paintings found on the first and second floors were moved under the direction of Kirk Varnedoe and paintings which had been on display were relegated to the store room until further notice so that paintings which had not yet been on show could be hung. So for the first time James Pollock had his own room – up until now a privilege enjoyed only by Matisse's work.

Also on show are works by Frida Kahlo, Florenze Stettheimer and Jakob Lawrence. The chronological order means that now European and American artists appear together whereas, for example, Giacometti's entire works are now in two departments: on the first floor the pre-war sculpture, on the second the later works. An accurate description of the individual galleries will only be possible when the alterations have finished.

Museum of Modern Art

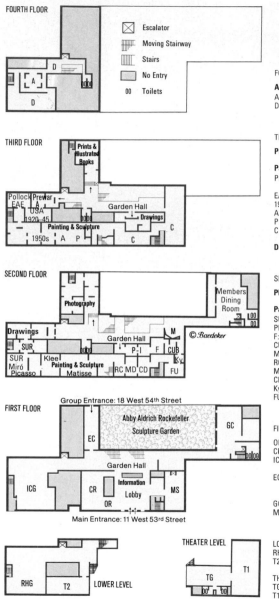

Museum of Modern Art ('M.O.M.A.')

Legend:
- ⊠ Escalator
- ⸬ Moving Stairway
- ⸬ Stairs
- ▨ No Entry
- 00 Toilets

FOURTH FLOOR

Architecture & Design
A: Architecture
D: Design

THIRD FLOOR

Prints & Illustrated Books

Paintings & Sculpture
Prewar A: Europe and America to 1940
EAE: Early Expressionism
1950s: America in the 50s
A: Abstract Expressionism to 1960
P: Pop Art
C: Contemporary Art

Drawings

SECOND FLOOR

Photography

Painting & Sculpture
SUR: Surrealism
PI: Post Impressionism
F: Fauvism
CUB: Cubism
M: "Waterlilies" Monet
RC: Russian Constructivism
MD: Mondrian
CD: Collage and Dadaism
Ky: Kandinsky
FU: Futurism

FIRST FLOOR

OR: Office Reception
CR: Check Room (Cloakroom)
ICG: International Council Galleries
EC: (Temporary Exhibitions) Edward John Noble Education Center
GC: Garden Café
MS: Museum Store

LOWER LEVEL
RHG: René d'Harnoncourt Galleries
T2: Roy & Niuta Titus Theater 2

THEATER LEVEL
TG: Theater Gallery
T1: Roy & Niuta Theater 1

Abby Aldrich Rockefeller Sculpture Garden: Picasso's "Billy goat"

Main works are:
  Cézanne "Baigneur" (*c.* 1885) and "Nature morte aux pommes" (1885–98), Degas "Chez la modiste" (*c.* 1882), Gauguin "Nature morte aux trois chiots" (1888) and "Lune et terre" (1893), Edvard Munch, Seurat "Port-en-Besin" (1888), Toulouse-Lautrec "La Goulue au Moulin Rouge" (1891–92), Henri Rousseau, Modigliani "Grand nu" (1919) and above all "Starry Night" (1889) by Vincent van Gogh, the only oil painting by this artist in the museum.

Post-Impressionism
École de Paris

Georges Braque, Vuillard, Léger "Trois Femmes" (1921), Chagall "I and the Village" (1911), Dérain, Dufy, Lipchitz, La Fresnaye. In an adjoining room are two panels of a triptych "Waterlilies" by Monet (*c.* 1920).

Cubism

Important artists and works include: Gustav Klimt, Kirchner "Street in Dresden" (1908), Oskar Kokoschka "Double Portrait of Hans Tietze and Erica Tietze-Conrat" (1909) and a self-portrait from 1913, Lehmbruck, Macke, Emil Nolde, Schmitt-Rottluf, Heckel, Franz Marc "Bull" (1911) and "Stables" (1913), Schlemmer "Bauhaus stairs" (1932), Edvard Munch, Roualt "Le christ raillé par ses soldats" (1932), Balla "Street light" (1909), Boccioni "Football players" (1913), Carra, Severini.

Expressionism, Futurism, Blaue Reiter

Gabo, Lissitsky, Malevich "Red Square, Black Square" (1914/15), Moholy-Nagy, Pevsner, Piet Mondrian "Broadway Boogie Woogie" (1942/43), van Doesburg.

Constructivism, de Stijl

The museum owns the largest collection of works by this artist including "La Danse" (1909) and the panorama "The Pool" from 1932 (in its own room on the second floor).

Henri Matisse

Museum of Modern Art

Vassilij Kandinsky, Paul Klee

Among the numerous works by both these artists "The Archer" and a set of four panels by Kandinsky (1914) together with "The Twittering Machine" by Paul Klee (1922) stand out.

Pablo Picasso

Only part of the seven or so works which make up this collection can be exhibited. Condsidered to be specially important is "Les Desmoiselles d'Avignon" (1907) which is regarded as the first Cubist painting. Also important are "The Women at the Fountain", "Ma Jolie" (1911/12), "Harlequin", the bronze sculpture "She-Goat" (1950) and the huge works in plaster "Head of a Woman" and "Head of a Warrior", gifts from the artist's wife.

Dadaism

The main representatives of this style are Max Ernst "Woman, Old Man and Flower" and "The Blind Swimmer" (1934), Picabia, Kurt Schwitters "The Circling", Hans Arp, Duchamp.

Joan Miró

The paintings by the Spaniard Joan Miró are a link between Dada and the Surrealist department. They include: "Catalonian Landscape" (1923/24), "The Hunter", "The Origins of the World" and "Hirondelle/Amour" from 1933 and 1934.

Surrealism

The Surrealist movement is well represented by Hans Arp, André Breton, Max Ernst "2 enfants sont menacés par un rossignol" (1924), Giovanni Giacometti, Man Ray, Meret Oppenheim, Tanguy "Multiplication of the Arcs" (1954), Salvador Dali "The Persistence of Memory" (1931), Delvaux "Phases of the Moon" (1939), De Chirico, Magritte "The Menaced Assassin" and "Le faux miroir" (1928), Masson, Matta and Tchelichev "Hide and Seek" (1952).

Photography

The Photographic Department adjoins the painting and sculpture collections and following the renovations now has well-designed galleries where work from early 1839 through classical photography to that of contemporary photographers is presented. This includes work by Eugéne Atget, Laszio Moholy-Nagy, Cartier-Bresson, Walker Evans, Man Ray, Dorothea Lange, Gertrude Kasebier, Berenice Abbot and Edward Steichen. The latter, from Luxembourg, laid the foundation of the photographic collection which MOMA began much earlier than other museums.

Third Floor

The rooms on this floor are almost exclusively devoted to American painting.

As well as the departments which are briefly described below there are numerous sculptures by Rodin, Maillol, Calder, Marini, Moore and Picasso for which there was no space in the Sculpture Garden and two large rooms of contemporary art.

Pre-war American

Among the most important painters and paintings are Bearden, Burchfield, Blume "Eternal City" (1934–37), S. Davis, Demuth, Dove "Grandmother" (1925), Edward Hooper "House by the Railroad" (1925), Marin "Lower Manhattan" (1922), O'Keefe, Prendergast, Sheeler and Weber.

Post-war European and American

This department contains chiefly works from the 50s and 60s including work by Albers, Francis, Liberman, Mitchell, Newman, Reinhardt "Abstract Painting" (1961), D. Smith, Vasarely, Johns, Krasner, Louis, Ossorio, Pousette-Dart, Bacon "Painting" (1946), Dubuffet, Stella and all the important pop artists such as James Dine, Claes Oldenburg, Roy Lichtenstein "Drowning Girl" (1963), James Rosenquist, Robert Rauschenberg, Tom Wesselman and of course Andy Warhol, although only represented by his less striking works.

This first important American school is represented by its main protagonist Jackson Pollock, the inventor of "Action Painting", with "She Wolf" (1943). Also de Kooning, "Woman, I" (1950–52), Gottlieb, Kline, Motherwell, Guston.

Abstract Expressionism

These departments show sketches, (Dubuffet, Klee, Matisse, Picasso, Schwitters, Kupka) book illustrations and prints (van Gogh, Degas, Edvard Munch "Madonna", 1895–1902; Beckmann, Feininger, Klee, Villon) and theatrical art, including 67 decorations and costume sketches by Marc Chagall for the ballet "Aléko".

Drawings and prints

Fourth Floor

The development of design since the late 19th c. of furniture (Gerrit Rietveld "Red and Blue Chair", 1918), everyday objects (Vico Magistretti "Atollo" table lamp, 1977), cars (Pininfarina "Cistalia 202", 1946) and architecture (Mies van der Rohe "Office block in Friedrichstrasse", Berlin 1921; Le Corbusier, Frank Lloyd Wright).

Architecture and Design

Museum of Television and Radio   E 6

This museum was founded in 1976 by Philip Johnson and John Burgee. The imposing entrance hall leads to the Steven Spielberg Gallery, used for temporary exhibitions. In the two cinemas and small projection rooms displays are given of material selected from the museum's archives, which contain more than 25 television programmes, 15,000 radio programmes and some 10,000 commercials. On the third floor visitors can use one of the many computers and, with the help of the museum catalogue, compile their own programmes.

Address
25 West 52nd Street

Subway station
Fifth Avenue
(lines E, F)

The museum is open Tues., Wed., Fri. and Sat. noon–6pm; cinema shows Fri. to 9pm. There is a charge for admission.

★New York Aquarium

One of the attractions of Coney Island (Brooklyn), New York City's only bathing beach by the sea, is the Aquarium with its large collection of marine fauna. Efforts have been made to recreate the natural living conditions of the creatures found in the Bermuda Triangle, in the native waters of America and in the display on the Red Sea.

Situation
Surf Avenue and West 8th Street, Coney Island, Brooklyn

During the warmer months (June to September) dolphin and sealion shows take place in the Aquatheater, during the colder months beluga whales are on show. Spectators can watch the daily feeding of sharks, penguins, seals, walruses, whales and electric eels.

Subway stations
West 8th Street
(lines D, F)

The exhibition space was nearly doubled in July 1989 with the opening of the George D. Ruggieri Discovery Cove. On display are the coastal ecosystems and hundreds of species of marine life showing us how marine mammals adapt to their wet surroundings and man's relationship to the sea. (Admission fee; free entrance for Senior Citizens on weekdays after 2pm.)

Opening times
Daily
10am–4.45pm

★New York Botanical Garden

The New York Botanical Garden, established in 1891 on the model of the Royal Botanical Gardens at Kew in London, occupies an area of 117 ha (292 acres) at the north end of Bronx Park.

Situation
Bronx Park, Bronx

New York Historical Society

Subway stations
Bedford Park
Boulevard
(lines C, D)

It is one of the oldest and largest gardens of its kind in the United States. Some historic buildings have been preserved in the gorge formed by the Bronx River which runs through the gardens. Hemlock Forest is the remains of the forest which covered the peninsula at the time the Indians occupied Manhattan. There are about 12 outdoor gardens with azaleas, rhododendrons and chrysanthemums to walk through. The "Enid A. Haupt Conservatory", inspired by the Crystal Palace in Kew Gardens, has tropical plants and waterfalls alongside desert landscapes.

The nearby museum, library, herbarium and research laboratory are a reminder that the gardens serve scientific as well as recreational purposes.
Conducted tours take place at the weekend from 10.30am–3.30pm (Information: tel. 220 8747; admission fee to the conservatory).

Opening times

Gardens: Apr.–Oct.: daily 8am–7pm; Nov.–Mar.: daily 8am–6pm; Conservatory: Nov.–Mar. Tues.–Sun. 10am–5pm; Apr.–Oct. 10am–6pm.

New York Historical Society   D 4

Address
170 Central Park
West and 77th
Street

Subway station
81st Street
(lines B, C, K)

Bus 10

Opening times
Tues.–Sat.
10am–5pm,
Sun. 1–5pm

Admission fee

Guided tours
Daily no charge

The New York Historical Society, founded in 1809, is one of the city's oldest learned institutions, and its museum is the oldest in New York State. The museum moved to its present site in 1908, but was considerably extended 30 years later.
Among the museum's treasures are 432 of John James Audubon's 1065 watercolours of American birds (near the entrance); a large collection of views of New York from the 17th to the 19th c.; silver by New York silversmiths; domestic interiors of the colonial period; portraits of prominent New Yorkers; popular arts and crafts, and much else. There is also a visual presentation of the city's history from the Dutch colonial period to the end of the 19th c. The Society's library and photographic archives are essential sources for all students of the history of the State and City of New York. Throughout the year temporary exhibitions concerned with the fields of work of this institution take place and films are shown. Following a crisis in 1988/89, which nearly led to its closure, the society was reorganised, a new committee elected and a new director appointed. During 1990 some of the galleries are being used by the Jewish Museum which is undergoing rebuilding.

★ New York Public Library   E 7

Situation
Fifth Avenue and
42nd Street

Subway stations
42nd Street
(lines B, D, F)
Fifth Avenue
(line 7)

Buses
1, 2, 3, 4, 5, 104

Opening times
Mon.–Wed.
10am–8.45pm,
Thur.–Sat.
10am–5.45pm

The New York Public Library, the largest library in the United States after the Library of Congress in Washington, is – in spite of its name – a private institution, though it now receives more than half its funds from public sources. It was originally formed by the amalgamation of three private libraries (the Astor library, established by John Jacob Astor in 1849, and the Lenox and Tilden libraries), and the imposing building of Vermont marble in which it is housed was erected between 1897 and 1911 to the design of the New York architects Carrère and Hastings, half the cost of building it being met by the Scottish-born steel magnate Andrew Carnegie. The site had previously been occupied by a reservoir, which supplied New York with water, and, in the city's early days, a paupers' cemetery.
The main entrance to the Library, a typical example of the "Beaux Arts" school of architecture, is on Fifth Avenue. There are regular exhibitions of material from the Library's collection in the entrance hall, the recently opened Gottesman Hall and the corridors.
On the second floor are various special departments (Slavonic, Jewish, economic and social sciences, etc.), on the third the large Reading Room with seating for 550 readers. Here, too, is the catalogue of the library's total

New York Public Library

stock of over 9 million volumes and 14 million manuscripts, any one of which can be brought from the book-stacks within a matter of minutes from the presentation of an application slip made out from a new computer-catalogue. Also in the Reading Room is a reference library of some 40,000 volumes, including telephone directories for the whole of the United States.

On the same floor are manuscripts (the Berg Collection) and rare books, which can be consulted only by special arrangement. Among the special treasures found in the Library are a Gutenberg bible, a letter from Christopher Columbus and a handwritten outline of the US Declaration of Independence by Jefferson.

Conducted tours Mon., Tues. and Wed. at 11am and 2pm (Astor Hall entrance)

The New York Public Library has over 80 branch libraries in Manhattan, the Bronx and Staten Island (Brooklyn and Queens have their own library service and central library). Among these are:

Branch libraries

The Mid-Manhattan Library at 455 Fifth Avenue, a reference library of over 400,000 volumes.

The Donnell Library Center at 20 West 53rd Street, mainly an art, film and video library.

The Library and Museum of the Performing Arts in the Lincoln Center (see entry), a reference and lending library in the fields of theatre, film, music and the dance.

The Library for the Blind and Physically Handicapped, 166 Avenue of the Americas, with over 50,000 volumes written in Braille.

The Schomburg Center for Research in Black Culture (see entry).

Newspaper department, 521 West 43rd Street.

Hectic dealing on the New York Stock Exchange

★New York Stock Exchange   E 11

Address
20 Broad Street

Subway stations
Wall Street
(lines 1, 2, 3, 4, 5),
Broad Street
(lines J, M, R)

Opening times
Mon.–Fri.
9am–3.15pm

Trading in over 4400 stocks and shares the New York Stock Exchange is the largest in the United States and despite several crises the most important in the world. Founded in 1792 it is also the oldest exchange trading in stocks and bonds.

On the Visitors' Balcony, which affords a good view of the circular trading floor, there is a small exhibition (with film shows) explaining the mysteries of trading on the Stock Exchange.

A ticket for the films and tours is available free of charge from the Visitor Center but it is necessary to collect one early as entry is often only after a two hour wait.

The building, with its façade in the style of a Roman temple, was designed by George B. Post and built in 1903.

The New York Stock Exchange is only one of New York's numerous financial and commercial exchanges. Among the others are the American Stock Exchange at 86 Trinity Place and the Coffee, Sugar and Cocoa Exchange in the World Trade Center (see entry).

Old Merchant's House   E 9

Address
29 East 4th Street

Subway station
Astor Place (line 6)

This early 19th c. house, one of the few buildings of the period to be preserved in its original state, was built by a well-to-do businessman named Seabury Tredwell in 1832 in what was then one of New York's most fashionable residential areas. Nowadays, however, this area between Lafayette Street and the Bowery (see entry) is in need of restoration.

The original furniture of the house has been preserved, and visitors are shown clothes belonging to Tredwell's daughter Gertrude, who died in 1933 at the age of 93.

Buses
1, 5, 6, 101, 102

Old Merchant's House is open to the public on Sun. 1–4pm (at other times by prior telephone appointment tel. 777 1089).

Admission fee

★ Pierpont Morgan Library   E 7

The Pierpont Morgan Library is much more than a library: it is a museum of art and bibliographical treasures assembled from 1890 onwards by the banker J. Pierpont Morgan and his son.

Address
29 East 36th Street

The Library is housed in a Renaissance-style palazzo built for the elder Morgan in 1903–06 by the well-known firm of New York architects McKim, Mead and White, with an extension added in 1928 after the collections had been opened up to the public for the first time in 1924. Today the museum is also a philological research library with a Reading Room only available to scholars and students with special permission.

Subway station
33rd Street (line 6)

Buses
1, 2, 3, 4

Opening times
Tues.–Sat.
10.30am–5pm,
Sun. 1–5pm

The Library is closed on Saturdays and public holidays in July and throughout August.

As well as the Reading Room the Library has three galleries in the East Room with extremely rare manuscripts and prints. Morgan senior brought together an extraordinary hoard of treasures only a few of which, however, can be seen behind glass to the left of the Reading Room and in the corridor to the galleries. Of particular note are a Gutenberg bible, a Mainz Psalter from 1495, a sacrament from the Weingarten monastery, a Constance missal, Catherine of Cleves' Book of Hours, a Venetian illuminated bible from 1471, a papal bull from Hadrian IV, 1155, and books by the first English printer William Caxton. Among the many manuscripts and autographs are those of Macchiavelli, Byron, Keats, Dickens and Heine together with handwritten scores by Mozart, Bach, Beethoven, Schubert, Brahms, Chopin and Berlioz. Also book covers and illustrations (by Dürer, among others), engravings and etchings (over 250 by Rembrandt), Assyrian-Babylonian cuneiform tablets, scroll seals and papyrus.

East Room

The West Room houses a permanent exhibition with the outstanding paintings by Lucas Cranach the Elder of the wedding portraits of Martin Luther and Katharina von Bora. Also a Tintoretto ("Portrait of a Moor"), a painting by Hans Memling ("Man with a Carnation"), two 15th c. Bohemian panels and Italian small sculptures of the Donatello School. Another jewel in this room is a Stablo triptych, a fine work in gold and enamel by Godefroi de Claire (c. 1150).

West Room

There is an Exhibition Hall in which there is always (except during the summer) a superb display of material from the Library's own resources or of items loaned for the purpose.

Poe Cottage

This little wooden house, built in 1812, was the last home of Edgar Allan Poe, the first American writer to achieve world fame. Anxious to get away from crowded Manhattan, Poe rented the house, then situated in the village of Fordham, in 1846 for 100 dollars a year. Soon afterwards his wife died of tuberculosis, and in 1849 Poe himself, a notorious alcoholic, died on his way back from a lecture tour in the South.

Situation
Grand Concourse and East Kingsbridge Road (Bronx)

Subway station
Kingsbridge Road (lines 4, D)

In 1902 Poe Park was laid out, and the cottage was moved across the road to its present site in the park. The interior has been faithfully restored to its original state. Here Poe wrote some of his best known poems, including "Annabel Lee", "Ulalume" and "Eureka". (Open: Wed.–Fri. 9am–5pm, Sat. 10am–4pm, Sun. 1–5pm.)

P.S.1 Museum (Institute for Contemporary Art)

Address
46–01 21st Street
Long Island City
(Queens)

Subway stations
Hunter's Point
(line 7),
23rd Street/Ely
Avenue (lines E, F)

Opening times
Wed.–Sun.
noon–6pm

"P.S.1" stands for Public School 1, an old elementary school dating from 1890 which stood empty for many years before being leased by the city for a token rent to the Institute for Art and Urban Resources. Since 1975 the former classrooms have been used as studios for artists, who are thus provided with a cheap place to work (though not to live).

P.S.1 puts on a full programme of exhibitions, in which displays of "Minimal" art predominate. It also provides a setting, particularly at weekends, for a variety of performances and "happenings". Thus in the course of a very few years this disused school building has developed into an international centre of creative artistic activity. Admission fee is discretionary.

Public Library

See New York Public Library

★Richmondtown Restoration/ Staten Island Historical Museum

Address
441 Clarke Avenue
(Staten Island)

Boat
Staten Island ferry
from Battery Park,
then bus S54, S14
(to Center Street)

Opening times
Wed.–Fri.
10am–5pm,
Sat. and Sun.
1pm–5pm

Events
Tel. 718 351 1617

In the district of Richmondtown, the old centre of Staten Island, 27 houses dating back to 1695 have been carefully restored and now give visitors a vivid impression of life in the colonial period. The oldest of the houses is the Voorlezer's House, with a single room, which is the oldest surviving schoolhouse in America.

The former County Building which dates from 1848 houses the Historical Society Museum and has collections of early American tools and equipment. Together with the Third County Court House (1837) built in Greek Revival style and St Andrew's Church from 1708 there are interesting old shops and workshops, including Dunne's Saw Mill (1800), Carriage House and Stephen's Store. The mausoleum of the Vanderbilt (see Famous People) family can be found in the Moravian Cemetery, established by the religious community of Moravian Brothers. Demonstrations of old handicrafts take place regularly as can be seen from the map available in the museum showing which of the 27 houses are open to visitors.

★Rockefeller Center   D/E 6

Situation
Fifth Avenue
between 47th and
52nd Streets

The Rockefeller Center, a complex of 21 high-rise office blocks on Fifth Avenue (48th–51st Streets) and Avenue of the Americas (47th–52nd Streets) is the largest comprehensively planned skyscraper city in the world, a development which has transformed the face of Manhattan over

Rockefeller Center: GE Building (formerly the RCA Building) ▶

St Bartholomew's Protestant Episcopal Church

Subway station
47th–50th Street
(lines D, F)
49th Street
(lines N, R)

Buses
5, 6, 7 (uptown,
Avenue of the
Americas), 1, 2, 3,
4, 5 (downtown)

Conducted tours
GE Building:
Oct.–Mar., daily
10.30am–7pm,
Apr.–Sept.,
10am–9pm

the past 50 years. The initiative for its construction came from America's wealthiest citizen, John D. Rockefeller Jr (to whom New York also owes Rockefeller University, Fort Tryon Park and the Cloisters (see entry), the United Nations Headquarters Building (see entry), for which he provided the site, and Riverside Church).

The Center, built on land belonging to Columbia University, originally consisted of 14 tower blocks between Fifth Avenue and the Avenue of the Americas and between 48th and 51st Streets, but further development from 1954 onwards took it beyond these limits. In 1985 the area was sold to the Rockefeller Center.

In addition to countless offices with a working population of a quarter of a million, the Rockefeller Center contains 30 restaurants, dozens of shops on ground-floor level and in the underground passages; television studios, several exhibition halls and a whole museum of mural paintings, sculpture and reliefs (over 100 works of art by more than two dozen artists).

At the end of 1989 51% of the Rockefeller Center was acquired by the Japanese Mitsubishi Estate Company. The 88 members of the Rockefeller family wanted to change their share into cash in view of the high property prices in Manhattan.

NBC Studio Tour
Mon.–Fri.
10 a.m.–4 p.m.
(charge)

The main building in the Rockefeller Centre is the 250m (820ft) high GE Building (General Electric Building; formerly known as the RCA – Radio Corporation of America – Building), containing the studios of the NBC (National Broadcasting Corporation) which are open to visitors. The main hall is decorated with murals by José M. Sert. On the 70th floor is the viewing platform which is, however, reserved for guests of the famous "Rainbow Room" on the 65th floor.

Radio City Music
Hall

Conducted tours
Daily (charge)
Tel. 632 1041

North-west behind the GE Building stands the Radio City Music Hall built in 1930 in Art-Deco style.
   It has 6200 seats, the largest concert hall in the world, and has revues and shows with famous celebrities and rock stars. (See Practical Information, Nightlife.)

Rockefeller Plaza

In front of the GE Building lies the Rockefeller Plaza, leading to the Sunken Plaza with the golden bronze figure of Prometheus by Paul Manship (1934). Sunken Plaza is a popualr meeting place in summer for shop and office workers; in winter an ice rink is set up with a 20m (66ft) high Christmas tree towering above it. Flower shows are held in summer in the Channel Gardens which lead to Fifth Avenue between the British Empire Building and the Maison Française.

St Bartholomew's Protestant Episcopal Church   E 6

Address
109 East 50th
Street

Subway stations
51st Street (line 6),
Lexington Avenue
(lines E, F)

This church, occupying the block between 50th and 51st Streets, was built by Bertram Goodhue in 1919. It is in an eclectic Byzantine style, with a Romanesque doorway (by McKim, Mead and White) modelled on that of St-Gilles in Arles which came from the previous church at the corner of Madison Avenue and 44th Street. The Byzantine-style interior has an altar by Lee Larrie (best known for his sculpture in the Rockefeller Center).

Opening times: daily until dusk.

St Mark's in the Bowery   F 9

This is New York's second oldest church, built in 1799 on the site of an earlier chapel erected by Peter Stuyvesant, Dutch governor of New York, on his farm. Stuyvesant and his family are buried in the crypt. Thirty years later a neo-Classical tower was added to the colonial-style church, and 26 years after that a Romanesque portico with cast-iron railings.

The church was devastated by fire in 1978 but was reopened in 1981 after restoration (mainly by volunteer helpers). Regular exhibitions take place in a newly formed gallery; open Wed.–Sat. noon–5pm, Sun. 1–5pm.

St Mark's (which is Episcopalian) achieved some prominence in the heyday of the hippie movement, the main centre of which was St Mark's Place, only two blocks away. In 1965 the Genesis Theater, which stages only plays by young US writers, was opened in the church. Recently an art gallery has been added with temporary art and historical exhibitions.

Situation
Second Avenue
and 10th Street

Subway station
Astor Place (line 6)

Bus 15

Opening times
Daily until dusk

★St Patrick's Cathedral   E 6

This Roman Catholic cathedral, seat of the Archbishop of New York, was designed by James Renwick in High-Gothic style and built of light-coloured marble between 1858 and 1888. It has two towers with spires rising to a height of 100m (330ft). The Lady Chapel at the east end was added in 1901–05.

Situation
Fifth Avenue,
between 50th and
51st Streets

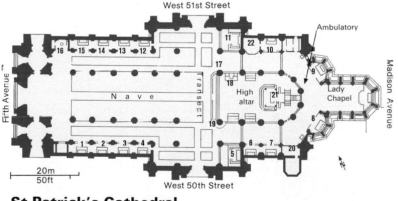

West 51st Street / West 50th Street

St Patrick's Cathedral

ALTARS
1 St Anthony of Padua
2 St John the Evangelist
3 St Elizabeth Ann Seton
4 St Rose of Lima
5 Sacred Heart
6 St Andrew
7 St Teresa of the Infant Jesus

8 St Elizabeth
9 St Michael and St Louis
10 St Joseph
11 Holy Family
12 Holy Relics
13 St Augustine
14 St John Baptist de la Salle
15 St Brigid and St Bernard

16 Baptistery
17 Statue of St Patrick
18 Archbishop's Throne
19 Pulpit
20 Archbishop's Sacristy
21 Entrance to crypt and
   sacristies
22 Organ

St Paul's Chapel

Subway station
Fifth Avenue
(lines E, F)

Buses
1, 2, 3, 4, 5

Opening times
Daily 7am–8pm

The cathedral was dedicated to St Patrick in 1910. The dignified interior is 93m (305ft) long and 38m (125ft) wide across the transept. It can seat a congregation of 2500.

The vaulting is borne on massive marble columns. Notable features of the interior are the stained glass, the canopied High Altar (dedicated 1942), the numerous side altars and the effigy of St Elizabeth Ann Seton (1774–1821), foundress of the order of the Sisters of Charity, who became the first woman saint of the United States in 1975.

The cathedral's organ has more than 9000 pipes.

St Paul's Chapel   E 11

Situation
Broadway and
Fulton Street

Subway stations
Fulton Street
(lines 4, 5, J),
Broadway-Nassau
(line A)

Opening times
Daily 7am–4pm

Built in 1764–66, this is the oldest church in Manhattan; and, unlike other buildings of the period (e.g. see Fraunces' Tavern), it has remained substantially unchanged.

It was designed by the Scottish architect Thomas McBean and was probably modelled on St Martin-in-the-Fields in London (designed by James Gibb, with whom McBean may have worked as a pupil). The spire and portico were added in 1796.

In the north aisle is George Washington's private pew marked with a "G". The little churchyard attracts many people, particularly in spring and autumn, to enjoy this oasis of peace.

Conducted tours by arrangement (tel. 602 0800).

Schomburg Center for Research in Black Culture

★Schomburg Center for Research in Black Culture

With the opening of its new premises in a five-storey building in Harlem (see entry) in 1980 the Schomburg Center for Research in Black Culture, founded in 1925 as a branch of the New York Public Library (see entry) and now the largest establishment of its kind in the world, has at last found a worthy home.

Address
515 A. Clayton Powell Avenue and 135th Street

Subway station
135th Street (lines 2, 3)

The nucleus of the Schomburg Center was the collection of 5000 books, 300 manuscripts, 2000 etchings and portraits and much other material assembled by Arthur A. Schomburg, a Puerto Rican banker living in New York. From 1932 until his death in 1938 Schomburg himself was the keeper of the collection.

Bus 1, 2

Opening times
Mon.–Wed. noon–8pm,
Thur.–Sat. 10am–6pm

The collection has now grown to over 80,000 volumes, over 200,000 manuscripts, 3000 prints and posters, 15,000 microfilms and 50,000 photographs. The Center also possesses a large store of material on the history, culture and folk traditions of the West Indies, records of African folk music and works of art by African painters and sculptors.

A visit to the Center will be a rewarding experience for anyone interested in the culture of black Africa and of black Americans.

The building itself, with an octagon at one end and a tower at the corner of 135th Street, can be seen as a symbol of the gradual rehabilitation of Harlem.

The tables, chairs and desks in the reading rooms and archive rooms are mostly made of African timber.

Sculpture in New York

In addition to the older monuments and statues there are numerous examples of modern sculpture in Manhattan.

At 140 Broadway is Isamo Noguchi's "Cube" (1973), 7m (23ft) high.

Financial District

In front of the Police Headquarters is Bernard Rosenthal's "Five in One" (1974). The five interlocking discs represent New York's five boroughs.

Police Plaza

Jean Dubuffet's "Four Trees" (1972), a monumental piece of sculpture 14m (46ft) high and weighing 25 tons which Dubuffet described as "a monument to the spirit, a landscape of the mind".

Chase Manhattan Plaza

Rudolph de Harak's "Helix" (1969), a spiral of stainless steel 7m (22ft) high, and William Tarr's "Rejected Skin" (1971), a piece of abstract sculpture made from rejected aluminium left over from the construction of a building.

77 Water Street

Yu Yu Yang's "Queen Elizabeth I Memorial" (1974), two stainless-steel units commemorating the liner, not the queen.

Wall Street Plaza

In Astor Place is Bernard Rosenthal's "Alamo" (1967), the first work of modern sculpture set up in a New York Street.

East Village

At 100 Bleecker Street is the "Bust of Sylvette", designed by Picasso and executed by the Norwegian sculptor Carl Nesjar (1968). This piece of concrete sculpture, weighing 60 tons, stands four storeys high, in front of the New York University residences. In spite of its great size this sphinx-like figure has a curious grace.

World Trade Center Plaza: "Globe" by Fritz König

At the end of 1989 a sculpture by the pop artist Jim Dine "Looking at the Avenue" was erected. It consists of three bronze sculptures (4m (13ft), 6m (19ft) and 7.5m (25ft) high), variations of the famous Venus de Milo, not only without arms but also heads.

1271 Avenue of the Americas

At No. 1271 is William Crovello's "Cubed Curve" (1971). The steel curves, painted blue, of this piece of sculpture form an effective counterpoint to the straight lines of the Time-Life Building behind it.

At No. 1221 is Athelstan Spilhaus's "Sun Triangle" (1973). Various parts of this modern sun-dial of stainless steel point to the position of the sun at noon at the solstices and equinoxes.

Lincoln Center

In front of the Library and Museum of the Performing Arts is Alexander Calder's "Le Guichet" ("The Ticket Window", 1972), a typical Calder "stabile" of blackened steel.

Outside the Vivian Beaumont Theatre is Henry Moore's "Reclining Figure" (1968), a two-part work of sculpture in blackened bronze, reflected in the water of the pool in which it stands. It is illuminated after dark.

Park Avenue 92nd Street

At 92nd Street is Louise Nevelson's "Night Presence IV" (1972), 7m (22ft) high, made of steel alloyed with nickel and copper, which are gradually giving it a brownish-black hue.

Skyscrapers

Skyscrapers: original American architecture

The real architectural history of America begins with the building of skyscrapers which was made possible by the new technolgy of the second half of the 19th c. As more traditional building materials gave way to steel the epoch making era of skyscraper building began. Whereas thick load-

Fifth Avenue:
"Atlas"

Chase Manhattan Plaza:
Jean Dubuffet's
"Four Trees"

Park Avenue:
Louise Nevelson's
"Night Presence IV"

bearing walls were necessary for the first skyscrapers built of stone the new construction method using a steel framework made it possible to build real "skyscrapers"; shortly after the turn of the century the use of concrete opened up new horizons. The exteriors still were imitations of traditional European designs (for example, the "Gothic" Woolworth Building, 1913).

Not until the Thirties did a functional architectural style develop: the famous Empire State Building (1931, see entry) seems quite modern; the clear lines of the Rockefeller Center (1940, see entry) are an example of advanced spatial planning within a large city.

As they developed the features of the Manhattan skyscrapers were less to do with the architect's ideas than the building regulations. Whereas the earlier skyscrapers were mainly built like towers (Chrysler Building, Empire State Building, see entries) the later ones were in the form of blocks and wedges. As a response to the shortage of daylight falling in the abyss-like gorges which resulted between the buildings the authorities introduced the Zoning Law resulting in the stepped style of architecture which is typical of Manhattan. Further restrictions were introduced in the early Sixties limiting the area which could be built upon and providing larger open spaces (plazas). This permitted a 20% increase in the height restriction.

Typical features

In the Eighties New York was gripped by a building boom which resulted in skyscrapers such as the former AT & T Building – now the Sony Building (see entry) –, the Trump Tower (see entry) or the World Financial Center in Battery Park City (see entry) which dramatically altered the skyline of the city, not always to the joy of its inhabitants.

Building boom

Skyscrapers

Flatiron Building

Crown Building

Skyscrapers in Lower Manhattan

Many of the new buildings have enormous luxurious public lobbies in common. The unusual side of the boom is the fact that most owners of the lower buildings sell the air rights over their properties to the builders of skyscrapers thus profitting from being in the shade. The Museum of Modern Art (see entry) financed the building of its extension in this way. The following skyscrapers are of historical or architectural interest:

1 Madison Avenue. 213m/760ft. 50 floors.
Built in 1893 by Napoleon LeBrun (23 and 25 floors). The tower was added 16 years later, which made it the highest building in the world (213m/700ft) for two years.

Metropolitan Life Building

Fifth Avenue and 23rd Street. 76m/248ft. 20 floors.
Built in 1902 by D. H. Burnham. The diagonal alignment of Broadway made it necessary, as at Times Square (see entry), to erect a triangular building with an acutely angled apex, making it look even narrower in perspective and giving it the name "Iron Building".

Flatiron Building

233 Broadway. 242m/792ft. 60 floors.
Built in 1913 by Cass Gilbert, this was the highest building in the world (241m/790ft) until the completion of the Chrysler Building (see entry) some 17 years later. The architectural critic Paul Goldberger called it "the Mozart among skyscrapers". The Gothic detailing is well adapted to the vertical form of the building, and the tower stretches naturally and organically up from the base. The three-storey lobby is also of notable quality.

Woolworth Building

375 Park Avenue (53rd Street). 160m/525ft. 38 floors.
Built in 1958 by Mies van der Rohe and Philip Johnson. It shows the form, later so popular, of a glass-walled skyscraper with a plaza, though the layout of the plaza later became much more interesting.

Seagram Building

1 Chase Manhattan Plaza. 248m/813ft. 60 floors.
Built in 1960 by Skidmore, Owings and Merrill. Situated near Wall Street (see entry), this building marked the beginning of the modernising process of the Financial District. Notable features are the sunken plaza with fountains (by Isamo Noguchi) and a sensational piece of sculpture by Jean Dubuffet called "Four Seasons" (see Sculpture).

Chase Manhattan Bank

200 Park Avenue (48th Street). 246m/809ft. 59 floors.
Built in 1963 by Emery Roth and Sons, Pietro Belluschi and Walter Gropius. Its construction gave rise to fierce criticism, since it blocked the previously open view of Park Avenue. The building, which PanAm sold to an insurance corporation in 1980 for 400 million dollars, can also be entered from Grand Central Station. In the large lobby are works of art by Josef Albers, Gyorgy Kepes and Richard Lippold.

MetLife Building

The skyscraper towers above the massive Grand Central Station, one of New York's two main railway stations. The ceilings designed like a starry sky and the largest clock to be found inside a building in the world are worth seeing. Guided tours take place on Wednesdays at 12.30pm and are free of charge.

Grand Central Station

767 Fifth Avenue. 215m/705ft. 50 floors.
Built in 1968, on a site previously occupied by the Savoy Plaza Hotel, by Emery Roth and Sons in collaboration with Edward Durell Stone. Destroying as it does the harmony of Grand Army Plaza, it can be cited as an example of how not to build a skyscraper.

General Motors Building

The fifty tallest skyscrapers in New York City	Height (metres)	(feet)	Floors
World Trade Center (2 towers)	419·7	1377	110
Empire State Building	381·0	1250	102
with aerial tower	448·7	1472	
Chrysler Building, 405 Lexington Avenue	318·8	1046	77
American International Building, 70 Pine Street	289·6	950	67
40 Wall Tower	282·5	927	71
Citicorp Center Tower, 575 Lexington Avenue	278·9	915	46
GE Building	259·1	850	70
1 Chase Manhattan Plaza	247·8	813	60
MetLife Building	246·3	809	59
Cityspire, 150 West 56th Street	243·5	799	70
Woolworth Building, 233 Broadway	241·4	792	60
1 Worldwide Plaza	237·1	778	47
1 Penn Plaza	232·9	764	57
Carnegie Tower	230·4	756	59
Exxon, 1251 Avenue of the Americas	228·6	750	54
Equitable Center Tower West, 787 Seventh Avenue	228·6	750	58
60 Wall Street	227·1	745	50
1 Liberty Plaza	226·4	743	50
Citibank, 399 Park Avenue	225·8	741	57
World Financial Center Tower C	225·2	739	54
1 Astor Plaza	222·5	730	54
Solow Building	220·9	725	50
Marine Midland, 140 Broadway	220·7	724	52
Metropolitan Tower, 146 West 57th Street	218·2	716	66
Union Carbide, 270 Park Avenue	215·5	707	52
General Motors Building, 767 Fifth Avenue	214·9	705	50
Metropolitan Life, 1 Madison Avenue	213·4	700	50
500 Fifth Avenue	212·4	697	60
Chemical Bank Building, 277 Park Avenue	209·4	687	50
55 Water Street	209·4	687	53
1585 Broadway	208·8	685	42
Chanin, Lexington Avenue and 42nd Street	207·3	680	56
Four Seasons Hotel	207·0	679	52
Gulf & Western Building, 15 Columbus Circle	207·0	679	44
McGraw Hill, 1221 Avenue of the Americas	205·4	674	51
Citicorp (Queens)	205·1	673	50
Lincoln Building, 60 East 42nd St	205·1	673	53
1633 Broadway	204·2	670	50
Trump Tower, 725 Fifth Avenue	202·3	664	68
599 Lexington Avenue	199·0	653	47
Museum Tower Appartments, 15 West 53rd Street	198·1	650	58
712 Fifth Avenue	198·1	650	56
American Brands, 245 Park Avenue	197·5	648	47
Sony Tower, 570 Madison Avenue	197·5	648	37
World Financial Center Tower B	196·5	645	50
General Electric, 570 Lexington Avenue	195·1	640	50
Irving Trust, 1 Wall Street	195·1	640	50
345 Park Avenue	193·2	634	44
Grace Plaza, 1114 Avenue of the Americas	192·0	630	50
1 New York Plaza	192·0	630	50
Home Insurance Building, 59 Maiden Lane	192·0	630	44

Columbus Circle. 207m/679ft. 44 floors.
Built in 1969 by Thomas E. Stanley. This is another skyscraper built without regard to its immediate surroundings and which disfigures the skyline of western Manhattan.

Gulf and Western Building

1114 Avenue of the Americas. 192m/630ft. 50 floors.
Built in 1974 by Skidmore, Owings and Morrill, who, as in another of their buildings at 9 West 57th Street, sought to achieve the setting-back of the upper floors by adopting a curved form.

W. R. Grace Building

645 Fifth Avenue. 189m/620ft. 50 floors.
Built in 1976 by Skidmore, Owings and Merrill. This was the first skyscraper to combine shops, offices and owner-occupied apartments in the same building. The public arcade within the building, however, has failed to achieve the intended effect of lively activity.

Olympic Tower

Lexington Avenue. 279m/915ft. 46 floors.
Built in 1978 by Hugh Stubbins, this was the most discussed building of the 1970s (between 53rd and 54th Streets). In addition to shops and restaurants it also incorporates a church (St Peter's, Lutheran) designed by the same architect. The sloping tower of this building, the fifth tallest in Manhattan, is visible from many parts of the city. It was originally planned to use solar energy for the heating of the building, but the structure proved insufficiently strong to support the installation.

Citicorp Building

Madison Avenue. 183m/600ft. 53 floors.
This building, completed in 1984 to the design of Edward Larrabee Barnes, stands at the corner of 57th Street and is an important addition to the skyscraper landscape of New York. Built of dark green granite it stands 53 storeys high, with a further four storeys of glassed-in garden and an exhibition hall for IBM products. IBM Gallery – see entry.

IBM Tower

West 53rd Street. 198m/650ft. 58 floors.
The 58-storeys-high skyscraper erected over the Museum of Modern Art is the work of the Argentinian architect, Cesare Pelli. It houses not only additional exhibition rooms for the museum, but also 260 private apartments.

Museum Tower

★SoHo

E 10

The name of this Manhattan district has nothing to do with Soho in London: it is an acronym for So(uth) of Ho(uston Street). This area of about a square mile is bounded on the north by Houston Street, on the west by West Broadway (SoHo's main street), on the south by Canal Street and on the east by Broadway.

Location
Between Avenue of the Americas, Broadway, Houston and Canal Street ("downtown")

Some twenty five years ago it was a quiet backwater of warehouses and small factories, but today it is New York's liveliest artists' quarter. It all began when artists took to renting the large areas of space available in disused warehouses and converting them into studios and living accommodation. In the course of time they were followed by numerous galleries, smart shops, restaurants and jazz and rock clubs, and SoHo became a tourist Mecca. Nowadays it hums with life and activity, particularly on Saturday afternoons, except during the quiet summer months.

Subway stations
Spring Street (lines A, E), Bleecker Street (line 6)

Nowhere else in America is there such a concentration of 100-year-old cast-iron buildings as can be seen in SoHo (off West Broadway, particularly

Cast iron houses

in Greene Street but also in Broome Street). The use of cast-iron made it possible to produce at low cost columns, arches, doorways and other constructional elements – indeed entire façades – the first use of standardised and prefabricated elements in building. This gave rise to an abundance of interesting detail which can still be admired. Fifteen years ago a proposal was put forward to demolish almost all the old buildings in this quarter to make way for a new road, but fortunately the plan was frustrated at the eleventh hour and the whole of SoHo is now under statutory protection as a national monument.

A stroll through SoHo is an experience not to be missed. Here you can see the very latest trends in American art and will encounter a seemingly endless range of galleries, boutiques and other interesting shops, restaurants and places of entertainment (see Practical Information, Galleries).

★★Solomon R. Guggenheim Museum   E 3

Location
1071 Fifth Avenue
& 89th Street

Subway stations
86th St.
(lines 4, 5, 6)

Bus
1, 2, 3, 4

Opening times
Mon.–Wed.
10am–6pm,
Fri.–Sun.
10am–8pm

Admission fee

Information
Tel. 360 3555

This art museum is based on the private collection of paintings of the coal and steel industrialist of Swiss origin, Solomon R. Guggenheim (1861–1949), which he donated to his foundation in 1937 "for the promotion of art and art education". In 1943 Guggenheim commissioned the architect Frank Lloyd Wright (1869–1959) to build a museum worthy of the works of arts in the "Solomon R. Guggenheim Collection of Non-Objective Paintings" which had only been temporarily housed since 1939. It took fourteen years before the municipal authorities approved the plans and building began in 1957. Wright died six months before it was completed in 1959. The only museum building and work by Wright in New York is an architectural masterpiece with its aesthetic form complementing its function. "A museum", postulated Wright, "is an organic structure consisting of a single large room on one continuous floor". He broke away from the room layout of traditional museums and created a single cylindrical, 28m (92ft) high interior where daylight shines through a glass dome. A 432m (1417ft) long spiral ramp with an angle of 3% winds conically upwards, becoming wider, leading to the works of art in over 70 niches and small galleries. Lighting is by natural daylight and indirect sources of light along the ramp; some works are specially illuminated. This layout forces an open and systematic presentation of the exhibits and at the same time points the visitor, after having taken the lift, in the direction of the logical sequence of exhibits which runs from top to bottom.

Thanks to renovation work completed in 1992 by the architect Charles Gwathmey numerous design faults which had become apparent since 1959 have been overcome and an additional 4,500sq.m (48,438sq.ft) of exhibition space has been provided in the ten storey annexe connected to the main building. A basement has been built under the entire complex to create room for workshops and storage. Until now the top part of the spiral was used for storage but it is now accessible to visitors so that they can experience the full effect of the ramp as Wright intended. Even so there is still insufficient room for the 8000 or more paintings and sculptures but with the opening of the Guggenheim Museum SoHo (see below) further exhibition space has been created.

Museum collection

Special exhibitions and continual rearrangements mean that only a general overview of the most important artists and their works is possible:

The largest Kandinsky colletion in the world including "Light picture No. 188" (1913), "Autumn" (1914), "Winter" (1914), "Two Red Pages, No. 437", (1928). Also Henri Rousseau "Artillerymen" (1895), "A Football Game" (1908); Delaunay "Eiffel Tower" (1904, 1910, 1912), "Saint Séverin" (1912); Braque "Violin and Palette" (1910), "Piano and Harp" (1910);

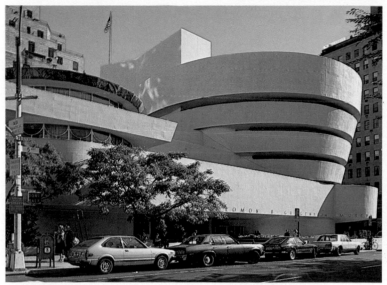

Solomon R. Guggenheim Museum:

Picasso "Harmonica Player" (1911), "Mandolin and Guitar" (1924); Léger "Smoker" (1911), "The Big Parade" (1954); Chagall "Paris through the Window" (1913), "The Green Violinist" (1918); Marc "Sleeping Horses" (1913); Mondrian "Composition 7" (1913); Kokoschla "Travelling Knight" (1915), Feininger "Gelmeroda IV" (1915); Modigliani "Act" (1917), "Yellow Sweater" (1919); Klee "Dance to my Song, you Monster" (1922); "Revolution of the Viaduct" (1937); Miró; Rauschenberg "Red Painting" (1953); Pollock "Ocean Greyness" (1953); Dubuffet "Door with Seagrass" (1957), "Nunc Stans" (1965). And the last work of Andy Warhol, a series of prints with Mercedes cars has found a place here.

The Munich art dealer Justin K. Thannhauser, who died in 1976, bequeathed his collection of 75 Impressionict and Post-impressionist masterpieces to the museum. They include: "The Chess Players" (*c.* 1863) by Daumier, "Les Coteaux de L'Hermitage à Pontoise" (1867) by Pissaro, Renoir's "Woman with a Parrot" (*c.* 1872), Manet's "In Front of the Mirror" (1878), "Madame Cézanne" (1885–87) and "The Watchmaker" (1895–1900) by Cézanne, van Gogh's "Hills at Saint-Rémy" (1889), "Au Salon" (1893) by Toulouse-Lautrec, Picasso's "Le Moulin de la Galette" (1900), "Two Harlequins" (1905) and "Three Bathers" (1920) as well as several works by Braque, Degas, Derain, Gauguin, Matisse, Modigliani and Vuillard. *Thannhauser Collection*

In another gallery art between the two world wars is on display, chronologically a continuation of the Thannhauser Collection. They include works by Kandinsky ("Several Cicles"), Mondrian ("Compositions"), Miró, Chagall, ("Green Violinist") and Léger ("Woman Holding a Vase"). *Art between the wars*

Among the sculptures are "The Dancers" by Degas (1882–95), "Sorcière" (1916) by Brancusi, "Mendrano" (1915) by Archipenko, "Growing" (1938) by von Arp and a "Mobile" by Alexander Calder. *Sculpture*

South Street Seaport Museum

Guggenheim
Museum SoHo

The Guggenheim Museum SoHo opened in 1992, which adjoins the museum, is located at 575 Broadway/corner of Prince Street (open: Sun., Mon.–Wed. 11am–6pm, Thur.–Sat. 11am–8pm).

★South Street Seaport Museum

F 11

Location
On East River

Subway stations
Fulton Street
(lines 2, 3, 4, 5, J, M, Z)
Broadway-Nassau
(lines A, C)

Bus
15, 2nd Avenue to
Fulton Street

South of Brooklyn Bridge (see entry) South Street Seaport, the heart of New York harbour, was once the "gateway" to New York and the surviving or restored buildings to be seen here bear witness to the early years of the overseas trade which was the basis of the city's growth and prosperity.

In the 1860s, however, when sail gave place to steam, the main port activity moved to the Hudson River, where there was room for the construction of large piers. The East Side quarter fell into decay with only the fish market remaining.

Opening times: Daily Jan.–Mar., Mon.–Sat. 10am–5pm Sun. 11am–6pm; Apr.–Dec., Mon.–Sat. 10am–9pm Sun. 11am–7pm

Historic Ships

Piers 15 and 16

The main attraction of the museum are the historic ships moored at these piers. At Pier 15 are the three-master "Wavetree" from 1885, the small

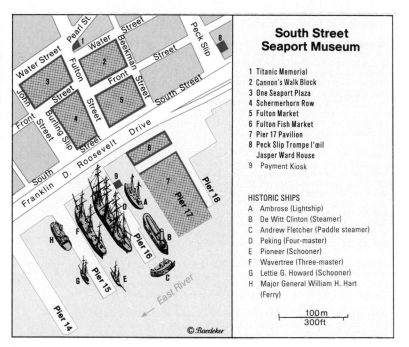

South Street Seaport Museum

1 Titanic Memorial
2 Cannon's Walk Block
3 One Seaport Plaza
4 Schermerhorn Row
5 Fulton Market
6 Fulton Fish Market
7 Pier 17 Pavilion
8 Peck Slip Trompe l'œil
   Jasper Ward House
'9 Payment Kiosk

HISTORIC SHIPS
A Ambrose (Lightship)
B De Witt Clinton (Steamer)
C Andrew Fletcher (Paddle steamer)
D Peking (Four-master)
E Pioneer (Schooner)
F Wavertree (Three-master)
G Lettie G. Howard (Schooner)
H Major General William H. Hart
   (Ferry)

100m
300ft

© Baedeker

114

schooner "Lettie G. Howard" and the "Major General William H. Hart", a ferry built in 1925 which plied between Manhattan and Governor's Island, now occupied by the Pioneer Marine School, a school of seamanship.

Between May and mid-September the "Pioneer", a sailing ship built in 1885, departs from here on two and three hour cruises around the port. They are, however, very expensive. (tel. 669 9400 for information).

Harbour tours

Shorter cruises can also be made on the paddle-steamer "Andrew Fletcher" (Pier 16) and the "De Witt Clinton", a steamer built around the turn of the century.

The showpiece at Pier 16 is the four-master "Peking", built in 1911 by Blohm & Voss at Hamburg. Together with her sister ship "Passat" and the "Pamir", sunk in 1957 she belonged to the "Flying P Liners", in total seventeen large sailing vessels from the Hamburg shipping line Laeisz, which travelled between Europe and South America. The "Peking" which could carry 4700 tons, was sold to England in 1932 and served under the name of "Arethusa" as a stationary school ship. In 1975 she was transferred to New York. The "Ambrose" a lightship from 1907 is also moored here.

Historic Buildings

The blocks around Front Street, Fulton Street and Water Street have been renovated and house a multitude of shops and restaurants. In Cannon's Walk Block between Water and Front Street is the old printing factory "Browne and Co.", the Trans-Lux Seaport Theater with the multi-media show "Seaport Experience" and the Museum Gallery.

South Street Seaport Museum

Statue of Liberty and American Museum of Immigration

Visitor Center	The Visitor Center and Museum Shop are at No. 12 Fulton Street (tel. 669 9424).
Fulton Market	The Fulton Market Building from 1883 has an exhibition of small wooden boats.
Pier 17	In 1985 the old Pier 17 was built over; the resulting "town" of shops and restaurants has since become very popular. From spring to the fall many shows take place in the open.
Peck Slip Trompe l'oeil	At Peck Slip square the artist Richard Haas has painted a house with a mural which presents the observer with a façade of shops and Brooklyn Bridge.

★★Statue of Liberty and American Museum of Immigration

Situation
Liberty Island

Boat
Ferry from Battery Park (from 9am hourly, on the hour; more frequently in summer; for information tel. 269 5755)

In Upper Bay, about 4km (2 miles) south-west of the Battery, the "Statue of Liberty Enlightening the World" (a national monument since 1924) towers above the foundations of a fort built in 1811 on Liberty Island (Indian "Minissais", later "Bedloes Island"). The statue and base, with a combined height of 93m (305ft), make up this internationally famous symbol of the USA as the stronghold of freedom and democracy .

This monumental statue, dedicated to the USA on its 100th anniversary from the people of France, was originally designed by Frédéric Auguste Bartholdi (1834–1904; from Colmar) for the northern entrance to the Suez Canal; it was erected at the entrance to New York harbour on October 28th 1886 in the presence of the US President Cleveland, F.A. Bartholdi and F. de Lesseps, the designer of the Suez Canal.

Liberty Island, with the Statue of Liberty

It consists of a steel frame (by Gustav Eiffel) covered in copper plates and measures 46m (151ft) to the tip of the flame held in the raised right hand, which is illuminated at night, and weighs 225 tons. The goddess of freedom wearing a radiant diadem stands on the broken chains of slavery and in the left hand holds the Declaration of Independence with the historical date "July 4th 1776". The massive star-shaped granite base was designed by Richard M. Hunt. The money for its construction had to be raised through donations. In total it took twenty years from planning to its unveiling in New York.

Opening times
Daily 9am–5pm or 6pm in summer;

For information
tel. 363 3200

Engraved into the base are the words composed by Emma Lazarus from the New to the old World:

"Give me your tired, your poor
Your huddled masses yearning to be free
The wretched refuse of your teeming shore.
Send these, the homeless, tempest-tost to me,
I lift my lamp beside the golden door!"

For millions of immigrants coming to the United States by boat the Statue of Liberty was their first view of the New World and embodied their hopes – before they were subjected to the immigration process on Ellis Island (see entry), as experienced by Egon Erwin Kirsch.

Following a three year renovation period the 100th birthday of "Miss Liberty" was celebrated in the presence of President Reagan and the French President Mitterand on July 3rd and 4th 1986 with a Hollywood-style party, including fireworks and a laser show.

The Statue of Liberty is open to visitors again. A small exhibition relates the history of the statue.

There are usually two long queues waiting to visit the statue. One is for the lift to the viewing platform on the base with an exceptionally fine view of New York. The other is for those not daunted by the demanding climb to the head to get a view of New York and its surroundings through the windows in the crown. However, this pleasure is often spoiled by people pushing impatient to have their turn.

Tour

American Museum of Immigration

The idea of establishing a museum of immigration was first put forward in 1954, the foundation stone was laid eight years later and the museum was opened in 1972.

Opening times
Daily 9am–5pm

In addition to its permanent display of drawings, photographs, models and audio-visual presentations illustrating the different stages of the immigration movement, the Museum puts on special exhibitions on various aspects of the history of immigration. It covers the whole range from the first Indians who moved into the American continent from Asia to the immigrants of many nationalities and adherents of persecuted religious groups who came into the United States in the 19th and 20th c. A special exhibition is devoted to the large group of immigrants who were brought in against their will – the negroes who were shipped to America from Africa as slaves.

Following the renovation of Ellis Island the immigration museum has been extended and moved there in the autumn of 1990.

Studio Museum in Harlem   E 1

Address
144 West 125th
Street

Subway station
125th Street
(lines 2, 3)

Admission fee

This museum, founded in 1970, is the only museum exclusively devoted to work by contemporary black artists. It has no permanent collection but puts on periodic special exhibitions, often including work by Harlem artists. It also serves as a cultural centre for black artists in all fields: the museum itself is on the ground floor of a two-storey building, the upper floor of which has been converted into a large studio for the use of the black community.

A sculpture garden was opened next to the museum building in 1993.
Opening times: Wed.–Fri. 10am–5pm, Sat. and Sun. 1–6pm

Theodore Roosevelt Birthplace   E 8

Address
28 East 20th Street

Subway station
23rd Street (line 6)

Opening times
Wed.–Sun.
9am–5pm

Admission fee

This house, between Broadway and Park Avenue South, is not the actual house, built in 1848, in which Theodore Roosevelt, 26th President of the United States and the only President born in New York, came into the world in 1858. The original house was destroyed, probably during Roosevelt's lifetime, and in 1923 four years after his death was rebuilt in its earlier form.

Roosevelt lived here until he was fifteen years old. The interior has been decorated and furnished as it was in Roosevelt's early days. A museum housing memorabilia on "Teddy" Roosevelt was also opened.

Theodore Roosevelt is also commemorated by an equestrian statue (by James Earle Fraser) in front of the American Museum of Natural History (see entry).

★Times Square   D 6

Location
Intersection of
Broadway and
Seventh Avenue
between West
42nd and West
47th Streets

Subway station
Times Square
(lines 1, 2, 3, 7,
N, R)

Buses
104, 106

Until 1904 the long intersection of Broadway and 7th Avenue between West 42nd and West 47th Street was called Longacre Square and was home to coachmen, saddleries and horse stables. When the "New York Times" built their new office block "Times Tower", the second highest building in the city at that time, at the southern end of the square the new name was quickly adopted. Today its headquarters are not far away at 229 West 43rd Street. A huge news board is illuminated above "One Times Square" (between Broadway & 7th Avenue and West 42nd & West 43rd Street).

The opening of the Metropolitan Opera in 1883 also at the southern end of the square and the founding of the Olympia Theatre two years later led to the square becoming the entertainment quarter of New York.

During the Twenties there were eighty theatres in the "Theatre District". The stars stayed in the Astor and other elegant hotels. Advertising signs such as the giant smoker who blew smoke into the air every five seconds were an attraction in their own right, giving the square the nickname "The Great White Way".

Times Square
today

The former glory has faded. Of the remaining 35 theatres located chiefly in the side streets around Times Square the oldest is the "Lyceum" (149 West 45th Street) from 1903 – all older theatre buildings have since been demolished. The district around 42nd Street (between 7th and 8th Avenue) and along 8th Avenue (between 42nd and 50th Street) has developed into an entertainment quarter with a dubious reputation. Among the many cinemas, night clubs and bars pornography, prostitution and drugs have become established – a problem common to many cities. Despite this – or perhaps because of it – Times Square has become a major attraction for tourists, especially in the evening. Visitors here should keep their bags

Times Square

fastened and not stop when approached by suspicious characters who may be up to no good.

In recent years the State and City of New York have jointly considered the future of the square and presented the suggestions of famous architects to the public. In 42nd Street and around Times Square 75 new sites are planned with hotels, office blocks, shopping centres and even theatres. In 1985 one of the largest of New York's hotels, the Marriot Marquis with more than 1800 rooms, was built between 45th and 46th Street. Despite its impressive atrium it resembles a gigantic bunker and can hardly be said to contribute to the intended rehabilitation of the square.

Whereas the side of Times Square adjoining 47th Street is taking its future shape with the construction of three hotels – Holiday Inn-Crown Plaza, Embassy Suites and Ramada Renaissance; building on the south side past 42nd Street still has not started despite advanced planning. Intended demolition/renovation projects include the old Times Building and the houses between 43rd and 42nd Street on Broadway as well as the block between 7th and 8th Avenue. Owing to problems of finance it will probably be some time before office blocks and a fourth large hotel are built on the south side of Times Square.

Tribeca   D/E 10

Tribeca – an acronym for "**Tri**angle **Be**low **Ca**nal Street" – is one of the most recent of New York's artists' quarters – rents in the adjoining district of SoHo (see entry) to the north having become too high for young artists trying to make a name for themselves.

Here, as in SoHo, whole floors of disused warehouses and factories have been converted into living accommodation; and here, too, numbers of

Situation
South of SoHo ("downtown")

Subway station
Canal Street
(lines A, C, E)

restaurants, bars, discos and jazz and rock clubs have sprung up. There are also a number of galleries, mostly on upper floors.

Trinity Church   E 11

Situation
Broadway and
Wall Street

Subway stations
Wall Street
(lines 4, 5),
Rector Street
(lines 1, R)

Buses
1, 6

Opening times
Museum:
Mon.–Fri.
9am–3.45pm; Sat.
10am–3.45pm;
Sun. 1pm–3.45pm

Guided tours of
the church
Mon.–Fri. 2pm

Museum

Cemetery

The present-day church, wedged in between the tower blocks, is the third church of this name to be erected on this site. The first Trinity Church from 1698 was a narrow building without a tower where services for slaves and free Blacks were held as early as 1705. The church burnt down in 1776. The second was built between 1788 and 1790 but demolished in 1839 as it was so dilapidated. On Ascension Day 1846 the present day Trinity Church was consecrated, designed in the "Gothic Revival" style of the English architect Richard Upjohn. Until the turn of the century its tower was the tallest building in New York. The bronze doors on the three entrances from Broadway depict biblical scenes (main entrance and north doorway) and events from the history of the United States and the Trinity community (south doorway). They were a present from the Astor family and were designed by Richard Morris Hunt (1828–95) but only made in this century. The west doorway is by the Viennese artist Karl Bittner. Following extensive restoration work, completed in 1992, the exterior façade is resplendent in its light brown sandstone.

In the interior the stained glass and the back of the altar with scenes from the life of Christ carved in stone from Caen (France) are of particular interest. Additions from this century are the All Saints Chapel and the Bishop Manning Memorial Wing.

There is a museum which houses numerous interesting documents about the early history of New York and also about the church which received its estates in 1705 from the English Queen Anne and which, owing to the considerable size of its property, is the richest episcopal parish of the city. St Paul's Chapel (see entry) also belongs to the parish of Trinity

The picturesque cemetery is the oldest in New York. The earliest gravestone dates from 1681. Many historic personalities are buried here including, in a pyramid shaped tomb, Alexander Hamilton (see Famous People), the first Finance Minister of the USA, who was killed in a duel by his opponenet Aaron Burr (see Morris Jumel Mansion Museum), and Robert Fulton (see Famous People), who built the first usable steamship.

Trump Tower   E 6

Address
725 Fifth Avenue
& 56th Street

Subway station
Fifth Avenue
(lines E, F, N, R)

Opening times
Daily 8a.m–10pm

Of the three skyscrapers completed in 1984 between 54th Street and 57th Street and between Fifth Avenue and Madison Avenue, Trump Tower is without doubt the most spectacular. The glass building, 68 storeys high, owes its origin to plans by Der Scutt and is named after the property speculator Donald J. Trump.

The atrium is by far the finest of all New York buildings. Here Breccia marble was used for the walls and the floor and this radiates a colourful mixture of pink, peach and orange.

Restaurants and numerous shops can be found here and above them are offices and apartments, of which the largest in the topmost storey cost an unbelievable 10 million dollars.

The site was formerly occupied by the fashion house Bonwit and Teller which now has a larger store on the ground floor and which is directly connected with the equally attractive "glass garden" of the IBM building (see Skyscrapers).

The atrium of Trump Tower

Ukrainian Museum   F 8

This museum, situated in an area still largely occupied by Ukranians, was founded in 1976. It is mainly devoted to Ukranian folk arts and crafts, including many examples of the famous *pysanky* (painted Easter eggs) as well as woven and embroidered textiles, pottery, wooden articles and metalwork. Most of the material dates from the 19th and 20th c.

Address
203 Second Avenue

Subway station
Union Square
(lines 4, 5, 6, N, R)

The museum is open Wed.–Sun. 1–5 p.m. Admission fee.

★United Nations Headquarters   F 6

The United Nations are committed to the goal of resolving disputes between nations by peaceful means so as not to endanger world peace and international security and justice. Their main bodies are the General or Full Assembly (UNGA) to which all member states belong, the Security Council (UNSC), its permanent members being the USA, Russia, People's Republic of China, Great Britain, France and 10 other countries voted in for two years by the General Assembly, the Economic and Social Council (ECOSOC), the Trusteeship Council (UNTC), the International Justice Court (IJC) with headquarters in The Hague (Netherlands) and the General Secretariat (UNSG) headed by the General Secretary (since January 1st 1992 the Egyptian Butros Ghali). Every state committed to the principles laid down in the UN charter can be accepted upon recommendation of the Security Council and agreement of the General Assembly. The original 51 members have increased to over 170 member states. The Federal Republic of Germany was accepted on September 18th 1973. The languages of the con-

Situation
First Avenue between 45th & 46th Street

Subway station
Grand Central
(lines 4, 5, 6, 7, S)

Buses
15, 104, 106

Opening times
Daily 8am–5.30pm

Conducted tours
9.15am–4.45pm

121

United Nations Headquarters

Admission fee
No children under 5; parties:
tel. 963 4440

ferences are Arabic, Chinese, English, French, Russian and Spanish. Since 1975 all important documents are also translated into German. Every year on October 24th, the official date of its foundation, "United Nations Day" is celebrated.

Meetings

During meetings it is possible to attend the conferences at 10.30am and 3.30pm daily. Visitors should enquire in the lobby of the General Assembly about one hour prior to the beginning of the meeting.

Buildings

The UN headquarters are built on a site previously occupied by slaughter-houses and light industry. The purchase was made possible by a munificence of John D. Rockefeller Jr, and the building costs were met by an interest-free loan of 67 million dollars from the United States. The site is extra-territorial and has its police force and postal sevice.

The flags of the member states arranged in English alphabetical order fly at this complex of buildings constructed between 1949 and 1953 to a design by Le Corbusier and Oskar Niemeyer under the direction of Wallace K. Harrison. The site is dominated by the glass façade of the relatively narrow

Secretariat Building

39-storey Secretariat Building (154m/505ft), seat of the UN administration and the General Secretary, whose office is on the 38th floor. In the Conference Room there is a notable Swiss world clock and a sculpture entitled "Single Form" by Barbara Hepworth (1963). The flat Conference Building is

General Assembly Building

connected to the rounded General Assembly Building with the domed eliptical auditorium in the centre. In the basement of the lobby is the UN gift shop, which sells craftwork and souvenirs from all the member states, and a bookshop. Stamp collectors would be interested in a visit to the UN post office, also in the basement, where letters can be franked with the special UN stamp. Letters and cards stamped here have to be posted from within the building. South-west of the General Assembly Building is the Dag Hammarskjöld Library, named after the second UN General Secretary, who died in an air crash in the Congo. The building was a gift from the Ford Foundation and was built in 1961.

Sculpture

Contributions from artists from all the member states decorate the azalea gardens and buildings of the complex. They include a Soviet sculpture "Swords to Ploughshares", the bronze "Climber" by the East German artist

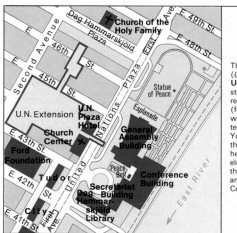

United Nations Headquarters

The **United Nations Organisation** (*UNO*), now generally known as the **United Nations** (*UN*), was constituted in 1945 at San Francisco, replacing the League of Nations (founded 1919). Its early meetings were held in London and at various temporary meeting-places in the New York area (Flushing, Lake Success); then in 1952 it moved into its present headquarters on East River. Its main elements are the General Assembly, the Security Council, the Economic and Social Council, the Trusteeship Council and the Secretariat.

200 m
600 ft

The United Nations Headquarters on East River

Fritz Cremer and the "White Horse" by the Düsseldorf artist E. von Janota-Bzowski.

Visitors to the UN headquarters should also visit the nearby squares and buildings. Between 42nd and 43rd Street stands the Ford Foundation with a winter garden which is an oasis of peace. On the corner of the United Nations Plaza & 46th Street is the African-American Institute (833 United Nations Plaza) which shows African art exhibitions on the ground floor. Temporary sculpture exhibitions are held on the Dag Hammarskjöld Plaza.

Surroundings

Urban Center   E 6

The Urban Center was formed at the end of 1980, when four organisations – the Municipal Art Society, the Architectural League, the New York branch of the American Institute of Artists and the Parks Council – took up their quarters at the north end of the famous row known as the Villard Houses, now incorporated in the new Palace Hotel. The main objective of these bodies is to promote the development of good architecture in an attractive environment, and they put on periodic ideas.

Situation
457 Madison Avenue and 51st Street

Subway stations
51st Street (line 6), Fifth Avenue (lines E, F)

The Villard Houses, in an Italian Renaissance style modelled on the Palazzo della Cancelleria in Rome, were built by the New York architects McKim, Mead and White in 1884 for Henry Villard (originally named Heinrich Hilgard), publisher of the "New York Post", who emigrated from Bavaria to the United States in 1860 and within a very short time had achieved an established position and a fortune. The Villard Houses lie immediately behind St Patrick's Cathedral (see entry). The Urban Center is open Friday to Wednesday from 1–5pm.

Buses
1, 2, 3, 4

Van Cortlandt Mansion and Museum

Situation
Bronx

Subway station
242nd Street/Van
Cortlandt Park
(lines 1, 9)

Admission fee

This well-preserved stone-built house, erected in 1748 for a well-to-do New York family, stands in north-west Bronx, at the south end of a park which now provides much-used facilities for a variety of ball games, but in the 18th c. was arable land.

The well-preserved furniture and furnishings date from the time when the house was built and latter part of the 18th c.

Opening times are: Tues.–Sat. 10am–4pm, Sun. noon–5pm; closed in February.

★Wall Street   E 11

Location
South of
Manhattan from
Broadway east to
East River

Subway stations
Wall Street
(lines 4, 5),
Rector Street
(lines N, R)

Bus
6

Wall Street has become a synonym for New York's Financial District, although this in fact extends in all directions from Wall Street.

The street takes its name from the wall built here to protect the Dutch settlement of New Amsterdam against British attack and Indian raids – a purpose which it failed to achieve. It is now a narrow canyon of a street built in 1700 into which the sun never penetrates, lined with banks, financial institutions and lawyers' offices; also two of the tallest skyscrapers in New York, which have no names other than their addresses of 40 and 60 Wall Street. On weekday afternoons Wall Street and the adjoining streets are so crowded with people that it is hardly possible to move; at weekends and on public holidays, however, the area is deserted.

At the corner of Wall Street and Broad Street are the fortress-like headquarters of the great banking house of J. P. Morgan, and diagonally opposite this is the New York Stock Exchange (see entry). A few yards north of Wall Street along Nassau Street is one of New York's most striking skyscrapers, the Chase Manhattan Bank (see Skyscrapers). Opposite the west end of Wall Street, on Broadway, stands Trinity Church (see entry).

Up and down Broadway – north as far as Fulton Street, south to Bowling Green – are more of the skyscrapers, housing banks and offices, which give the district its characteristic aspect.

★★Whitney Museum of American Art   E 4

Situation
Madison Avenue
and
75th Street

Subway station
77th Street (line 6)

Buses
1, 2, 3, 4

Opening times
Wed., Fri–Sun.
11am–6pm
Thurs. 1–8pm

Admission fee

The museum developed from the studio, which was already founded in 1908, of the wealthy sculptress and art patron Gertrude Vanderbilt Whitney (1877–1942) whose aim it was to promote, through meetings, exhibitions and sales, the work of unknown American artists and stimulate national artistic activity. The first studio museum which exhibited primarily the patron's own private collection, was established in 1931 in Greenwich Village 8 West 8th Street now the site of an alternative art school. The collection which was growing year by year was housed in 1966 in the building designed by the architects Marcel L. Breuer and Hamilton Smith on Madison Avenue. Since then three branches have been added and another building is planned which would increase the exhibition space considerably.

The five-storey inverted pyramid is covered with grey granite plates. The severity of the north front on East 75th Street is relieved by irregularly arranged prism windows of varying size. The Museum is entered by a concrete bridge, from which there is a view of the Sculpture Garden with the adjoining restaurant. On two of the four floors of display space there are regular special exhibitions, leaving too little room for the steadily growing permanent collection. Every two years in autumn there is an exhibition mainly devoted to items acquired during the preceding years.

Museum exhibits

The Whitney Museum is the only museum in New York exclusively devoted to 20th c. American art. It also possesses some 2000 paintings, drawings and prints bequeathed by Edward Hooper.

All important American artists are represented including:

Paintings

Albers "Homage to the Square: Ascending" (1953), Bellows "Dempsey and Firpo" (1924), Davis "Owh! in San Pao" (1951), de Koonong "Door to the River" (1960), Dine "The Toaster" (1962), Evergood "Lily and the Sparrows" (1939), Feininger "Gelmeroda VIII" (1921), Gorky "The Betrothal II" (1947), Gottlieb "Excalibur" (1963), Guston "Fial" (1956), Henri "Storm Tide" (1903), Johns "Studio" (1964), Kline "Mahoning " (1956), Kuhn "The Blue Clown" (1931), Lichtenstein "Little Big Painting" (1965), Lindner "Ice" (1966), Louis "Gamma Delta" (1959–60), Marin "Weehawken Sequence No. 5" (1903–04), Motherwell "The Red Skirt" (1947), O'Keefe "The White Flower" (1931), Pollock "Number 27" (1950), Prendergast "The Promenade" (1913), Reinhardt "Number 18" (1948–49), Rosenquist "U-Haul-It" (1967), Rothko "Four Darks in Red" (1958), Shahn "The Passion of Sacco and Vanzetti" (1931–32), Frank Stella "Agbatana I" (1968), Joseph Stella "Brooklyn Bridge" (1939), Warhol "Green Coca-Cola Bottles" (1962), Wes-

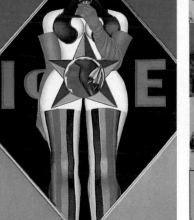

Whitney Museum: "Ice" by R. Linder . . .   *. . . "Ethel Scull" by A. Warhol*

125

selman "Great American Nude, Number 57" (1964), Wyeth "Spool Bed" (1947).

Sculpture

Among the sculptures are works by Archipenko "Torso in Space" (1936), Louise Bourgeois "One and Others" (1955), Calder "Indian Feathers" (1969), Johns "Lightbulb" (1969), Kienholz "The Wait" (1964–65), Reuben Nakian "Olympia" (1961), Louise Nevelson "Night – Focus – Dawn" (1969), Oldenbourg "Ice Bag – Scale C" (1971), Serra "Prop." (1968), Trova "Study/ Falling Man" (1966), Gertrude Vanderbilt Whitney "Mother and Child" (1935).

Branch Museum

There is a branch museum of the Whitney Museum at Philip Morris, Park Avenue & 42nd Street with a sculpture courtyard and adjoining gallery for temporary exhibitions (open: Mon.–Fri. 11am–6pm, Thur. until 7.30pm).

★★ World Trade Center   D/E 11

Situation
Between Church, Vesey, Dey and Liberty Streets

Subway stations
Cortlandt Street (lines 1, R), World Trade Center (line E) Chambers Street (line A)

Bus 10

The 420m (1378ft) high twin towers (110 floors) of the World Trade Center are the tallest buildings in New York. The New York Harbor Authority began planning in the early Sixties and work started in 1966 on the World Trade Center, designed by Minuro Yamasaki from Japan for the 21st century. The site with numerous workshops, small businesses and warehouses was in need of renovation. Officially opened on April 4th 1973 the International World Trade Center consists of the two imposing identical towers and a building in the corner between Washington St. and West Broadway together with the South-east Plaza Building, which houses the Commodity Futures Exchange (visitors' gallery) on the 9th floor, the North-east Plaza Building and the US Customs Building with a museum, and also a long building for an Information Center (with a computer centre) and a hotel.

Towers of the World Trade Center on the Manhattan skyline

The buildings surround the Austin J. Tobin Plaza with its greens and fountains and in the centre there is a bronze globe that moves almost undetectably by the Munich artist Fritz König.

Both the twin towers South Tower and North Tower have 21m (69ft) foundations dug into the slate rock and rise on 63m (206ft) square bases to form sharp-edged towers with finely structured aluminium façades (comprising about 43,600 windows opening only 55cm (22in.) wide) covering a framework of closely spaced steel columns. Altogether about 180,000 tons of steel and 4800km (2982 miles) of electric cable were required to construct the towers which sway above the 12m (39ft) high Gothic-like buttresses by up to 30cm (12in.). Approximately 50,000 people are employed in the offices of the authorities, public and private national and international commercial organisations, banks, insurance companies, property developers, haulage companies, scientific institutions and many others connected with world trade and about 80,000 visitors come every day. Each tower has 104 lifts (in three zones: 1st–43rd, 44th–77th and 78th–110th floor; 23 express lifts). The World Trade Center has its own post code NY 10048.

There is a comprehensive view of New York from the Observation Deck. On the 107th floor there is an exhibition on trade. Following a bomb attack in February 1993 the restaurant "Windows on the World" on the 107th floor of the North Tower had to be closed as did the Hotel Vista. Since the attack the security procedures throughout the entire complex of the World Trade Center have been tightened.

Opening times
Observation Deck:
daily
9.30am–9.30pm
Exchange:
Mon.–Fri.
9.30am–3pm
Conducted tours
by arrangement:
tel. 938 2018

Admission fee
to Observation
Deck

Yorkville   E/F 3/4

Yorkville used to be the German quarter of Manhattan, and 86th Street (between Lexington and Second Avenue) was known as "German Broadway". However, nowadays little remains apart from a handful of coffee houses and restaurants, a few shops and two abbatoirs. Only a few German-speaking residents remain as the urban development and demolition pushed up the rents.

At the turn of the century Germans began to settle here and numbers increased until the outbreak of the Second World War. Its rapid decline as a German quarter started around 1960. At the east end of 86th Street is Gracie Mansion (see entry), residence of the mayor of New York, and Carl Schurz Park.

Situation
Between 79th
Street, Park
Avenue, 90th
Street and East
River

Subway station
86th Street
(lines 4, 5, 6)

Bus 18

Practical Information

Airlines

Air Canada
Two branches, tel. 800 776 3000

Air France
666 Fifth Avenue, tel. 247 0100

Alitalia
666 Fifth Avenue, tel. 582 8900

American Airlines
Ten branches, tel. 1 800 433 7300

British Airways
530 Fifth Avenue, tel. 1 800 247 9297

Continental Airlines
tel. 1 800 525 0280

Delta Airlines
Eight branches, tel. 239 0700

KLM
437 Madison Avenue, tel. 800 374 7747

Lufthansa
tel. 1 800 645 3880

Swissair and Austrian Airlines
608 Fifth Avenue, tel. 1 800 221 4750

TWA
tel. 1 800 892 4141

United Airlines
Six branches, tel. 1 800 241 6522

Airports

The times quoted for the connecting services apply to weekdays. At weekends services are less frequent but still operate round the clock. **Note**

This, the largest of New York's three commercial airports, lies on Jamaica Bay, 26km (16 miles) from the city centre. Passengers arrive in the International Arrival Building, except those flying with American, United, Eastern, Delta, TWA or British Airways, which all have their own terminals. **J. F. Kennedy International Airport (JFK)**

◀ *General Sherman guards the entrance to Central Park*

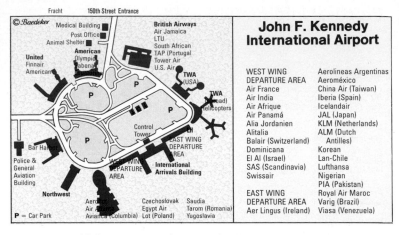

Fracht   150th Street Entrance

© Baedeker

Medical Building ■
Post Office ■
Animal Shelter ■
American
United
Finnair
American
Olympic
Sabena
Canadian

British Airways
Air Jamaica
LTU
South African
TAP (Portugal)
Tower Air
U.S. Air
TWA (USA)
TWA (road)
Helicopters
Control Tower
EAST WING DEPARTURE AREA
WEST WING DEPARTURE AREA
International Arrivals Building

P
P
P
P
P

Bar Harbor
Police & General Aviation Building
Northwest

Aeroflot
Air Atlanta
Avianca (Columbia)
Czechoslovak
Egypt Air
Lot (Poland)
Saudia
Tarom (Romania)
Yugoslavia

P = Car Park

John F. Kennedy International Airport

WEST WING DEPARTURE AREA	
Air France	Aerolineas Argentinas
Air India	Aeroméxico
Air Afrique	China Air (Taiwan)
Air Panamá	Iberia (Spain)
Alia Jordanien	Icelandair
Alitalia	JAL (Japan)
Balair (Switzerland)	KLM (Netherlands)
Dominicana	ALM (Dutch Antilles)
El Al (Israel)	Korean
SAS (Scandinavia)	Lan-Chile
Swissair	Lufthansa
	Nigerian
	PIA (Pakistan)
EAST WING DEPARTURE AREA	Royal Air Maroc
Aer Lingus (Ireland)	Varig (Brazil)
	Viasa (Venezuela)

By minibus	Minibuses on request (7am–11pm) to the largest hotels in Manhattan. Fare $15 per person, every 55 minutes.
Information	Central information office in the hall of the International Arrival Building, tel. 1 718 656 7990.
Disabled	Port Authority of New York and New Jersey, tel. 1 718 656 4476.
Lost Property	Contact the airlines or main lost property office, tel. 1 718 656 4120.
Connections within the airport	Yellow and white JFK Airline courtesy buses between terminals every 5–15 minutes.

Getting to and from Manhattan

By taxi
The fare at present ranges between $40 and $50, plus the tunnel or bridge toll and a tip (see Tipping).

By Carey Bus
To 125 Park Avenue; Port Authority Bus Terminal (Eighth Avenue, 41st Street); Hilton Hotel (West 53rd Street); Sheraton City Square (Seventh Avenue); and Marriott Marquis Hotel (Broadway).
   Fare at present $11. The buses run every 30 minutes 5am–10.30pm.

By service bus
Take the Q10 Green bus to its terminus at Kew Gardens; then subway line E or F to Manhattan.
   Fare $1.25 (plus $1.25 for subway). The cheapest way, but the slowest, and only possible if you have not much luggage. Duration of journey – about one hour.

By helicopter
To East 34th Street (East River) from TWA International Terminal/Gate 37.
   Fare at present $75 (plus tax). Quickest way (10 minutes). With some airlines this is included in the First Class or Business Class fare.

There are also connections with places outside New York including New Jersey, Westchester, Long Island, etc.

Information about departure times can be obtained from the transport companies (toll-free telephones in the arrival halls).

Taxi journeys to places outside New York cost twice the fare shown on the meter, plus bridge or tunnel tolls.

Connections with places outside New York

Carey Line buses run to LaGuardia Airport hourly 5am–1pm and half-hourly 1.30–9.20pm.

Salem Transportation Inc. have cars running to Newark Airport 9am–9pm.

Helicopter flights operate between all the airports 6am–9pm.

Connections with other New York airports

LaGuardia Airport, also in Queens, is only 13km (8 miles) from the city centre.

LaGuardia International Airport

Information desk "Apple Aide" in the Main Terminal. Open: Mon.–Fri. 9am–8pm, Sun. 2–6pm.

Information

Port Authority Police Headquarters, tel. 1 718 476 5115.

Disabled

Contact the airlines or tel. 1 718 476 5128

Lost Property

Yellow and white courtesy buses between terminals every 10–15 minutes.

Connections within the airport

By taxi
Fare about $20–30, plus bridge or tunnel toll and tip.

Getting to and from Manhattan

By service bus
QT bus (information tel. 1 718 335 1000) to Queensbridge/21st Street, connecting with lines B and Q into the city. Fare $6.25. Not recommended if you have heavy luggage.

By Carey Express Bus
Every 30 minutes (5am–1am) to same stops as from JFK. Fare $8.50. Journey time approx. 40 minutes.

Minibus
For times and destinations see JFK airport. Fare $12. Journey time approx. 45 minutes.

To J. F. Kennedy International Airport
Carey Bus every 30–60 minutes
New York helicopter on request.

Connections with other airports

To Newark: Salem Transportation: by limousine every 60–90 minutes (9am–9pm).
New York Helicopter: on request.

On Newark Bay (New Jersey), 24km (15 miles) from the city centre, but a quicker journey than to or from the other airports, since the traffic on the road is not so heavy.

Newark International Airport

Information desk in terminals A and B, gates 5 and 6; terminal C, gate 8.

Information

Tel. 1 201 961 2154.

Disabled

Contact the airlines or tel. 1 201 961 2230.

Lost Property

Auction rooms

Connections within the airport	Brown and white courtesy buses between terminals.
By taxi	Fare must be negotiated as the drivers are not required to turn on the meter for journeys between New York and New Jersey. Bridge or tunnel toll and tip not included. (See tipping.)
By service bus/train	Airlink bus every 20–30 minutes (6am–1pm) to Newark Penn Station, change for New Jersey Transit, Amtrak or PATH. Trains every 20–30 minutes (6.15am–12.45am) to Manhattan Pennsylvania station (NJ Transit, Amtrak) or World Trade Center (PATH). Not recommended if you have heavy luggage.
By express bus	New Jersey Transit every 15 minutes (6am–12pm) or every 30 minutes (midnight–6am) to the Port Authority Bus Terminal (Eighth Avenue and 42nd Street), fare $7. Journey time 25–35 minutes.
	Olympic trails bus every 20–30 minutes (5am–1am) from and to the World Trade Center and Grand Central Station; from and to Pennsylvania Station, 34th Street and Eighth Avenue, all journeys $7 single, $12 return. Journey time 25–35 minutes.
Minibus	Newark International/NYC minibus on request to the largest hotels in Manhattan, tel. 1 201 961 2535 from New Jersey or 718 361 9092 from New York. Fare $17 per person. Journey time approx. 55 minutes. Greyhound: information tel. 1 201 642 8205.
By helicopter	New York Helicopter from United Airlines terminal (Gate 21) to the heliport East 34th Street. Fare $75. Flight time approx. 10 minutes.
Connections to other New York airports	To J. F. Kennedy International Airport Salem Transportation: Limousines every 30–90 minutes. New York Helicopter on request
	To La Guardia Salem Transportation: Limousines every 60–90 minutes. New York Helicopter on request
Connections with places outside of New York	Information on connecting services to places outside New York is available from the individual transport companies. They can usually be contacted by toll-free telephones in the arrival halls.
Note	For taxi journeys beyond the city boundary the fare doubles outside the city. The fare displayed to the boundary, the double fare and all bridge and tunnel tolls are payable.

Auction rooms

Almost every day there are auctions of works of art, carpets, jewellery and miscellaneous objets d'art in New York. The major auctions, which are also great social occasions, are usually held in the evening at Sotheby's and Christie's.

There is always provision for viewing the objects to be sold before the auction.

Christie's, 502 Park Avenue (59th Street), tel. 546 1000
Christie's East, 219 East 67th Street, tel. 606 0400
Open: Mon.–Sat. 10am–5pm

William Doyle Galleries, 175 East 87th Street, tel. 427 2730
Open: irregularly

Phillips, 406 East 79th Street, tel. 570 4830
Open: Mon.–Sat. noon–5pm

Sotheby's, 1334 York Avenue, corner of 72nd Street, tel. 606 7000
Open: Tues.–Sat. 9.30am–5pm, Sun. 1–5pm

The "Arts and Leisure" supplement of the Friday edition of the "New York Times" has information on auctions.

Banks

Most banks are open Mon.–Fri. 9am–3pm Some are also open on Saturday mornings.

Banking hours

Exchange offices are usually open 9am–6pm.

Exchange offices (Bureaux de change)

In the International Arrival Building of J. F. Kennedy Airport:
Exchange office of Citibank and Perera Co. (open until midnight, except Sun.).

In New York City:
American Express, 374 Park Avenue, 150 East 42nd Street
Chequepoint USA, 651 Madison Avenue
Thomas Cook Travel, 2 Penn Plaza
Harald Reuter and Co., PanAm Building, 200 Park Avenue
Foreign currency can also be changed in various foreign banks on Fifth Avenue, as indicated by signs posted up.

Since there may be difficulty about changing foreign money in the United States (no provision for changing money in hotels, time-consuming checks by banks) and since you are likely to lose on the exchange, the best plan is to take US dollars with you – a limited amount in cash but most of your money in the form of dollar travellers' cheques, obtained either from your own bank or from a branch of American Express. Eurocheques and cheque cards are of no use.
    If your American Express cheques are lost or stolen you can usually have them replaced by the nearest American Express branch on presentation of the sales advice issued when you bought the cheques.
    Visa cheques are also widely used now.

Travellers' cheques

Bathing beaches

Since the New York boroughs of Brooklyn and Queens are situated by the sea, they have bathing beaches which are readily accessible free of charge but tend to be very overcrowded during the season.
    The Atlantic is slow to warm up, and the water is therefore rarely warm enough for bathing before the end of June. The season lasts only until the beginning of September, though bathing is usually possible until the end of that month.

Coney Island and Brighton Beach
Subway: line B, N, D or F to Stillwell Avenue or D and Q to Brighton Beach; line C and H to Rockaway and A and H to Far Rockaway.

Within the city

Beach on Long Island

Outside the city Jones Beach State Park
Long Island Railroad from Pennsylvania Station to Freeport, then bus connecting with train. Information about departures: tel. 739 4200.

Perhaps the most beautiful beach on the east coast of the United States 20km (12 miles) of sand, fresh-water and sea-water pools, restaurants, open-air theatre).

Fire Island
Long Island Railroad to Sayville, Bayshore and Patchogue, where there are also mainland ferryboat lines. Fifty kilometres (32 miles) of Nautical Sea-shore. Fishing, swimming and walking in natural unspoilt landscape, as well as numerous facilities.

Boat excursions

The only day trip, run by the Hudson River Day Line, is up the Hudson River to Bear Mountain and West Point, site of the United States Military Academy. From here it is possible to visit Hyde Park, former home of President F. D. Roosevelt, where his papers are preserved in a specially built library.

Departures from the end of May to mid September, Wed., Thur., Sat. and Sun. at 9.30am, from Pier 81 (end of 41st Street), returning at 7pm approx. Information: tel. 279 5151.

Circle Line Sightseeing Yachts
Pier 83, West 83rd Street & 12th Avenue (Hudson River)
Season: April–mid-November. Information: tel. 563 3200.

An interesting three-hour trip down the Hudson River into New York Bay to the Statue of Liberty (see A to Z, Statue of Liberty), up East River and around Manhattan returning to the pick-up point.

Circle Line Statue of Liberty Ferry
Battery Park, South Ferry
Season: daily, all year round
Information: tel. 269 5755
Trip to the Statue of Liberty on Liberty Island and to Ellis Island.

Seaport Line
Pier 16, South Street Seaport (East River)
Season: April–May, daily 2–4pm
Information: tel. 630 8888
A 90-minute trip to the Statue of Liberty on Liberty Island on the paddle steamer Andrew Fletcher and the steamer Dewitt Clinton.

Staten Island Ferry
The cheapest and best way to see New York from the sea (see Ferries).

Bookshops

Applause Theater Books, 211 West 71st Street
Argosy, 116 East 59th Street
Barnes & Noble, 105 Fifth Avenue; 128 and 600 Fifth Avenue
Citybooks, Municipal Building (New York)
Comic Art Gallery, 940 Third Avenue
Complete Traveller, 199 Madison Avenue
B. Dalton, 666 Fifth Avenue; 396 Avenue of the Americas;
    170 Broadway
Doubleday, 777 Third Avenue and 724 Fifth Avenue
Drama Bookshop, 723 Seventh Avenue
Gotham Book Mart, 41 West 47th Street
Hacker Art Books, 54 West 57th Street
Harper & Row, 10 East 53rd Street
McGraw Hill, 1221 Avenue of the Americas
New York Bound Bookshop, 50 Rockefeller Plaza
Jaap Rietman, 134 Sprig Street
Rizzoli, 31 West 57th Street; 454 West Broadway; 250 Vesey Street
Richard Stoddard, 18 East 16th Street
Science Fiction Bookshop, 163 Bleecker Street
Shakespeare & Co., 2259 Broadway and 716 Broadway
Strand's, 828 Broadway
Village Comics, 163 Bleecker Street
Waldenbooks, 57 Broadway; 931 Lexington Avenue;
    270 Park Avenue and 55 Water Street
Samuel Weiser, 132 East 24th Street
Wittenborn Art Books, 1018 Madison Avenue

General
bookshops

See Business hours

Shop hours

Breakdown assistance

If you have a breakdown in a hired car the car hire firm should be informed in the first place (see Car hire).

Breakdown
Assistance

Otherwise the "Yellow Pages" of the New York telephone directory give a full list of repair garages. (Automobile Repairing and Service.)

Spare Parts   Visitors bringing in their own car which is not a US make should ensure that
it is in perfect mechanical order, since spare parts not in accordance with
American standards may be difficult to obtain – though in the larger towns
there is usually a firm which sells or repairs foreign cars.

Business hours

Shops   There are no regulations limiting shop hours, and shops and restaurants in
New York can stay open as long as the owner likes: some shops, indeed –
including supermarkets – are open seven days a week and 24 hours a day.
    The large department stores tend to be open 9.45am–6.45pm, on Mon-
days and Thursdays (and during the pre-Christmas period every evening)
until 9pm, on Sundays from 11am or noon to 5pm. Many small shops keep
similar hours, particularly in areas where there are department stores. (See
Shopping.)

Chemists   Mon.–Sat. 9am–6pm
(drugstores)

Banks   Mon.–Fri. 9am–3pm

Museums   See the entries for particular museums and the list of museums on p. 155.

Post Offices   Post Offices are usually open Mon.–Fri. 8am–6pm, Sat. 9am–1pm.

Car hire

There is little point in driving your own car or a hired car in New York City,
with its heavy traffic and inadequate parking facilities, and the best way of
getting about is by public transport or by taxi; but if you want to see
something of the surrounding area or to continue your journey to some
other part of the United States a car is essential.
    To hire a car it is necessary to be at least 21 years old (in some cases 25)
and to produce a valid driving licence: British licences and those of certain
other countries are acceptable. It is useful also to have a credit card (American Express, Mastercharge or Visa), since otherwise it may be necessary to
put down a considerable sum as surety.
    There are numerous car hire firms in New York, some internationally
known, others local; some of them also hire out cars with drivers. All well
known car hire firms have a toll-free telephone service (Hot Lines) and are
listed in the "Yellow Pages" telephone directory under the heading "Automobile renting and leasing".
    You can arrange for a hire by telephone, by ringing one of the large car
rental firms at the following numbers:
Alamo: (1 800) 327 9633
Avis: (1 800) 331 1212
Budget Rent-a-Car: (1 800) 527 0700
Dollar Rent-a-Car: (1 800) 800 4000
Hertz: (1 800) 654 3131
National Car: (1 800) 227 7368

Note   It is advisable to contact several companies and compare costs. There are
usually special offers for weekly rates. Some companies charge an amount
per mile as well as daily hire charge (some have a certain mileage free),
others charge extra if the car is returned to another depot.

Chemists

See Drugstores

Churches and synagogues

Over a hundred different religious denominations are represented in New York. Some hotels have lists giving the times of services (usually at 11am on Sunday).

Cathedral Church of St John the Divine. See A to Z

123 East 55th Street
Subway: Lexington Avenue (lines E and F); 51st Street (line 6)
New York's oldest synagogue, a Moorish-style building designed by Henry Fernbach (1872). The interior is more attractive than the exterior, apart from the two domes topped by stars.

Central
Synagogue

Broadway and 10th Street
Subway: Astor Place (line 6), 8th Street (lines N, R)
A neo-Gothic building erected by James Renwick, an engineer and amateur architect, in 1846. One of New York's more beautiful churches, it has considerable grace and sensitivity.

Grace Episcopal
Church

Washington Square South
Subway: 8th Street (lines N, R), 4th Street (lines A, C, D, E, F)
Built in 1892 by McKim, Mead and White: in an eclectic Romanesque style with Italian Renaissance features, it dominated the square for many years before being dwarfed by surrounding buildings. The marble Washington Arch in the square was built by the same architects in the same year.

Judson Memorial
Church

1 East 29th Street; subway station 28th Street (line 6)
Built between 1849–56 the church's official name is the "Episcopal Church of the Transfiguration". It acquired its everyday name in 1870 when the priest of a nearby rich church refused to bury the actor George Holland and suggested the "little church around the corner", which became the church of artists and actors and is very popular for weddings. Broadway celebrities are depicted in the stained glass.
   The Serbian-Orthodox Church of St Sava is nearby (15 West 25th Street).

Little Church
Around the
Corner

3rd Avenue & 96th Street (line 6)
Consecrated in the autumn of 1991 with an adjoining cultural centre, it is the first mosque visible from afar in New York. It was financed chiefly with money from the Emir of Kuwait.

Mosque of
New York

Mulberry/corner of Prince Street
Subway station: Prince Street (lines N, R)
Built in 1809 it was designed by J. F. Mangin. Following a fire in 1866 it was rebuilt. It is the earliest Roman Catholic cathedral in New York.

Old Patrick's
Church

409 Riverside Drive; subway station: 116th Street (line 1, 9)
Guided tours; Sun. 12.30pm
Built in 1929 in Riverside Park it is an inter-denominational church of the Baptist Church and the United Church of Christ. The 59m (193ft) high tower based on that of Chartres Cathedral houses a carillon with 74 bells, the largest in the world. The interior contains impressive 16th c. stained glass from Bruges and a Madonna by J. Epstein.

Riverside
Church

St Bartholomew's Protestant Episcopal Church. See A to Z

Churches and synagogues

St Mark's in the Bowery. See A to Z

St Patrick's Cathedral. See A to Z

St Paul's Chapel. See A to Z

St Peter's Church Lexington Avenue and 54th Street
Subway: Lexington Avenue (lines E and F), 51st Street (line 6)
One of New York's few modern churches, built by Hugh Stubbins in 1977 together with the Citicorp skyscraper. It occupies the same site as its neo-Gothic predecessor, which sold its rights to the air space above the site to Citicorp. The church, surmounted by a vaulted granite roof, has something of a sculptured effect. A notable feature of the interior is the Erol Baker Chapel, decorated by the sculptress Louise Nevelson.

St Thomas's Church Fifth Avenue and 53rd Street
Subway: Fifth Avenue (lines E and F)
A Gothic church built by Bertram Goodhue in 1914, showing a mingling of English and French stylistic elements; an asymmetric building, designed to fit into a street intersection, which asserts its position alongside the neighbouring skyscrapers. The interior contains fine snow-white retables behind the altar by Goodhue and the sculptor Lee Lawrie.

Temple Emanu-El Fifth Avenue and 65th Street
Buses: 1, 2, 3, 4
A synagogue belonging to the wealthiest Jewish community in New York, built by Robert D. Kohn, Charles Butler and Clarence Stein in 1929. It is one of the city's largest places of worship (larger than St Patrick's Cathedral), with seating for 2500. Notable features are the neo-Romanesque arch over the entrance and the Byzantine-influenced interior.

Temple Emanu-El, the synagogue of New York's wealthiest Jewish community

See A to Z

See Music

Cinemas

New York's cinemas are too numerous to count. Its 50 first-run cinemas are concentrated in the area of Times Square, on 57th Street and on Third and Second Avenues between 57th and 72nd Streets, so that visitors to New York are likely to come across a good many of them in the course of their sightseeing. Programmes are listed in the newspapers. Some cinemas offer "Double Features": two films for the price of one.

The following cinemas show chiefly older films:
Angelika, corner of Houston and Mercer Street, tel. 995 2000
Biograph Cinema, 225 West 57th Street, tel. 586 1900
Carnegie Hall Cinema, Seventh Avenue & 57th Street, tel. 265 2520
Cinema Village, 22 East 12th Street, tel. 924 3363
Quad Cinema, 34 West 13th Street, tel. 255 8800
Theatre 80 St Marks Place, 80 St Marks Place, tel. 254 7400

Older films

The cinema in the Museum of Modern Art (see A to Z), 11 West 53rd Street, shows foreign films old and new, usually as part of a series, with a programme which changes daily.

Foreign films

Mainly showings of avant-garde films:
Anthology Archives, 32 Second Avenue, tel. 505 5181
Film Forum, 209 West Houston Street, tel. 727 8110
Millennium Film Workshop, 66 East 4th Street, tel. 673 0090
Public Theatre, 425 Lafayette Avenue, tel. 598 7100
Whitney Museum of American Art (see entry)

Experimental films

Held annually from end September to mid October in the Alice Tully Hall (see A to Z, Lincoln Center): a programme of some 20 films new to New York, mostly from Europe. Commercial films are shown but only those of artistic merit that are not often shown in cinemas. No prizes are awarded.

New York Film Festival

Climate

New York City lies in roughly the same latitude as Naples in Italy, but in summer (June to mid September) New York is hotter and in winter (December to March) considerably colder – mainly as a result of the wind – than Naples. In general it has long periods of clear weather (250–300 days), since depressions usually pass over quickly and anticyclones remain constant. The best times to visit New York are in May and from mid September to the beginning of December. The height of summer should be avoided if possible: in air-conditioned buildings it is tolerable, but the high humidity of the air makes it oppressively close in the streets. In summer hotel rooms tend to be rather too cool, while in winter they are usually overheated.

Snow rarely falls before January. The highest summer temperature ever recorded in New York was 41 °C (106 °F), the lowest winter temperature −24 °C (−11 °F); but such extreme temperatures seldom occur.

Temperatures

Conversion table (F/C)	°F	°C	Conversion factors:
	0	−18	°F to °C: (°F−32)×⅝
	10	−12	°C to °F: °C×⅘+32
	20	−5	
	32	0	Relationship °F/°C:
	50	10	°F:°C=9:5
	68	20	°C:°F=5:9
	86	30	
	95	35	
	212	100	

Weather information Weather forecasts are included in almost all the news bulletins given at regular intervals on radio and television.
For recorded reports tel. 976 1212

Consulates

United Kingdom: 845 Third Avenue, tel. 752 8400
Canada: 1251 Avenue of the Americas, tel. 586 2400

Credit cards

It is advisable to have one or more of the major credit cards (American Express, Mastercharge, Visa, Diner's Club, Carte Blanche), which are often regarded as a better indication of creditworthiness than the possession of cash. They can be used for the payment of bills of all kinds (in hotels, restaurants and shops), for the purchase of air tickets, in place of a deposit when hiring a car or as evidence of identity.

Currency

The US unit of currency is the dollar ($), which contains 100 cents. There are notes (bills) for 1, 2, 5, 10, 20, 50 and 100 dollars and coins in denominations of 1 cent (a penny), 5 cents (a nickel), 10 cents (a dime), 25 cents (a quarter) and – less commonly found – 50 cents (a half-dollar) and a dollar.
The exchange rate of the dollar against sterling (and other currencies) fluctuates considerably.
Since it is not so easy to change money in New York (or elsewhere in the United States) as in Europe, it is a good idea to get some dollar bills and small change before arriving in New York.

Import and export of currency There are no restrictions on the import or export of either American or foreign currency; but if you are taking in more than 10,000 dollars a customs declaration must be filled in on the aircraft.

Travellers' cheques See Banks

Customs regulations

Visitors to the United States may take in, duty free, personal effects including clothing, articles of personal adornment, toilet articles and hunting, fishing and photographic equipment; one litre of alcoholic beverages (wine, beer, spirits) if over 21; 300 cigarettes or 50 cigars or 3 lb of tobacco, or proportionate amounts of each; and gifts up to a total value of 100 dollars. Items which cannot be taken into the United States include meat, fruit, vegetables and ornamental plants.

Department stores

Abraham and Straus,
Avenue of the Americas and 32nd Street

Bloomingdale's
Lexington Avenue and 59th Street
Open: Mon. and Thurs. 10am–9pm, Tues., Wed., Fri. and Sat. 10am–6.30pm; Sun. noon–5pm

Lord and Taylor
Fifth Avenue and 38th Street
Open: Thurs. 10am–8pm, Mon., Tues., Wed., Fri. and Sat. 10am–6pm; closed Sun.

Macy's
Broadway and 34th Street
Open: Mon., Thurs. and Fri. 9.45am–8.30pm, Tues. and Wed. 9.45am–6.45pm, Sat. 9.45am–6pm, Sun. noon–5pm

Saks Fifth Avenue
Fifth Avenue and 50th Street
Open: Thurs. 10am–8.30pm, Mon.–Wed., Fri. and Sat. 10am–6pm; closed Sun.

Doctors

See Emergency calls

Drinks

The most popular drink at breakfast and at other meals is coffee ("sanka" or "decaf"=decaffeinated). Refills are poured without any extra charge. Tea made with tea bags and drinking chocolate are also popular as are other refreshing drinks, even iced coffee, tea and chocolate. Non-alcoholic drinks include coke, tonic, fruit juices, brightly coloured sodas, milk and milk shakes.

Vending machines sell "root beer", a light alcoholic drink originally made from the roots and bark of the sassafras tree but nowadays made from water, sugar, colouring and spices and containing no alcohol.

The ice-cold beer is lighter than in Europe and served in a glass or tankard. The most well-known brands are Budweiser, Schlitz, Falstaff, Pabst, Coors, La Crosse, Löwenbrau (brewed in the USA) and Miller along with imported European beers.

Before meals cocktails are often drunk. Americans prefer whisky (Bourbon, Scotch, Canadian, Rye, Irish and Blended), vodka, gin, rum, brandy, vermouth and cordial.

Iced chilled water is available free of charge with meals in cafés and restaurants.

Drugstores

The American drugstore is a very different kind of place from a European chemist's shop or pharmacy. In most drugstores the supply of medicines on prescription is only a small part of their business, and many of them are more like small department stores offering a wide range of wares, including facilities for eating and drinking.

Information
For a list of drugstores in New York consult the "Yellow Pages" telephone directory.

Opening times
Usually 9am–6pm Some stay open until 9pm or even midnight.

All-night pharmacy
The following Manhattan pharmacy is open 24 hours a day: Kaufman Pharmacy, 50th Street and Lexington Avenue, tel. 755 2266. Subway station 51st Street (line 6).

Emergency service
There is no organised night emergency service. In case of emergency it is always possible to go to the nearest hospital (see Hospitals), since all hospitals have pharmacies. Alternatively telephone 265 3546 or 755 2266.

Electricity

110–115 volt, 60 cycle AC. If you have an electric razor, hair-drier or iron you should take an adapter with you. If you forget or lose your adapter you can get one in a hardware store or a department store. (The hotel porter will be able to tell you where to go.)

Emergency calls

Police, fire, ambulance
Dial 911.

To call a doctor
In Manhattan telephone 879 1000.

To call a dentist
Telephone 679 3966.

Events

Note
A complete list of events with precise dates is available from the New York Convention and Visitors Bureau (see Tourist Information).

January
Chinese New Year celebrations in Chinatown. The time, determined by the Chinese lunar calendar, ranges between the end of January and mid February. Information: tel. 397 8222.
Mid January: National Boat Show in the Jacob K. Javits Convention Center.
National Hunting, Fishing, Camping and Sportsmen Expo in Jacob K. Javits Convention Center.

February
Mid February: Black History Month: events in all five boros on the Black history and culture.
Mid February: Westminster Kennel Club Dog Show in Madison Square Garden. A two-day show of all breeds.

New Year celebrations in Chinatown

17 March: St Patrick's Day, with New York's largest and most spectacular parade by Irish Americans along Broadway from 44th to 86th Street, starting at 11am. Many decorated floats and bands.   *March*

New York Flower Show at the Passenger Ship Terminal Pier 90.

Greek Independence Day Parade on Fifth Avenue.

Easter Day: Easter Parade on Fifth Avenue (49th to 59th Street), noon–4pm   *March or April*

From April to mid May there is a magnificent display of spring flowers in the Rockefeller Center on Fifth Avenue.   *April*

End of April: Greater New York International Auto Show in Jacob K. Javits Convention Center.

Ringling Brothers and Barnum and Bailey Circus in Madison Square Garden. This three-ring circus, continuing into June, puts on its show in New York's largest auditorium.

Fourth Sunday. Parade on Fifth Avenue commemorating the murdered black leader and Nobel prizewinner Martin Luther King.   *May*

Ninth Avenue International Festival, held on Ninth Avenue, between 37th and 59th Streets, on a weekend in May (information: tel. 687 1300). An occasion displaying all the ethnic variety of Ninth Avenue, with its numerous shops and stalls.

Last Monday: Memorial Day, a parade to honour those who lost their lives in war, on Riverside Drive.

Washington Square Outdoor Art Show. On three weekends during May painters, sculptors and other artists and craftsmen offer their work for sale around Washington Square (see A to Z; Greenwich Village), particularly in University Place, Fifth Avenue and the adjoining side streets (also takes place in September).

52nd Street Fair: many stalls between Lexington and Seventh Avenue.

143

Good Friday procession in Lower East Side

June	First Sunday: Puerto Rican Day; parade on Fifth Avenue. Second Tuesday evening: Museum Mile Festival on Fifth Avenue from 82nd to 104th Streets. Mid June to September: Brooklyn Festival in Prospect Park (Brooklyn); music, theatre, dance.
End of June to August	Shakespeare in the Park; free performances in the Delacorte Theater in Central Park (plays by William Shakespeare and others). June/July: open-air concerts and performances in the Rockefeller Center and World Trade Center; Concerts by the Metropolitan Opera and the New York Philharmonic in the parks.
June to July	Other events: JVC Jazz New York Festival in the concert halls and squares. Feast of St Anthony in Little Italy, Sullivan Street. Flag Day Parade from Fulton and Water Street to the Fraunces' Tavern Museum.
July	4 July: Independence Day, with celebrations in Battery Park, noon–7pm (information: tel. 687 1300), a nautical event on the Hudson (information: tel. 687 1300), and a firework display on the Hudson at 9.15pm, seen at its best from Riverside Park between 80th and 105th Street.
July to August	Summer Gardens Concerts in the Museum of Modern Art. Summerpier Jazz Concerts in South Street Seaport. Other events: Festa Italiana in Carmine Street/Bleecker Street; a week-long Italian festival.
August	Early to mid-August: Harlem Week.

Mid-August: Lincoln Center Out of Doors Festival; daily street festivals on the Lincoln Center Plaza.
End of August: Greenwich Village Jazz Festival.
End of August: Avenue of the Americas Festival between 35th and 50th Street.

First Sunday: West Indian American Day Carnival on Eastern Parkway and September Utica Avenue in Brooklyn, with an exotic parade.
First three weekends: Washington Square Outdoor Art Show (see May).
Third Saturday: Steuban Parade by German Americans on Fifth Avenue (from 44th to 86th Street).
Mid September: Feast of San Gennaro (St Januarius) in Little Italy (Mulberry Street, Lower Manhattan), a colourful fiesta with many stalls, sideshows, etc.
Mid September: "New York is Book Country". Fifth Avenue, 48th to 57th Streets.
Mid-September: National Antique Show in the Jacob K. Javits Convention Center.
End of September to mid-October: New York Film Festival (see Cinemas).

Other events:
African American Day Parade on 111th Street and Adam Clayton Powell Boulevard.

Columbus Day Parade of Italian Americans on Fifth Avenue (varying dates). October
Mid October: Hispanic American Day Parade on Fifth Avenue.
Mid October: Pulaski Day Parade by Poles.
31st October: Halloween Parade in Greenwich Village.
Last Sunday: New York City Marathon, run on a 26-mile course through the five boroughs, starting from the Staten Island side of the Verrazano Narrows Bridge and ending at the Tavern-on-the-Green in Central Park. Some 15,000–20,000 runners take part.

Early November: International Horse Show in Madison Square Garden. November
Fourth Thursday: Thanksgiving Day. A Thanksgiving Parade is organised by Macy's, the great department store, mainly intended for children; it starts from Central Park (West 77th Street) at 9.15am, heads south to Columbus Circle and then along Broadway to end at 34th Street in front of the store.
Veterans' Day Parade to commemorate end of First World War on Fifth Avenue.

Beginning of December: A huge Christmas tree is erected in the Rockefeller December Center, where there is carol singing and other events
31 December: Tens of thousands of New Yorkers gather in Times Square to see the New Year in. During the last minute of the old year a large ball illuminated by nearly 200 bulbs descends a flagpole on top of the 1 Times Square Building.
December to January: The New York City Ballet (see Music) perform the Nutcracker Suite.

To find out what is going on in New York consult the newspapers ("Daily What's on? News", "New York Times,", "New York Post"); the following publications are also useful:
"Village Voice" and "SoHo Weekly News" (both weekly) give the complete programmes of the small "off-Broadway" theatres.
The "Big Apple Guide" is published annually by the New York Convention and Visitors Bureau (see Tourist information).
"Village Voice", which is published each Wednesday prints more or less completely the programmes of the off-off-Broadway theatres.

Ferries

Manhattan to Staten Island	Staten Island Ferry

Staten Island Ferry
Departures from Battery Park every 20 minutes Mon.–Fri., every 30 minutes; Sat. and Sun., every 45–60 minutes between midnight and 5am. Information: 248 8097.
The crossing takes about half an hour each way. The return fare is 25 cents, making this one of the cheapest as well as most rewarding trips in New York, offering – particularly on the return journey – a magnificent view of the skyscrapers of lower Manhattan.

Manhattan to Statue of Liberty and Ellis Island
Departures from Battery Park every 30 minutes 9am–4pm. Information: tel. 269 5755.

Food

Even if you lack time, money or appetite for a meal in one of New York's countless restaurants (see entry) you need never go hungry, since there are plenty of opportunities all over the city for picking up a hamburger, a hot dog or one of the other popular forms of "fast food".

Hamburgers
A hamburger is a sandwich consisting of a patty of ground or chopped meat, seasoned with onions, cheese, etc., between two halves of a roll.

Hot dogs
A hot dog is a frankfurter, with mustard and sauerkraut, served in a split roll.

Pizzas
A pizza consists of a flat dough base spread with tomato sauce, pieces of sausage, cheese and seasoning, and is eaten hot.

Sandwiches
The most popular American form of sandwich is made of rye bread and corned beef, roast beef or pastrami (a highly seasoned cut of smoked beef), with a slice of gherkin and a cup of coffee.

Brunch
A New York speciality is brunch, a cross between breakfast and lunch which is served in many hotels and restaurants on Saturdays and Sundays from about 11 a.m. to the early afternoon.

Galleries

New York has over 500 art galleries, mostly concentrated in two areas of the city, between 57th and 86th Streets (particularly in 57th Street and Madison Avenue) and in SoHo (on West Broadway and adjoining streets). The following are some of the principal galleries, listed in alphabetical order. Some of them specialise in particular genres or periods.

Uptown galleries
Aberbach Fine Art, 988 Madison Avenue, tel. 988 1100
A.C.A. Galleries, 41 East 57th Street, tel. 644 8300
Babcock Galleries, 20 East 67th Street, tel. 767 1852
I. N. Bartfield, 30 West 57th Street, tel. 245 8890
Grace Borgenicht, 725 Fifth Avenue, tel. 247 211
Carus Gallery, 872 Madison Avenue, tel. 879 4660
Cordier and Ekstrom, 417 East 75th Street, tel. 988 8857
Terry Dintenfass, 50 West 57th Street, tel. 581 2268
André Emmerich Gallery, 41 East 57th Street, tel. 752 0124
David Findlay Galleries, 984 Madison Avenue, tel. 249 2909

Wally Findlay, 17 East 57th Street, tel. 421 5390
Forum Gallery, 1018 Madison Avenue, tel. 772 7666
E. & I. Frankel, 1020 Madison Avenue, tel. 879 5733
James Goodman Gallery, 41 East 57th Street, tel. 593 3737
Graham Gallery, 1014 Madison Avenue, tel. 535 5767
Daniel B. Grossman, 1100 Madison Avenue, tel. 861 9285
Hirschl & Adler Galleries, 21 East 70th Street, tel. 535 8810
Hirschl & Adler Folk, 851 Madison Avenue, tel. 988 3655
Hirschl & Adler Modern, 851 Madison Avenue, tel. 744 6700
Leonard Hutton Galleries, 33 East 74th Street, tel. 249 9700
Martha Jackson Gallery, 521 West 57th Street, tel. 586 4200
Sidney Janis Gallery, 110 West 57th Street, tel. 586 0110
Kennedy Galleries, 40 West 57th Street, tel. 541 9600
Knoedler and Co., 19 East 70th Street, tel. 794 0550
Monique Knowlton, 19 East 71st Street, tel. 794 9700
Kraushaar Galleries, 724 Fifth Avenue, tel. 307 5730
La Boëtie, 9 East 82nd Street, tel. 535 4865
Lafayette Parke, 58 East 79th Street, tel. 517 5550
Marlborough, 40 West 57th Street, tel. 541 4900
Pierre Matisse Gallery, 41 East 57th Street, tel. 355 6269
Achim Moeller, 52 76th Street, tel. 988 8483
Tibor de Nagy Gallery, 41 West 57th Street, tel. 421 3780
Naga Antiques, 145 East 61st Street, tel. 593 2788
Newhouse Galleries, 19 East 66th Street, tel. 879 2700
Pace Gallery of New York, 32 East 57th Street, tel. 421 3292
Perlis Galleries, 1016 Madison Avenue, tel. 472 3200
Royal-Athena, 153 East 57th Street, tel. 355 2034
Serge Sabarsky Gallery, 58 East 79th Street, tel. 628 6281
Saidenberg Gallery, 1018 Madison Avenue, tel. 288 3387
Holly Solomon, 724 Fifth Avenue, tel. 757 7777
Spencer A. Samuels, 72 East 78th Street, tel. 288 9333
Schaeffer Galleries, 983 Park Avenue, tel. 535 6410
Schlesinger, 24 East 73rd Street, tel. 734 3600
Robert Schoelkopf Gallery, 50 West 57th Street, tel. 765 3540
Solomon & Co. Fine Art, 959 Madison Avenue, tel. 737 8200
Ira Spanierman, 50 East 78th Street, tel. 879 7085
Tsuru, 22 East 66th Street, tel. 772 6422
Weintraub Gallery, 988 Madison Avenue, tel. 879 1195
Wildenstein and Co., 19 East 64th Street, tel. 879 0500
Daniel Wolf, 52 West 78th Street, tel. 772 7721
Zabriskie, 724 Fifth Avenue, tel. 307 7430

Mary Boone Galleries, 417 West Broadway, tel. 431 1818
Leo Castelli Gallery, 420 West Broadway, tel. 431 5160
Leo Castelli Gallery, 578 Broadway, tel. 431 6279
Paula Cooper Gallery, 155 Wooster Street, tel. 674 0766
Dannenberg Gallery, 484 Broome Street, tel. 219 0140
John Gibson, 568 Broadway, tel. 925 1192
Ronald Feldman Fine Arts, 31 Mercer Street, tel. 226 3232
Gimpel/Weitzenhoffer, 415 West Broadway, tel. 925 6090
O. K. Harris, 383 West Broadway, tel. 431 3600
Nancy Hoffman, 429 West Broadway, tel. 966 6676
Ingber, 415 West Broadway, tel. 941 7878
Louis Meisel, 141 Prince Street, tel. 677 1340
Pleiades Gallery, 164 Mercer Street, tel. 266 9093
Sonnabend Gallery, 420 West Broadway, tel. 966 6160
Staempfli, 415 West Broadway, tel. 941 7100
Edward Thorp, 103 Prince Street, tel. 431 6880
Vorpal SoHo, 411 West Broadway, tel. 334 3939
Ward-Nasse, 178 Prince Street, tel. 925 6951

SoHo galleries

John Weber Gallery, 142 Greene Street, tel. 966 6115
Witkin, 415 West Broadway, tel. 925 5510
André Zarre, 48 Greene Street, tel. 966 2222

Opening times   With few exceptions Tues.–Sat. 10am to 5 or 6pm

Photograph   Exhibiting only photographs, either historical or contemporary.
galleries

Fourth Street Photo Gallery
67 East 4th Street, tel. 673 1021
Open Sun.–Thurs, 2–8pm, Fri. and Sat. 3–10pm

Lieberman & Saul
560 Broadway, tel. 431 0747

Neikrug Gallery
224 East 68th Street, tel. 288 7741
Open Wed.–Sat. 1–6pm

Nikon House
620 Fifth Avenue (49th Street), tel. 586 3907
Open Tues.–Sat. 10am–5pm

SoHo Photo
15 White Street, tel. 226 8571
Open Fri.–Sun. 1–6pm, Tues. 7–9pm

Getting to New York

Practically all visitors to New York now go by air. Only a few arrive in the last remaining transatlantic liner, Cunard's "Queen Elizabeth 2", or call in at New York in the course of a cruise. The return journey can be made on Concorde.

Most international flights land at the J. F. Kennedy International Airport (see Airports) and discharge their passengers through the International Arrival Building. American, United, Eastern, Delta, TWA and British Airways have their own terminals.

Visitors arriving in New York will be well advised to come equipped with at least some American currency (dollar bills, coins) to cover small outgoings like tips, bus or taxi fares, telephone calls, etc. It is usually difficult and time-consuming to change large banknotes.

Hospitals

All major hospitals have casualty and emergency departments.

Manhattan   Columbia Presbyterian Medical Center, 622 West 168th Street, tel. 305 2555
Lenox Hill Hospital, 100 East 77th Street, tel. 439 3030
Manhattan Eye, Ear and Throat Hospital, 210 East 64th Street, tel. 838 9200
Mount Sinai Medical Center, 100th Street and Fifth Avenue, tel. 241 6500
New York Hospital, 525 East 68th Street, tel. 746 5454
St Luke's and Roosevelt Hospital Center, 58th Street and Ninth Avenue,
tel. 523 4000

Emergency calls   See Emergency calls

Hotels

New York has many hundreds of hotels, with over 100,000 beds in Manhattan alone; but it is still difficult at certain times to find accommodation, since the city attracts more than 17 million visitors a year, including two million from outside the United States. New York offers a wide range of accommodation for every taste and every purse, from luxury hotels to modest establishments in the less expensive parts of the city.

Almost all the hotels listed below have rooms with private bath, air conditioning and colour television. Breakfast is never included in the room charge. Guests are not required to have breakfast in the hotel – many of the smaller hotels, indeed, do not serve breakfast – but can go out to a nearby coffee shop or cafeteria. Almost all hotels, particularly the larger ones, have one or more restaurants, with prices which vary in line with room charges. All hotels have safes in which money, jewellery and other valuables can be deposited. It is usually not necessary to leave your key at the reception desk every time you leave the hotel. Bills can be paid by traveller's cheque or credit card (American Express, Mastercharge, Visa, Diner's Club, Carte Blanche). Room charges are subject to a tax which at the time of going to press is at the rate of 8.25% plus 6% municipal hotel tax plus $2 per night; in addition for rooms costing over $100 per night, there is a further tax of 5%, making a total addition to the bill of some 20% or more.
Advance reservation of rooms is strongly recommended.

In view of the continuing rise in hotel tariffs as a result of inflation the list of hotels given below does not attempt to show precise scales of charges. Hotels are listed in alphabetical order in four groups: | Price categories

Luxury hotels (single rooms $200–$250, double rooms $250–$400).

Hotels with a high standard of amenity (single rooms $125–$175, double rooms $150–$200).

Good quality hotels (single rooms $80–$120, double rooms $100–$150).

Reasonably priced hotels (single rooms $60–$90, double rooms $70–$100).

Several luxury hotels, and quite a few others, have special offers at the weekend (Friday, Saturday and sometimes Sunday) with price reductions up to 50%. To obtain these special rates advance booking is necessary. | Special offer

★Omni Berkshire Place (415 r.), 21 East 52nd Street, tel. 753 5800 | Luxury hotels
★Carlyle (500 r.), 35 East 76th Street, tel. 744 1600
★Doral Tuscany (250 r.), 120 East 39th Street, tel. 686 1600
★Dorset (190 r.), 30 West 54th Street, tel. 247 7300
★Drake Swissotel (650 r.), 440 Park Avenue, tel. 421 0900
★Embassy Suites (460 suites), Broadway & 47th Street, tel 719 1600
★Essex House (580 r.), 160 Central Park South, tel. 247 0300
★Four Seasons (370 r.), 57 East 57th Street, tel. 758 5700
★Grand Hyatt (1400 r.), 42nd Street and Lexington Avenue, tel. 883 1234
★Halloran House (650 r.), 525 Lexington Avenue, tel. 755 4000
★Helmsley Park Lane (640 r.), 36 Central Park South, tel. 371 4000
★Holiday Inn Crowne Plaza (770 r.), 1605 Broadway, tel. 977 4000
★Mack Lowe (250 r.), 145 West 44th Street, tel. 768 4400
★Marriot Marquis (1850 r.), 1535 Broadway, tel. 398 1900
★Mayfair Regent (201 r.), 610 Park Avenue, tel. 288 0800
★New York Helmsley (800 r.), 212 East 42nd Street, tel. 490 8900
★New York Hilton (1800 r.), 1335 Avenue of the Americas, tel. 586 7000
★Palace (1100 r.), 455 Madison Avenue, tel. 888 7700
★Parker Meridien (450 r.), 118 West 57th Street, tel. 245 5000

149

Horse-drawn cabs await guests in front of Plaza Hotel

★Peninsula (250 r.), 2 West 55th Street, tel. 247 2200
★Pierre (200 r.), Fifth Avenue and 61st Street, tel. 838 8000
★Plaza (800 r.), Fifth Avenue and 58th Street, tel. 759 3000
★Ramada Renaissance (900 r.), 714 Seventh Avenue, tel. 765 7676
★Regency (500 r.), 540 Park Avenue at 61st Street, tel. 759 4100
★Rihga Royal (250 r.), 151 West 54th Street, tel. 937 5454
★Ritz-Carlton (200 r.), 112 Central Park South, tel. 757 1900
★Royal Concordia (506 suites), 151 West 54th Street, tel. 307 5000
★Sheraton Center (1850 r.), 811 Seventh Avenue, tel. 581 1000
★Sherry-Netherland (370 r.), 781 Fifth Avenue, tel. 355 2800
★Stanhope (130 r.), 995 Fifth Avenue, tel. 288 5800
★United Nations Plaza-Park Hyatt (428 r.), 1 United Nations Plaza, tel. 355 3400
★Vista International (800 r.), 3 World Trade Center, tel. 938 9100
★Waldorf Astoria (1750 r.), 301 Park Avenue, tel. 355 3000
★Westbury (325 r.), Madison Avenue and 69th Street, tel. 535 2000

High amenity hotels

Bedford (200 r.), 118 East 40th Street, tel. 697 4800
Doral Inn (700 r.), 541 Lexington Avenue, tel. 755 1200
Doral Park Avenue (200 r.), 70 Park Avenue, tel. 687 7050
Elysee (110 r.), 60 East 54th Street, tel. 753 1066
Helmsley Middletowne (192 r.), 148 East 48th Street, tel. 755 3000
Loew's New York (765 r.), Lexington Avenue and 51st Street, tel. 752 7000
Omni Park Central (1450 r.), 7th Avenue and 56th Street, tel. 484 3300
Roosevelt (1107 r.), Madison Avenue and 45th Street, tel. 661 9600
San Carlos (150 r.), 150 East 50th Street, tel. 755 1800
Sheraton City Squire (730 r.), 790 Seventh Avenue, tel. 581 3300
Sheraton Park Avenue (150 r.), 45 Park Avenue, tel. 685 7676
St Moritz on the Park (770 r.), 50 Central Park South, tel. 755 5800
Warwick (500 r.), 65 West 54th Street, tel. 247 2700

Entrance of Waldorf-Astoria

Algonquin (200 r.), 59 West 44th Street, tel. 840 6800
Barbizon (360 r.), 140 East 63rd Street, tel. 715 0900
Beverly (300 r.), 125 East 50th Street, tel. 753 2700
Century Paramount (610 r.), 235 West 46th Street, tel. 764 5500
Executive (200 r.), 237 Madison Avenue, tel. 686 0300
Gorham (160 r.), 136 West 55th Street, tel. 245 1800
Helmsley Windsor (300 r.), 100 West 58th Street, tel. 265 2100
Howard Johnson Plaza (300 r.), Eighth Avenue and 51st Street, tel. 581 4100
Kitano (95 r.), 66 Park Avenue, tel. 685 0022
Lexington (880 r.), 511 Lexington Avenue, tel. 755 4400
Mayflower on the Park (570 r.), Central Park West and 61st Street,
   tel. 265 0060
Novotel/New York (470 r.), 226 West 52nd Street, tel. 315 0100
Roger Smith (180 r.), 501 Lexington Avenue, tel. 755 1400
Salisbury (220 r.), 123 West 57th Street, tel. 246 1300
Southgate Tower (523 r.), 371 Seventh Avenue, tel. 563 1800
Travel Inn (160 r.), 515 West 42nd Street, tel. 869 7171
Tudor (600 r.), 304 East 42nd Street, tel. 986 8800
Wyndham (200 r.), 42 West 58th Street, tel. 753 3500

Aberdeen (200 r.), 17 West 32nd Street, tel. 736 1600
Carter (610 r.), 250 West 43rd Street, tel. 944 6000
Collingwood Hotel, 45 West 35th Street, tel. 947 2500
Consulate (200 r.), 224 West 49th Street, tel. 246 5252
Diplomat (220 r.), 108 West 43rd Street, tel. 921 5666
Edison (1000 r.), 228 West 47th Street, tel. 840 5000
Esplanade (100 r.), 305 West End Avenue, tel. 874 5000
Excelsior (150 r.), 45 West 81st Street, tel. 362 9200
Henry Hudson (300 r.), 353 West 57th Street, tel. 265 6100
Iroquois (125 r.), 49 West 44th Street, tel. 977 2719

Good quality
hotels

Reasonably
priced hotels

Mansfield (200 r.), 12 West 44th Street, tel. 944 6050
Martha Washington (500 r.), 30 East 30th Street, tel. 689 1900
Penn Plaza (145 r.), 215 West 34th Street, tel. 947 5050
Pickwick Arms (400 r.), 250 East 51st Street, tel. 335 0300
Stanford (160 r.), 43 West 32nd Street, tel. 563 1500
Wellington (400 r.), 7th Avenue at 55th Street, tel. 247 3900
Wentworth (245 r.), 59 West 46th Street, tel. 719 2300

Youth hostels

Prices in youth hostels range between $25 and $40 for a single room and $35 to $50 for a double room. Enquire about discounts for groups and students.

YMCA Vanderbilt Branch (430 r.), 224 East 47th Street, tel. 755 2410
YMCA West Side (550 r.), 5 West 63rd Street, tel. 787 1301
Youth hostel (480 b.), Amsterdam Avenue and 103rd Street, tel. 932 2300

Bed and
Breakfast

Cheaper accommodation is available in private houses for the visitor who wishes to stay longer in New York and avoid the relatively high hotel costs. Further information from:

Bed & Bath & Beyond, 620 Avenue of the Americas, tel. 255 3550
Bed & Breakfast A New World, 150 Fifth Avenue, tel. 675 5600
Bed & Breakfast Hosts and Guests Inc., 322 West 72nd Street, tel. 874 4308
Bed & Breakfast in the Big Apple, 306 West 38th Street, tel. 594 5650
Bed & Breakfast Network of NY, 130 Barrow Street, tel. 645 8134

Insurance

It is essential to take out short-term health and accident insurance when visiting the United States, since the costs of medical treatment are high; and it is also advisable to have baggage insurance and (particularly if you have booked a package holiday) cancellation insurance. Arrangements can be made through your travel agent or insurance company; many companies running package holidays now include insurance as part of the deal.
Within the United States foreign visitors can effect insurance through American International Underwriters, 1200 19th Street, Suite 605, Washington, D.C. 20036; tel. 202 861 8664. (UK address: 120 Fenchurch Street, London WC3M 5BP).

Jazz

See Night Life

Language

British (and other) visitors may find it helpful to be reminded of some of the differences between American and British usage.

British	American
autumn	fall
bill	check
billion – 1000 million	billion
(now widely accepted in Britain, where traditionally a billion was a million million)	

British	American
biscuit	cracker, cookie
bonnet	hood (of car)
boot	trunk (of car)
braces	suspenders
caravan	trailer
carry-out	"to go" (in cafeteria, etc.)
cinema	movie (theater)
cloakroom	checkroom
cupboard	closet
dustbin	garbage can
first floor	second floor
flat	apartment
football	soccer
fortnight	two weeks
"gents" (lavatory)	men's room
graduation (university, etc.)	commencement
ground floor	first floor
handbag	purse
label	sticker
"ladies" (lavatory)	ladies' room, powder room
lavatory	rest room
lavatory (roadside)	comfort station
lift	elevator
lorry	truck
luggage	baggage
maize	corn
nappy	diaper
open square	plaza
pavement	sidewalk
personal call (on telephone)	person to person call
petrol	gas, gasoline
post	mail
post code	zip code
queue	(stand in) line
(railway) line, platform	track
refrigerator	icebox
return ticket	round trip ticket
reversed charge	collect (on telephone)
ring (up)	call (on telephone)
scone	biscuit
second floor	third floor
shop	store
single ticket	one way ticket
spanner	wrench
subway	underpass
summer time	daylight saving time
surname	last name
tap	faucet
tin	can (e.g. of food)
tram	streetcar
trousers	pants
trunk call	long distance call
underground	subway
viewpoint, viewing platform	observatory
Whitsun	Pentecost

It is perhaps worth a special reminder that in multi-storey buildings the Americans begin counting the storeys from street level, so that the

American first floor is the British ground floor, the American second floor is the British first floor, and so on.

Libraries and archives

Libraries

The principal New York libraries, apart from the Public Library (see A to Z, New York Public Library), are the following:

Frick Art Reference Library
10 East 71st Street, tel. 288 0700
Art

Grolier Club
47 East 60th Street, tel. 838 6690
Bibliophile editions

Institute of Fine Arts
1 East 78th Street, tel. 772 5800
Art

Museum of the City of New York
See A to Z

New York Historical Society
See A to Z

New York Law Institute
120 Broadway, tel. 732 8720
Law

New York Society Library
53 East 79th Street, tel. 288 6900
A subscription lending library founded in 1754

Pierpont Morgan Library
See A to Z

Walter Hampden Memorial Library
16 Gramercy Square South, tel. 228 7610
The theatre

For students and teaching staff only

Bobst Library, New York University
70 Washington Square South, tel. 998 2520

Columbia University Libraries, on University campus, tel. 854 3533

There are also numerous specialised libraries for particular disciplines, and each college has a library for its own students.

Archives

Library and Museum of the Performing Arts
See A to Z, Lincoln Center

Leo Baeck Institute
129 East 73rd Street, tel. 744 6400
German-Jewish history

Schomburg Center for Research in Black Culture
See A to Z

Zionist Archives and Library
515 Park Avenue, tel. 753 2167

Opening times vary, and some of the libraries and archives are not open every day. It is advisable to check by telephone that a particular establishment will be open before visiting it.

Opening times

Lost property

J. F. Kennedy Airport: apply to the airline concerned. If you lose something within the airport tel. 656 4120.
LaGuardia Airport: tel. 476 5128 or apply to the airline concerned.
Newark Airport: tel. (1201) 961 2230 or apply to the airline.

Airports

Tel. 869 4513. If the article has not turned up within 48 hours tel. 374 4925.

Taxis

Tel. 1 718 625 6200.

Subway and buses

Grand Central Station: tel. 340 2571.
Pennsylvania Station: tel. 239 6193.

Railway

New York Port Authority Bus Terminal, tel. 466 7000, ext. 219; Sat., Sun. and public holidays, tel. 564 9523, ext. 219.

Country buses

Markets

Ninth Avenue between 39th and 54th Streets
Union Square
Open all year round. Wed., Fri. and Sat. 7am until dusk.

Fresh vegetables

14th Street west of Seventh Avenue
"La Marqueta", Park Avenue, between 110th and 115th Streets (see A to Z, El Barrio).

Spanish produce

Annex Flea Market, 725 Avenue of the Americas
Antiques Market, 137 Ludlow Street
Canal Street Flea Market
Lord of the Fleas, 670 Broadway.

Flea markets

Movies

See Cinemas

Museums

The majority of museums in New York are privately owned and receive no money from public funds. Many do not charge an admission fee but request a "suggested contribution" towards maintenance and development costs. In this guide this is classified as an admission fee. Where this comment is missing there is no charge.

Admission fees

On certain days some museums have a "Pay-what-you-wish" tariff with payment left to the visitor's discretion. In many museums it is free at certain times (usually after 5pm on Tuesdays).

155

There are reduced admission fees in many museums, usually up to 50%, for students, OAPs, groups and disabled visitors.

Museums described in the A to Z section

American Craft Museum
American Museum of Immigration
American Museum of the Moving Image
American Museum of Natural History
Asia Society Gallery
Brooklyn Children's Museum
Brooklyn Museum
China House Gallery
Chinese Museum (see Chinatown)
The Cloisters
Cooper-Hewitt Museum
Dyckman House
Ellis Island Immigration Museum
Fraunces' Tavern Museum
Frick Collection
Guggenheim Museum (see Solomon Guggenheim Museum)
Guinness World Records Exhibit Hall
Hispanic Society of America
IBM Gallery of Science and Art
International Center of Photography
Jacques Marchais Center of Tibetan Art
Jewish Museum
Jumel Mansion (see Morris-Jumel Mansion)
Lower East Side Tenement Museum
Metropolitan Museum of Art
Museo del Barrio
Museum of African Art
Museum of American Folk Art
Museum of Modern Art
Museum of Television and Radio
Museum of the American Indian
Museum of the City of New York
New York Historical Society
New York Public Library
Old Merchant's House
Pierpont Morgan Library
Poe Cottage
Richmondtown Restoration
Schomburg Center for Research in Black Culture
South Street Seaport Museum
Staten Island Historical Museum (see Richmondtown Restoration)
Studio Museum in Harlem
Theodore Roosevelt Birthplace
Tibetan Museum (see Jacques Marchais Center of Tibetan Art)
Ukrainian Museum
Van Cortland Mansion and Museum
Whitney Museum of American Art

Other Museums, Collections and Monuments

Abigail Adams Smith Museum, 421 East 61st Street
Subway station: 59th Street (lines 4, 5, 6)
Open: Mon.–Fri. 10am–4pm,

Closed in August
House with a colonial style garden from 1799

American Numismatic Society, Broadway & 155th Street
Subway station: 157th Street (line 1)
Open: Tues.–Sat. 9am–4.30pm
Coins and medals

Americas Society, 680 Park Avenue
Subway station: 68th Street (line 6)
Open: Tues.–Sun. noon–6pm
Exhibitions on Central and South America, Canada and the Caribbean

Bible House/American Bible Society, Broadway & 61st Street
Subway station: 59th Street (lines 1, A, D)
Open: Mon.–Fri. 9am–4.30pm
Biblical history in many languages

Black Fashion Museum, 157 West 126th Street
Subway station: 125th Street (lines 2, 3)
Open: daily noon–8pm by prior arrangement
Tel. 666 1320
Costumes from theatre and film

Bronx Museum of Arts, 1040 Grand Concourse & 165th Street (Bronx)
Subway station: 161st Street (line 4)
Open: Sat.–Thur. 10am–4.30pm, Sun. 11am–4.30pm
Temporary exhibitions

Children's Museum of Manhattan, 212 West 83rd Street
Subway station: 86th Street (lines 1, 9)
Open: Tues.–Fri. 1–5pm, Sat. and Sun. 11am–5pm

Fire Department Museum, 258 Spring Street
Subway station: Spring Street (line 6)
Open: Tues. Fri. 9am–6pm, Sat. and Sun. 9am–2pm
History of the Fire Brigade

Forbes Magazine Galleries, 62 Fifth Avenue
Subway station: 14th Street (lines 4, 6, B, D, L, N, R)
Open: Tues., Wed., Fri., Sat. 10am–4pm
Private collection of the deceased multi-millionaire Malcolm Forbes

Fort Wadsworth Military Museum, Fort Tomkins (Staten Island)
Boat: Staten Island Ferry from Battery Park
Open: Mon., Thur., Fri., Sun. 1–4pm, Sat. 10am–4pm

Hall of Fame for Great Americans
Bronx Community College, 181st Street & University Avenue (Bronx)
Subway stations: Burnside Avenue, 183rd Street (line 4)
Open: daily 10am–5pm
Monuments to famous Americans

Harbor Defense Museum, Fort Hamilton (Brooklyn)
Subway station: 95th Street (Brooklyn; line R)
Open: Mon., Thur., Fri. 1–4pm, Sat. 10am–5pm
History of the coastal fort in New York

157

Intrepid Sea-Air Space Museum
Hudson River Pier, 46th Street & 12th Avenue
Subway station: 42nd Street and 8th Avenue (lines A, C, R), then bus 42
Open: May to Sept. daily 10am–5pm, Oct.– April Wed.–Sun. 10am–5pm
Over 70 aircraft, rockets, space capsules and the decommissioned aircraft
carrier INTREPID; D-Day exhibition

Isabelle Bacon Holy Land Museum
Marble Collegiate Church, Fifth Avenue & 29th Street
Subway station: 28th Street (line 6)
Open: Tues.–4pm, closed June–Aug.
Exhibits from the Holy Land

Museum of Bronx History, 3266 Bainbridge Avenue & East 208th Street
Subway station: 205th Street (line D)
Open: Mon.–Fri. 9am–5pm by prior arrangement
Tel. 881 8900; Sat. 10am–4pm, Sun. 1–3pm
History of the Bronx in a farmhouse from 1758

The Museum of the Staten Island Institute of Arts and Sciences
75 Stuyvesant Place (Staten Island)
Boat: Staten Island Ferry from Battery Park
Open: Tues.–Sat. 9am–5pm, Sun. 1–5pm
Exhibitions of natural history and fine art

National Academy of Design, 1083 Fifth Avenue/89th Street
Subway station: 86th Street (lines 4, 5, 6)
Open: Tues. noon–8pm (no charge after 8pm), Wed.–Sun. noon–5pm
American and European design, architecture, art

The New Muse Community Museum of Brooklyn
1530 Bedford Avenue (Brooklyn)
Subway station: Franklin Avenue (lines 2, 3, 4, 5)
Open: Tues.–Fri. 10am–5pm
Mainly Black art

New Museum of Contemporay Art, 583 Broadway
Subway station: Prince Street (lines N, R)
Open: Wed., Thur., Sun. noon–6pm, Fri., Sat. noon–8pm
Works mainly by young and unknown artists

New York Public Transit Exhibit
Boerum Place & Schermerhorn Street (Brooklyn)
Subway station: Mon.–Fri. 10am–4pm, Sat. 11am–4pm
Subway museum in disused station

Police Academy Museum, 235 East 20th Street
Subway station: 23rd Street (line 6)
Open: Mon.–Fri. 9am–3pm
One of the largest police museums in the world

Queens County Farm Museum
73–50 Little Neck Parkway, Floral Park (Queens)
Open: Sat., Sun. 11am–5pm
Agricultural history of New York on an old farm, out of town

Queens Museum, NYC Building, Flushing Meadow/Corona Park (Queens)
Subway station: Willets Point/Shea Stadium (line 7)
Open: Tues., Thur., Fri. 10am–5pm, Wed. 10am–8pm, Sat. and Sun.
noon–5.30pm. The museum contains a panorama of New York and a large
model of the five boros

Nicolas Roerich Museum, 319 West 107th Street
Subway station: 110th Street (line 1)
Open: Sun.–Fri. 2–4pm
Asian art and documents from and about Nicolas Roerich

Rotunda Gallery, Brooklyn War Memorial
Cadman Plaza West & Orange Street (Brooklyn)
Subway station: Borough Hall (lines 2, 4, 5)
Open: Tues.–Fri. noon–5pm, Sat. 11am–4pm
Closed July and Aug.
Temporary exhibitions

Staten Island Children's Museum, Snug Harbor Cultural Center
1000 Richmond Terrace (Staten Island)
Boat: Staten Island Ferry from Battery Park
Open: Wed.–Fri. 2–5pm, Sat., Sun. and pub. hols. 11am–5pm

Yeshiva University Museum, 2520 Amsterdam Avenue & 185th Street
Subway station: 181st Street (line 1)
Open: Tues.–Thur. 10.30am–5pm, Sun. noon–6pm
Closed on Jewish holidays
Jewish culture

Music

New York is a world centre for music. Together with two major opera companies, the New York Philharmonic and world-famous ballet ensembles, the city has a multiplicity of music and dance theatres and concert halls, only the most important of which are listed in this guide.

Information on the numerous events can be found in the newspapers and magazines (see entry) and by telephoning the TDF/NYC ON STAGE hotline, tel. 768 1818 (see Events).

Programme Information

New York has two major opera companies and a number of smaller companies which give only occasional performances. The two principal operahouses are part of the Lincoln Center for the Performing Arts (See A to Z).

Opera

Metropolitan Opera House
Broadway (between 61st and 66th Streets), tel. 362 6000
Subway: 66th Street (line 1, 9), 59th Street (lines A, C, D)
Buses: 5, 7, 104
Season: end September to April. Performances Mon.–Fri. (evenings), Sat. (afternoon and evening); closed Sun.
Founded in 1883 the "Met" is one of the most famous opera houses in the world. For conductors and singers it is the climax of their career to perform at the Metropolitan Opera. Some of the famous artists who perform here include James Levine, Luciano Pavarotti, Placido Domingo and Jessye Norman.
The repertoire is relatively small, and includes hardly any modern works, which appeal to the Met's audiences less than the operas of Wagner, Verdi, Puccini, etc.; but since the Met, like other cultural institutions in New York, is privately run and must cover 70% of its outgoings from box office receipts it has to have regard to box office appeal.

159

Music

New York City Opera
New York State Theater, Lincoln Center, tel. 870 9259. Transport details as for Metropolitan Opera House.
Season: July–November.
Six performances a week; closed Mon., Tues.

Founded in 1943, the New York City Opera like the Met, has a conventional repertoire, but it does make more attempt to present contemporary operas, particularly by American composers.

The City Opera gives six performances a week. It is closed on Mondays and Tuesdays but regularly gives two performances on Saturdays; it sometimes gives two performances on Sundays as well, in which event there are no performances on Thursday. Ticket prices are lower than those for the "Met" as international stars rarely perform here.

Ballet

New York is often called the ballet capital of the world, by virtue not only of its own great ballet ensembles and its many smaller companies but also of the visiting companies from the United States and many other countries which perform in the city.

Among directors of ballet and dance companies who have worked in New York have been such outstanding choreographers as Jerome Robbins, Robert Joffrey, Arthur Mitchell and Alwyn Nikolais. With the exception of the two principal companies, the American Ballet and the New York City Ballet, the New York companies concentrate mostly on the modern expressive style of dancing. The following companies give regular performances:

American Ballet Theater
Metropolitan Opera House, Lincoln Center, tel. 362 6000
Transport: see Metropolitan Opera above
Season: mid-April–mid-June.

New York City Ballet
New York State Theater, Lincoln Center, tel. 870 5570
Subway: see Metropolitan Opera above
Season: beginning of May to beginning of July, November to February.

Alvin Ailey American Dance Theater
City Center, 131 West 55th Street, tel. 767 0590
Subway: 57th Street (lines N, R)
Season: first half of May, second half of November.

Joffrey Ballet
City Center, 131 West 55th Street, tel. 265 7300
Subway: 57th Street (lines N, R)
Season: March, October.

Joyce Theater
175 Eighth Avenue, tel. 242 0800
Subway: 14th Street (lines A, C), 18th Street (lines 1, 9)

Other good dance companies, with no regular season, are the following:
Merce Cunningham Dance Company, tel. 255 8240
Dance Theater of Harlem, tel. 976 3470
Martha Graham Dance Company, tel. 838 5886
Feld Ballets, tel. 777 7710
Paul Taylor Dance Company, tel. 431 5562

Concerts

During the main season (October–April) there are some 150 concerts and recitals every week in New York, from the concerts given four times a week (Tues., Thurs., Fri. and Sat.) by the New York Philharmonic Orchestra in the Lincoln Center and the concerts by other major US and foreign orchestras, by way of choral events, chamber music, jazz and rock concerts to a host of solo recitals by pianists and singers.

Alice Tully Hall   Concert halls
Lincoln Center, Broadway and 64th Street, tel. 362 1911

Avery Fisher Hall
Lincoln Center, Broadway and 64th Street, tel. 874 6770

Brooklyn Academy of Music
30 Lafayette Avenue (Brooklyn), tel. 1 718 636 4100

Brooklyn Center for the Performing Arts at Brooklyn College
Nostrand and Avenue H (Brooklyn), tel. 1 718 951 4500

Carnegie Hall and Weill Recital Hall
154 West 57th Street, tel. 247 7800

Golden Center for Performing Arts
Queens College, Flushing (Queens), tel. 1 718 793 8080

Florence Gould Hall
French Institute, 55 East 59th Street, tel. 355 6105

Lehman Center for Performing Arts
Bedford Park Blvd. (Bronx), tel. 960 8833

Merkin Concert Hall,
129 West 67th Street, tel. 362 8719

92nd Street Y,
92nd Street and Lexington Avenue, tel. 966 1100

Carnegie Hall

Music

Regular concert series	Metropolitan Museum, Fifth Avenue and 82nd Street New School of Social Research, 66 West 12th Street YM-YWHA, 1395 Lexington Avenue (92nd Street)
Jazz concerts	The New York jazz scene is so varied and changes so rapidly that any information given here would be quickly out of date. The best plan for jazz enthusiasts, therefore, is to ring the Jazz Line (tel. 1 718 465 7500) for the latest news of what's on. Important jazz events are sometimes held in the concert hall mentioned above.
Rock 'n Roll	Information, tel. 540 7625
Jazz clubs	See Night life
Rock concerts	Well-known rock bands and singers perform in the following theatres: Madison Square Garden Seventh Avenue and 32nd Street, tel. 564 4400 (20,000 seats) Pennsylvania Station
Rock clubs	See Night life
Church music	There are recitals of church music in many New York churches, mainly at Christmas and Easter but by no means only then. They are listed in the Saturday edition of the "New York Times".
Concerts in the parks	Concerts and opera performances (admission free) are given by the New York Philharmonic and the Metropolitan Opera during the summer in Central Park and in parks in the other four New York boroughs. Information: tel. 755 4100 or 580 8700.

Madison Square Garden with Round Building

Newspapers and periodicals

In spite of its population of 7 million New York has only three dailies:

The "New York Times", the most respected American newspaper, appears seven times a week. On weekdays it runs to between 72 and 124 pages, on Sundays to between 300 and 500.

The "Daily News", until 1989 the American newspaper with the largest circulation, also appears seven times a week.

The "New York Post", American's oldest surviving newspaper, appears six times a week.

Even the strictly regional newspaper "USA Today" is obtainable in New York.

For information about events in New York the following weeklies are useful:
"New Yorker" (Monday)
"New York Magazine" (Monday)
"Village Voice" (Wednesday).

Night life

New York's wide variety of night life is concentrated in the areas around Times Square (see A to Z, Times Square; be careful!), Broadway and Greenwich Village (see A to Z, Greenwich Village). The list below only represents a small selection of venues. It is advisable to reserve a table in the clubs and bars offering entertainment. The minimum age for the consumption of alcoholic beverages is 21 and for admission to clubs between 18 and 23, depending on the type of establishment.

Radio City Music Hall
Avenue of the Americas and 50th Street, tel. 757 3100

Theatre revues

Adam's Apple, 117 First Avenue and 61st Street
Elaine's, 1703 Second Avenue
Friday's, 1152 First Avenue
Regine's, 502 Park Avenue

Bars and night clubs

Algonquin, 59 West 54th Street
The Ballroom, 253 West 28th Street
Caroline's, 332 8th Avenue
Chicago City Limits, 351 East 74th Street
Don't Tell Mama, 343 West 46th Street
Duplex, 61 Christopher Street
Improvisation, 358 West 44th Street
Stand-Up N.Y., 236 West 78th Street

Cabaret and shows

Parks

Discothèques | Not all the discos listed open every day. On some days admission is free.
Cat Club, 76 East 13th Street
Danceteria, 30 West 21st Street (on five floors)
Limelight, 47 West 20th Street (in a former church)
Palladium, 126 East 14th Street
> Housed in a former theatre this discothèque was designed by the Japanese architect Arata Isozaki. The graffiti artist Keith Haring designed the bar, the drinks coupons are by Andy Warhol and the staff wear clothes by the Paris fashion designer Azzedine Alaia. Above the dance floor are two video units each with 25 monitors and the background scenery from the theatre which constantly changes. The Palladium can accommodate 3500 guests.

Roseland, 239 West 52nd Street
Underground, 860 Broadway, tel. 254 4005

Jazz Clubs | Arthur's Tavern, 57 Grove Street
Blue Note, 131 West 3rd Street
Bradley's, 70 University Place and 10th Street
Condon's, 117 East 15th Street
Fat Tuesday's, 190 Third Avenue
Kelly's Village West, 46 Bedford Street
Knitting Factory, 47 East Houston Street
Michael's Pub, 211 East 55th Street
Nick's Grove, 207 East 84th Street,
Red Blazer Too, 349 West 46th Street
Sweet Basil, 88 Seventh Avenue South (near Bleecker Street)
Village Gate, 160 Bleecker Street
Village Vanguard, 11th Street and Seventh Avenue South
Zinno, 126 West 13th Street

Rock, Pop, Folk | Back Fence, 155 Bleecker Street
The Baja, 246A Columbus Avenue
Bottom Line, 15 West 4th Street
CBGB, 315 Bowery (Bleecker Street)
Mudd Club, 77 Water Street
Rock 'n' Roll Café, 149 Bleecker Street
Tramps, 456 West 21st Street

Parks (and open spaces)

Battery Park
Subway stations: South Ferry (line 1), Bowing Green (lines 4, 5), Whitehall Street (lines N, R); Bus: 6
Situation: Southern end of Manhattan.
Battery Park is traversed by wide pathways and enjoys magnificent views of Liberty Island and the Statue of Liberty (see A to Z, Statue of Liberty), Ellis Island (see A to Z, Ellis Island), Governor Island, the harbour and docks as well as Verrazano Bridge (see A to Z, Bridges).

In the park are the Castle Clinton National Monument (see A to Z) and several other monuments, including one of the Italian sailor Giovanni di Verrazano, who is said to have landed here in 1524, the poetess Emma Lazarus (1849–87), the Swedish-American engineer and inventor John Ericson (1803–89) and the "East Coast War Memorial" which commemorates the 4956 who died in the Second World War.

Bronx Park
(See A to Z, Bronx Zoo)

Carl Schurz Park
Bus 19
Situation: On East River near East 86th Street
The park is named after the German-American journalist and politician Carl Schurz (1829–1906), (see Facts and Figures, Famous People). In the north of this well-tended park stands Gracie Mansion (see A to Z), built around 1799, the residence of the mayor of New York.

Central Park
(See A to Z)

City Hall Park
(See A to Z, City Hall)

Clove Lakes Park
Staten Island ferry from Battery Park, then the bus
Situation: in the north of Staten Island
Clove Lakes Park has various recreational amenities.

Damrosch Park
(See A to Z, Lincoln Center for the Performing Arts)

Flushing Meadow Park/Corona Park
Subway stations: 111st Street/Main Street, Flushing (line 7)
Situation: In the north of Queens from Flushing Bay to Jamaica
This large site was the showground of the World Exhibitions in 1939/40 and 1964/65. Today it offers a variety of recreational and sports facilities (see Sport) including the National Tennis Center and Shea Stadium with a seating capacity of 55,000 and Louis Armstrong Stadium (18,000 seats). The US Open, the International American tennis Championships are held here annually. Other places of interest are Queens Museum (see Museums), the New York City Building, the former United Nations Assembly and the 42m (138ft) high dome "Unisphere".

Fort Green Park
Subway stations: DeKalb Avenue (lines B, D, N, R)
Situation: In the north-west of Brooklyn
The 44m (144ft) high Martyrs' Monument by Standford White is located here. It commemorates the 11,000 American soldiers who died in British imprisonment during the War of Independence.

Fort Tryon Park
Subway stations; 190th Street, Dyckman Street, 207th Street/Washington Heights (line A)
Situation: North-west tip of Manhattan
This park has good views of the opposite bank of the Hudson River, "The Pallisades". The main attraction of the park is The Cloisters Museum (see A to Z, The Cloisters).

Gramercy Park
Subway stations: 23rd Street (line 6)
Situation: Between East 20th and East 21st Streets
Access to this park is restricted to residents living close by. The houses themselves are interesting.

Morningside Park
Subway stations: 125th Street (lines A, C, D)
Situation: North-west of Central Park
Built on terraces the park has an impressive view over Harlem and East River. Even during the day it is not absolutely safe. Caution is required.

Pelham Bay Park
Subway stations: Pelham Bay Park (line 6), then by bus which stops in the
park
Situation: North-east of Bronx on Long Island Sound
This spacious park has a golf course and Bartow Pell Mansion lies in its
grounds, built in 1830 in "Greek Revival Style" with contemporary
furniture.

Prospect Park
Subway stations: Grand Army Plaza (line 2), Prospect Park (line D)
Situation: In the heart of Brooklyn
Donated by the Litchfield family in 1858 it is a large nature park with old
trees, wide green spaces, playgrounds and a small zoo.

It was designed by the architects of Central Park (see A to Z). To the south
is the extensive Swan Lake where there is rowing in summer and ice-
skating in winter.

Two interesting buildings are Litchfield Mansion, the former residence of
the patron, and Lefferts Homestead, a farmhouse from 1776 which was
moved here in 1918 and established as a museum. To the north of the park
is the oval Grand Army Plaza with the Soldiers' and Sailors' Arch, an
impressive 24m (78ft) high triumphal arch by McMonnies in honour of the
dead of the War of Succession and a Kennedy memorial. Brooklyn Library
(see Libraries and Archives) is housed in the Ingerson Building (Art Deco),
to the south-east, built in 1941.

Riverside Park
Subway stations: Several stations between 72nd and 25th Streets (lines 1,
2, 3, 9)
Situation: Along the east bank of the Hudson River
Also designed by the architects of Central Park it is traversed by the Henry
Hudson Parkway. There is a line of monuments running north to south
through the park. First the Jewish Martyrs' Memorial (83rd Street) for the
Jewish vicitims of Nazi oppression, followed by the Soldiers' and Sailors'
Monument (89th Street), a circular column to comemorate the dead of the
War of Succession, Jeanne d'Arc on horseback, made partly out of stone
from Rheims Cathedral, the Firemen's Memorial (100th Street) in honour of
the New York Fire Service and finally the statue of the German General
Franz Sigel on horseback, from the Civil War (106th Street).

To the north of the park is Grant's Tomb (General Grant National Memorial 1891–97) made of marble and granite, a mausoleum in Roman style for
the General of the Union forces, Ulysses Simpson Grant (1822–85), who
later became the 18th President of the USA, and his wife who rest here in
porphyry sarcophagi.

Van Cortlandt Park
(See A to Z, Van Cortlandt Mansion and Museum)

Postal services

The US Post Office is responsible only for postal services.
The telephone and telegraph services (see entries) are run by private
enterprise.

Postage rates Letters within the United States: 29 cents for the first ounce, plus 23 cents
for each additional ounce.
Air mail letters to Europe: 50 cents for each half ounce.
Postcards: 36 cents. Pre-stamped air mail letter forms cost 38 cents.
Stamps are most conveniently bought in a post office.

In midtown Manhattan: Post offices
General Post Office, Eighth Avenue and 33rd Street
Grand Central Post Office, Lexington Avenue and 45th Street
Times Square post office, 340 West 42nd Street
Rockefeller Center post office, RCA Building
Franklin D. Roosevelt post office, 909 Third Avenue (55th Street)
Bryant post office, 23 West 43rd Street
Empire State post office, 19 West 33rd Street
Columbus Circle post office, 27 West 60th Street.
    There are also post offices in Macy's and Bloomingdale's department
stores (see Department stores).

Usually Mon.–Fri. 8am–6pm, Sat. 9am–1pm. The General Post Office is   Opening times
open all the time.
    After closing time, stamps can be bought from coin-operated machines.
It is advisable to purchase stamps at a post office as most machines in
hotels levy a surcharge.

Poste restante letters should be marked "General Delivery".   Poste restante

This is a five-figure number following the two-letter abbreviation for the   Zip code (post
state: e.g. New York, NY 10017. The last figures of the number vary accord- code)
ing to the district.

These are painted blue, with the legend "US Mail" in white.   Letter-boxes

See Telephone   Telephone

See Telegrams   Telegrams

Public holidays

With the exception of Easter Day, Christmas Day and New Year's Day many
shops remain open on official holidays, though banks, the Stock Exchange,
government offices and schools are closed. On Christian festivals (Easter,
Christmas) there is no extra public holiday.
    Most official holidays vary slightly from year to year, being fixed for the
Monday before or after the actual day in order to make a long weekend.

New Year's Day (1 January); Martin Luther King Day (Monday following 15   Statutory public
January); Washington's Birthday (third Monday in February); Easter Day;   holidays
Memorial or Decoration Day (last Monday in May); Independence Day (4
July); Labor Day (first Monday in September); Columbus Day (second
Monday in October); Veteran's Day or Armistice Day (11 November);
Thanksgiving Day (fourth Thursday in November); Christmas Day (25
December).

Radio and television

New York has seven television stations and some 50 radio stations, some of
them operating 24 hours a day. With the exception of one television station,
WNET, and two radio stations, WNYC and WBAI, they are all commercial,
financing their operations by the sale of transmission time and advertising
spots.

There are few live programmes on American radio. Most stations make   Radio
much use of records and tapes, sometimes specialising in a particular kind

167

of music (classical, jazz, rock). Some transmit programmes directed at particular ethnic groups; others send out news all day long.

Television — Some television stations admit an audience to the transmission or recording of certain programmes. For information apply to the following stations:

WABC (Channel 7), 1330 Avenue of the Americas, tel. 456 1000
WCBS (Channel 2), 51 West 52nd Street, tel. 975 4321
WNBC (Channel 4), 30 Rockefeller Plaza, tel. 664 4444
WNET (Channel 13), 356 West 58th Street, tel. 560 2000
WNEW (Channel 5), 205 East 67th Street, tel. 535 1035
WWOR (Channel 9), 1440 Broadway, tel. 764 6683
WPIX (Channel 11), 220 East 42nd Street, tel. 949 1100

There are also more than 30 commercial cable television networks offering programmes 24 hours a day, e.g. Channel 24 sport, Channel W Weather Reports, Channel O, P and Q Films, etc. Channels 16 and 17 are "Public Access" channels where anyone can buy airtime to broadcast (almost) anything.

Programme information — Television programmes and the programmes of the principal radio stations are given daily in the newspapers.

Railway and bus stations

Railways — Since the railway plays relatively little part in the transport network of the United States, visitors to New York will have little occasion to travel by train, except perhaps to the suburbs and between New York, Washington and Philadelphia. Passenger services are run (with large government subsidies) by the Amtrak corporation, to which practically all the private rail companies have leased their stations, track and rolling stock.

New York has two main-line railway stations:
Grand Central Terminal, 42nd Street and Park Avenue
Information: tel. 736 4545, daily 6am–1am
Surban services to the north only (see A to Z, Skyscrapers).

Penn Station, 33rd Street and Seventh Avenue
Information: tel. 736 4545, daily 5.45am–11.30pm
Services run by the Long Island Railroad (tel. 739 4200) and services to the southern and western United States.

Long-distance bus services — The main competition to air and rail services for long-distance travel in the United States is provided by country-wide bus services, which are cheaper than travelling by rail. Almost all the traffic is carried by Greyhound Lines.

All buses depart from and arrive at the central bus station:
Port Authority Bus Terminal, Eighth Avenue (40th–42nd Streets)
Information: tel. 564 8484
Greyhound: tel. 971 6363

The bus company offers short-term season tickets (Greyhound's "Ameripass") allowing unlimited travel on all its services for a week, two weeks or a month. For those who want to see America by bus this is much cheaper than buying a series of separate tickets.

Bus station — Port Authority Bus Terminal
Eighth Avenue (40th–42nd Street)
tel. 564 8484

Rent-a-Car

See Car hire

Restaurants

New York is reliably reported to have almost 15,000 restaurants, from the most exclusive establishments to the most modest coffee shops and cafeterias. There is a wide price range, from the luxury restaurants, where the standard meal may cost about 100 dollars a head, to the smaller places, where a satisfying meal can be had for a few dollars. Lunch is almost always cheaper than dinner. In reading the menus, which are almost always posted up outside the restaurant, remember to allow for tax at 8·25% and a tip of perhaps 15% of the bill. The prices of drinks are not usually posted up, but wine tends to be dear. There is, however, no obligation to order drinks. Iced water is always supplied free of charge.

Almost every national cuisine in the world is represented in New York. Thus in 55th and 56th Streets, between Fifth Avenue and the Avenue of the Americas, there is a choice of Japanese, Chinese, Korean, Italian and French restaurants. The cheapest Chinese food – and frequently the best – is to be found in modest establishments in Chinatown. For Near Eastern cuisine the best area is between 28th and 32nd Streets, on both sides of Lexington Avenue, where there are many Lebanese and Syrian restaurants. French and Italian restaurants – the most numerous of the foreign restaurants apart from the Chinese – are mainly to be found on East Side, where there is some competition between the traditional *haute cuisine* and the now fashionable *nouvelle cuisine*.

These are perhaps the more popular of the foreign cuisines which can be sampled in New York, but there are numerous other restaurants offering Argentinian, Brazilian, British, Czech, Danish, Filipino, Greek, Indian, Mexican, Persian, Russian, Thai, Turkish, Ukrainian and West Indian food – to mention only a few.

In many restaurants, particularly those in the higher price ranges, it is necessary to book a table by telephone.

All New York restaurants are listed in the "Yellow Pages" telephone directory. The following is only a brief selection.
    The list does not include hotel restaurants. (All the larger hotels have restaurants, often more than one.)

The various types of cuisine are distinguished as follows:

Af	=Afghanistani	K	=Korean
A	=American	M	=Mexican
C	=Chinese	M–T	=Mex-Tex
F	=French	O	=Oriental
FR	=fish restaurant	P	=Polish
G	=German	R	=Russian
Gr	=Greek	Sc	=Scandinavian
I	=Italian	Sp	=Spanish
In	=Indian	Sw	=Swiss
Ind	=Indonesian	T	=Turkish
Is	=Israeli	V	=Vietnamese
J	=Japanese		

Restaurants

The letters *L* (luxury) and *E* (expensive) give some indication of price level.

East Side of Manhattan (42nd–86th Streets)

Ambassador Grill (A), 44th Street, First Avenue (UN Plaza – A Park Hyatt), tel. 702 5014
Anatolia (I), 1422 Third Avenue, tel. 517 6262
Arizona 206 (A), 206 East 60th Street, tel. 838 0440
Azzuro (I), 245 East 84th Street, tel. 517 7068
Barclay (A), 111 East 48th Street (Hotel Inter-Continental), tel. 421 0836
Bistro du Nord (F), 1312 Madison Avenue, tel. 289 0997
Brasserie (F), 100 East 53rd Street, tel. 751 4840
Bukhara (In), 148 East 48th Street, tel. 421 1919
Chalet Suisse (S), 6 East 48th Street, tel. 355 0855
Christ Cella (A), 160 East 46th Street, tel. 697 2479
Coldwaters (FR), 988 Second Avenue/52nd Street, tel. 888 2122
Contrapunto (I), 200 East 60th Street, tel. 757 8616
Dawat (In), 210 East 58th Street, tel. 355 7555
Ecce Panis (I), 1120 Third Avenue, tel. 535 2099
Ferrier (F), 29 East 65th Street, tel. 772 9000
Four Seasons (A, T), 99 East 52nd Street, tel. 754 9494
Gian Marino (I), 230 East 58th Street, tel. 752 1696
Grand Central Oyster Bar (FR), Grand Central Station, tel. 490 6650
Japanese Restaurant Awoki (J), 305 East 46th Street, tel. 759 8897
La Côte Basque (F; *E*), 5 East 55th Street, tel. 688 6525
Lespinasse (F), 2 East 55th Street (Hotel Regis), tel. 753 4500
Living Room (A), 154 East 79th Street, tel. 772 8488
Lutèce (F; *L*), 249 East 50th Street, tel. 752 2225
Mitsukoshi (J), 461 Park Avenue (57th Street), tel. 935 6444
Mon Cher Ton Ton (F, I), 68 East 56th Street, tel. 223 7575
Oceana (FR), 55 East 54th Street, tel. 759 5941
Pamir (Af), 1437 Second Avenue, tel. 650 1095
Paper Moon Milano (I), 39 East 58th Street, tel. 758 8600
Piccolo Mondo (I), 1269 First Avenue, tel. 249 3141
Pronto (I), 33 East 60th Street, tel. 421 8151
Sakura of Japan (J), 581 Third Avenue, tel. 972 8540
Sichuan Palace (C), 310 East 44th Street, tel. 972 7377

West Side of Manhattan (42nd–73rd Streets)

Abruzzi (I), 37 West 56th Street, tel. 489 8110
Adrienne (FR) 2 West 55th Street (Peninsula Hotel), tel. 903 3918
American Festival Café (A), Rockefeller Plaza, 20 West 50th Street, tel. 246 6699
Aquavit (Sc), 13 West 54th Street, tel. 307 7311
Assembly Steak House (A), 16 West 51st Street, tel. 581 3580
Café de la Paix (F), St Moritz, 50 Central Park South, tel. 755 5800
Café Luxembourg (F), 200 West 70th Street, tel. 873 7411
Darbar (In), 46 West 56th Street, tel. 432 7227
Fontana di Trevi (I), 151 West 57th Street, tel. 247 5683
44 (V), 44 West 44th Street (Royalton Hotel), tel. 944 8844
French Shack (F), 65 West 55th Street, tel. 246 5126
Fuji (J), 238 West 56th Street, tel. 245 8594
Gallagher's Steak House (A), 228 West 52nd Street, tel. 245 5336
Houlihan's (A), 729 Seventh Avenue (51st Street), tel. 575 2012
Joe's Pier 52 (FR), 163 West 52nd Street, tel. 245 6652
La Caravelle (F), 33 West 55th Street, tel. 586 4252
La Cité (F), 120 West 51st Street, tel. 956 7100
La Strada (I), 134 West 46th Street, tel. 869 7188
Le Bernardin (FR), 155 West 51st Street, tel. 489 1515
Le Biarritz (F), 325 West 57th Street, tel. 757 2390
Mickey Mantle's (A), 42 Central Park West, tel. 688 7777
Les Pyrenées (F), 251 West 51st Street, tel. 246 0044
Nirvana (In), 30 Central Park South, tel. 468 5700

Palio (I), 151 West 51st Street, tel. 245 4850
Poiret (F), 474 Columbus Avenue, tel. 724 6880
Rainbow Room (F, I), 30 Rockefeller Plaza (65th Floor), tel. 632 5000
Rikyu (J), 210 Columbus Avenue, tel. 799 7847
Romeo Salta (I, T), 30 West 56th Street, tel. 246 5772
Russian Tearoom (R), 150 West 57th Street, tel. 265 0947
Sacred Cow Steak House (A), 228 West 72nd Street, tel. 873 4067
San Domenico (I), 240 Central Park South, tel. 265 5959
Sardi (A), 234 West 44th Street, tel. 221 8440
Shun Lee Café (C), 43 West 65th Street, tel. 595 8895
Tavern on the Green (A), Central Park West and 67th Street, tel. 873 3200
Top of the Sixes (A), 666 Fifth Avenue (53rd Street), tel. 757 6662
Wally's and Joseph's (A), 249 West 49th Street, tel. 582 0460
Yamaguchi (J), 35 West 45th Street, tel. 840 8185
Yellow Rose Café (A), 450 Amsterdam Avenue, tel. 595 8760

Ballroom (A), 253 West 28th Street, tel. 244 3005
Bianchi & Margherita, 186 West 4th Street, tel. 242 2756
Chanterelle (FR), 2 Harrison Street/Hudson Street, tel. 966 6960
Ecole (FR), 462 Broadway/Grand Street, tel. 219 3300
Farnie's (A), Second Avenue and 18th Street, tel. 228 9280
Fraunce's Tavern (A), Broad and Pearl Street, tel. 269 0144
Gotham (C), 12 East 12th Street, tel. 620 4020
Grand/Ticino (I), 228 Thompson Street, tel. 777 5922
Great Shanghai (C), 27 Division Street, tel. 966 7663
Hisae (FR), 35 Cooper Square, tel. 228 6886
Hudson River Club (FR), 4 World Financial Center, tel. 786 1500
La Colombe d'Or (F), 134 East 26th Street, tel. 689 0666
La Gauloise (F), 502 Avenue of the Americas, tel. 691 1363
Le Madri (I), 168 West 18th Street, tel. 727 8022
Minetta Tavern (I), 113 MacDougal Street, tel. 475 3850
Montrachet (F), 239 West Broadway, tel. 219 2777
One Fifth (A), One Fifth Avenue, tel. 727 1515
Park Bistro (F), 414 Park Avenue South, tel. 689 1350
Periyali (Gr), 35 West 20th Street, tel. 463 7890
Pete's Tavern (A), 129 East 18th Street, tel. 473 7676
Provence (F), 38 MacDougal Street, tel. 475 7500
Rectangles (Is), 159 Second Avenue, tel. 677 8410
Sal Anthony (I), 55 Irving Place, tel. 982 9030
Sevilla (Sp), 62 Charles Street, tel. 929 3189
Spain (Sp), 113 West 13th Street, tel. 929 9580
Swoots (FR), 2 Fulton Street, tel. 344 9189
Tai Hong Lau (C), 70 Mott Street, tel. 219 1431
Toots Shor (A), 233 West 33rd Street, tel. 563 7440
Union Square Café (A), 21 East 16th Street, tel. 243 4020
Windows on the World (A, T), World Trade Center, tel. 938 1111

Manhattan below
42nd Street

Security and crime

The visitor to New York may not want to heed the horror stories concerning crime in the city. The crime level is high but by no means the worst in the US. Crime in New York is concentrated in certain areas. If the visitor follows certain guidelines which apply to most cities he/she is in no greater danger than in any other city.

Avoid certain areas after dark. This includes parks, especially Central Park, the red-light areas around 42nd Street, between 7th and 8th Avenue, and 8th Avenue between 42nd and 50th Street, Harlem and Lower East Side. If

you are returning late take a taxi rather than the subway. Even the lesser-used subways can be dangerous.
- Avoid going out alone at night.
- Try not to appear and behave like a tourist. When visiting Harlem during the day, if you must take it, keep your camera out of sight and be discreet when taking photographs.
- Do not carry valuable objects or large amounts of money on your person. Keep them in your hotel safe.
- Avoid wearing striking jewellery, especially necklaces. Shoulder bags invite crime.
- When in the hotel lock your door from the inside and do not open it to strangers. Take the key with you.
- Do not let anyone help you with your luggage at the airport or in hotels, either to carry it into the taxi or up to your room.
- Do not trust strangers or slight acquaintances with personal valuables.
- In the event of any incident inform the police.

Shopping

New York is a shopper's paradise. There are the exclusive fashion and jewellery shops on Fifth Avenue (see A to Z, Fifth Avenue), exotic goods from Asia (see A to Z, Chinatown), hi-fi and photographic shops (see Practical Information, Customs Regulations) as well as shops offering a most unusual array of goods. Numerous shops are concentrated in shopping centres, malls and around markets. Opening times vary but they stay open late at least one evening a week. It is possible to shop at the weekend as there are no official trading laws governing opening and closing times.

Department stores	See Department stores
Markets	See Markets
Antiques	See Antiques
Bookshops	See Bookshops
Shopping centres	A and S, Avenue of the Americas and 32nd Street 575 Fifth Avenue, 575 Fifth Avenue (on four floors) Herald Center, 34th Street and Broadway (140 shops) The Market at Citicorp Center, Lexington Avenue and 54th Street Rockefeller Center (see A to Z, Rockefeller Center) South Street Seaport and Pier 17 (see A to Z, South Street Seaport Museum) Trump Tower (see A to Z, Trump Tower) World Trade Center Shopping Concourse (see A to Z, World Trade Center)
Specialist shops	The following is a selection of specialist shops.
Chocolates	Godiva Chocolatier, 701 Fifth Avenue, 793 Madison Avenue, 560 Lexington Avenue and 245 Columbus Avenue Teuscher Chocolates of Switzerland, 620 Fifth Avenue and 25 East 61st Street
Fashion houses	Bergdorf-Goodman, Fifth Avenue and 58th Street Henri Bendel, 10 West 57th Street
Fashion for the family	Alexander's, Lexington Avenue and 58th Street Lord and Taylor, Fifth Avenue and 39th Street Saks Fifth Avenue, Fifth Avenue and 50th Street

Macy's: New York's largest department store

Ashanti Larger Sizes, 872 Lexington Avenue	Fashion for
Benetton, 601 Fifth Avenue and 20 other stores in Manhattan	women
Charivari for Women, 2307 Broadway	
Escada, 7 East 57th Street	
Ferragamo, 717 Fifth Avenue	
The Forgotten Woman, 60 West 49th Street	
Galeries Lafayette, 46 East 57th Street	
Lerner Shops, 17 West 34th Street and 3 other stores	
Petite Pleasures, 1192 Madison Avenue	
Plymouth, 30 Rockefeller Plaza and twelve other shops in Manhattan	
Brooks Brothers, 346 Madison Avenue	Fashion for men
The Cockpit, 595 Broadway	
Ferragamo, 730 Fifth Avenue	
F. R. Tripler & Co., Madison Avenue and 46th Street	
Wallachs, 150 Broadway and 555 Fifth Avenue	
Barney's, Seventh Avenue and 17th Street	Fashion for
Jaeger International Shop, 818 Madison Avenue and two other shops	women and men
Made in the USA, 130 East 59th Street and 155 Spring Street	
Riding High, 1147 First Avenue	
Strawberry, 501 Madison Avenue and 12 other shops in Manhattan	
Antonovich Furs, 333 Seventh Avenue	Furs
The Fur Vault, 581 Fifth Avenue and 333 Seventh Avenue	
Caswell Massey Co. Ltd., 518 Lexington Avenue	Gifts and
Forbidden Planet, 821 Broadway and 227 East 59th Street	souvenirs
Jerry Ohlinger's Movie Material Store Inc., 242 West 14th Street	

Let there be Neon, 38 White Street
Quong Yuen Shing & Co., 32 Mott Street (Chinatown)
Star Magic-Space Age Gifts, 743 Broadway, 560 Lexington Avenue and
    275 Amsterdam Avenue
Statue of Liberty Giftshop, Liberty Island
Steuben Glass, 715 Fifth Avenue
Think Big! 390 West Broadway, 313 Columbus Avenue
Treat Boutique, 200 East 86th Street

Jewellers

The best known jewellers are concentrated in the area of Fifth Avenue and
57th Street:
Bulgari, Fifth Avenue and 61st Street
Cartier, 653 Fifth Avenue (52nd Street)
Aaron Faber, 666 Fifth Avenue (53rd Street)
Michael C. Fina, 580 Fifth Avenue (47th Street)
Fortunoff, 681 Fifth Avenue (55th Street)
Mikimoto (America), 608 Fifth Avenue (42nd Street)
Tiffany and Co., 727 Fifth Avenue (57th Street)
Van Cleef and Arpels, 744 Fifth Avenue (57th Street)
David Webb, 445 Park Avenue
Harry Winston, 718 Fifth Avenue (56th Street)
    Every type of jewellery can also be found in 47th Street, between Fifth
Avenue and the Avenue of the Americas. There are about two dozen
jewellers' shops on this block.

Pipes and
smokers' articles

Alfred Dunhill of London, 620 Fifth Avenue (50th Street)
Nat Sherman, 711 Fifth Avenue (55th Street)

Records

Colony Records, 1619 Broadway (49th Street)
Sam Goody, 51 West 51st Street
Sam Goody, 575 Fifth Avenue
Sam Goody, 666 and 1011 Third Avenue
Sam Goody, 390 and 901 Avenue of the Americas
Sam Goody, 230 East 42nd Street
Sam Goody, 11 Fulton Street
HMV, 2081 Broadway and 1280 Lexington Avenue
Tower Records, 692 Broadway and 1965 Broadway (the largest and most
    modern record shop)

Stamps

United Nations Postal Administration,
First Avenue and 46th Street
UN stamps for collectors

Toys

F. A. O. Schwarz, 787 Fifth Avenue (58th Street)
The Enchanted Forest, 85 Mercer Street (SoHo)
Toys R Us. 1293 Broadway/33rd Street

Sightseeing

The following recommendations are intended to help the first-time visitor
to New York see the most of the city in a short time.
    The distances between the places of interest are too far to walk but all
places are easily accessible by public transport.

Day One

A visit to New York should begin with an overall view of the city and this is
best achieved from the Empire State Building. From here a stroll past the
many luxury shops on Fifth Avenue brings one to the Rockefeller Center
(about 1·5km (1 mile)) with the GE Building and Radio City Music Hall.
Opposite, between East 50th Street and 51st Street, stands St Patrick's
Cathedral. Some of the most notable skyscrapers are to be found here such

as the Sony Building (Madison Avenue and 55th Street) and Trump Tower (Fifth Avenue and 56th Street). If time and energy permit round off the day with a visit to the United Nations Assembly on East River (subway or bus). Central Park is only a few blocks away to the north of the Rockefeller Center.

The second day is spent exploring the southern tip of Manhattan. It begins with a boat trip to New York's most famous landmark, the Statue of Liberty with the American Museum of Immigration inside its base. From South Ferry it is a 10 minute walk to the tallest building in New York, the World Trade Center. Visitors should not miss a visit to the viewing platform in the south tower. From here head east to Broadway and turn right. A few hundred yards further on turn off east, opposite Trinity Church, down skyscraper-lined Wall Street, the main artery of the financial district, to the heart of the financial world, the New York Stock Exchange. Wall Street joins South Street at East River which leads north to South Street Seaport Museum. Near the museum ships are restaurants and cafés in which to relax. Day Two

The third day is spent visiting the museums according to personal interest. However, the Metropolitan Museum of Art is an essential part of the itinerary, for which several days would not even suffice. Select the departments you wish to see in advance. If, afterwards, you still have the time and energy, a refreshing walk through Central Park brings you to the American Museum of Natural History or a few blocks south to the Frick Collection. Modern art enthusiasts should head for the Museum of Modern Art in East 53rd Street. This can be followed by travelling from Madison Avenue (bus lines 1, 2, 3, 4) to 90th Street to the Solomon R. Guggenheim Museum or a visit to the Whitney Museum of American Art (76th Street). Those less interested in art may like to spend the day in the other districts shopping or just strolling around. Chinatown with its exotic charm is particularly interesting. Equally inviting are the districts of Little Italy, SoHo and Greenwich Village to the north. Day Three

The fourth day is spent visiting the more outlying sights. Those who still have an appetite for museums could take the subway (line A) or bus to The Cloisters in north Manhattan (medieval art) or to Brooklyn Museum (line 2) in Brooklyn. A more relaxing time may be had at the Bronx Zoo or Brooklyn Botanic Garden. Day Four

There are many companies in New York which organise a whole variety of guided tours ranging from the standard bus tour and private tours in limousines to organised shopping trips. A visit to a restaurant or show is often included in the tour. General

A number of organisations conduct guided walks: On foot

Accent on Language Custom Tours
160 East 52nd Street, tel. 355 5170
Private tours in a chosen language.

Friends of Cast-Iron Architecture
221 West 19th Street, tel. 886 3742
Walks in spring and autumn through parts of the city, particularly in SoHo, where there are 19th c, cast-iron buildings.

Municipal Art Society
457 Madison Avenue between 50th and 51st Streets, tel. 935 3960
Guided walks from May to the beginning of September introducing the participants to the architecture of New York and changes in the face of the city.

Sightseeing

Museum of American Folk Art
Columbus Avenue and 65th Street, tel. 595 9533
Visits by small groups to New York buildings or houses of particular interest are organised at irregular intervals.

Museum of the City of New York
103rd Street and Fifth Avenue, tel. 534 1672
Walks through different parts of Manhattan on Sundays at 11am from April to October.

By bus

Gray Line
900 Eighth Avenue between 53rd and 54th Streets,
tel. 397 2620, 1 800 669 0051
A programme of eighteen tours of Manhattan, lasting from $2\frac{1}{2}$ to $8\frac{1}{2}$ hours.

Short Line Tours
166 West 46th Street, tel. 354 5122
A programme of eight day and evening tours of Manhattan.

Boat excursions

See Boat excursions

Ferries

See Ferries

Helicopter trips

Island Helicopters, tel. 683 4575
Sightseeing flights lasting 5–7, 10–12, 15–17 or 30 minutes, daily 9am–9pm (6pm Jan.–Mar.). Departure from Heliport, East River (end of East 34th Street).

Manhattan Helicopter Tours, tel. 247 8687
Depart from Heliport West 30th Street and 12th Avenue
Daily 9am–6pm

Special interests

There are a variety of specialised programmes, some of them tailored to individual requirements. To avoid unpleasant surprises, enquire about cost in advance.

Art Tours of Manhattan, Inc.
63 East 82nd Street, tel. 677 6005
Guided tours of museums, galleries, the artists' quarter of SoHo and artists' studios.

Backstage on Broadway Tours
228 West 47th Street, tel. 575 8065
Behind the scenes of a Broadway show under the guidance of an actor.

Harlem Spiritual Inc.
1697 Broadway, tel. 757 0425
Tour of Harlem with church visits (Sun. 8.45am–12.45pm)
"Soul Food" lunch (Thur. 9am–1.30pm) and Gospel singing (Wed. 9am–1pm).

Harlem, Your Way
129 West 130th Street, tel. 690 1687
Conducted walks of Harlem (Mon.–Sat. 12.30pm);
Church visits and gospel singing (Sun. 10.45am).

Hello New York
430 East 86th Street, tel. 861 1323
Conducted tours by bus of the principal sights.

Inside New York
203 East 72nd Street, tel. 570 2988
Behind the scenes of the New York fashion industry.

Young Visitors
175 West 88th Street, tel. 595 8100
Tours for children and student groups, introducing them to the history of
New York and the ethnic composition of its population.

Sport

New York offers endless scope for every kind of sport and recreation.
Anglers and golfers are catered for in the Bronx, Brooklyn, Queens and
Staten Island; but the main centre of sporting activity in New York is Central
Park (see A to Z) in the heart of Manhattan. Here there are facilities for roller
skating and ice skating, riding, cycling, rowing and playing tennis. (In
addition, there are many tennis courts, both public and private, in all parts
of the city.)

For information about sports facilities and particular sporting events
telephone 755 4100.

Some of the principal sports grounds are listed below.

N. Y. Mets, Shea Stadium, Flushing (Queens), tel. 1 (718) 507 8499   Baseball
N. Y. Yankees, Yankee Stadium, Bronx, tel. 293 4300

N. Y. Knicks, Madison Square Garden, Seventh Avenue and 32nd Street,   Basketball
  tel. 465–JUMP
N. Y. Nets, Rutgers Center, Piscataway, New Jersey, tel. 1 (201) 935 8888

Yankee Stadium: Venue of Baseball

Street names and numbers

Football, American	N. Y. Giants, Giants Stadium, Meadowlands, New Jersey, tel. 1 (201) 935 8222
	N. Y. Jets, Shea Stadium, Flushing (Queens), tel. 1 (718) 421 6600
Ice Hockey	N. Y. Islanders, Nassau Coliseum, Uniondale (Long Island), tel. 1 (516) 694 5522
Horse-racing	Aqueduct Racetrack, Ozone Park (Queens), tel. 1 (718) 641 4700
	Belmont Raceway, Belmont (Long Island), tel. 1 (718) 641 4700
	Meadowlands Racetrack, Meadowlands, New Jersey, tel. 1 (201) 935 8500
	Roosevelt Raceway, Westbury (Long Island), tel. 1 (516) 222 2000 (trotting)
	Yonkers Raceway, Yonkers, NY, tel. 1 (914) 968 4200 and 562 9500 (trotting)
Betting	Bets on horse-races can be placed at offices of the state-sponsored Off-Track Betting Corporation (OTB) which can be found all over the city. Information: tel. 752 1940.
Tennis	April/May: Tournament of Champions, West Side Tennis Club, Forest Hills (Queens)
	August/September: U.S. Open Tennis Championships, USTA National Tennis Center, Flushing Meadows/Corona Park (Queens)
	November/December: Masters, Madison Square Garden

Street names and numbers

Thanks to the regular grid plan adopted by the city fathers in 1811 for the layout of Manhattan N of Washington Square it is easy for visitors to find their way about the city. The streets running up the whole length of Manhattan from south to north are called avenues, those cutting across the island from east to west are plain streets. The main exception to this regularity is Broadway, Manhattan's longest street, which cuts across the rectangular grid in its course from south to north of the island.

The main avenues are numbered, from First Avenue in the east to Twelfth Avenue in the west, but some bear names, and a few in southern Manhattan are known by letters. The streets are numbered consecutively from south to north. Fifth Avenue divides Manhattan into two parts, East Side and West Side, and the streets east and west of this divide are called, for example, East 42nd Street and West 42nd Street.

The Manhattan avenues are very long, and if you are looking for a particular number it is helpful to know roughly where it is located. This can be achieved by using the following table.

Take the number you are looking for, drop the last digit, divide the remainder by 2 and add or subtract the key number shown against the avenue in the table. The result will give you the number of the cross street nearest the building you are looking for.

First Avenue	+3	Eighth Avenue	+10
Second Avenue	+3	Ninth Avenue	+13
Third Avenue	+10	Tenth Avenue	+14
Fourth Avenue	+8	Amsterdam Avenue	+60
Fifth Avenue to 200	+13	Broadway	
201–400	+16	(23rd–192nd St)	−30
401–600	+18	Madison Avenue	+26
601–775	+20	Lexington Avenue	+22
776–1286	−18	Central Park West	
(do not divide by 2)		(divide number by 10)	+60
1287–1500	+45	Columbus Avenue	+60
Avenue of the Americas	−12	Park Avenue	+35
Seventh Avenue		Riverside Drive	
(to 110 St)	+12	(divide number by 10)	+72
(from 110th Street)	+20	West End Avenue	+60

Example: To find the situation of 825 Madison Avenue, drop the final 5 to give 82; divide by 2 to give 41; and add the 26 shown in the table to give 67. Thus 825 Madison Avenue lies at the intersection with 67th Street.

Taxis

In New York there are about 11,000 taxis. They are licensed by the New York City Taxi and Limousine Commission which can be contacted for lost property (tel. 840 4734) or complaints (tel. 221 8294). Quote the licence number (not registration number) of the taxi.

General

There is no difficulty about getting a taxi in Manhattan, except at rush hours and if it is raining. Taxis, which are painted a distinctive yellow, can be hailed in the street if the little glass dome on the roof is illuminated. If a taxi is off duty or on radio call it will not stop.

The fare is $1·50, plus 25 cents for each fifth of a mile. There is a 50 cents surcharge between 8pm and 6am

Telegrams

Telegrams are almost invariably telephoned, since there are very few telegraph offices where they can be handed in.

Western Union, tel. 325 6000

International telegrams

Telephone

New York: 212 (Brooklyn, Queens and Staten Island: 1 718)
To the United Kingdom: 011 44
To Canada: as for a long-distance call within the United States (i.e. dial 0 followed by the local dialling code)

Dialling codes

Local calls from coin-operated telephones cost 25 cents; each succeeding 5 minutes 5 cents.

Tariffs

Long-distance, and particularly international, calls cannot be dialled from coin-operated telephones, which accept no coins larger than 25 cents. If you have a friend whose telephone you can use this is preferable to telephoning from a hotel, which normally adds a surcharge to the cost of a call. A three-minute call to Europe costs some $5 between 7am and 1pm (direct dialling), rather less in the afternoon and evening and during the night.

Telephone: 1 800 874 4000.

International Information Service

Certain numbers (in the form 800 123 4567) can be dialled free of charge (e.g. for hotel reservations, information, etc.). Dial 1, followed by the number.

Toll-free calls

In Manhattan and Bronx: tel. 411; in the other three boros; tel. 555 1212; outside New York: tel. 1 – Area Code – 555 1312.

Free enquiries

179

Television

Television

See Radio and Television.

Theatres

The theatrical life of New York is rich and varied, and can no longer be thought of merely as Broadway, as it used to be. It is still true, however, that the 35 or so theatres around Broadway and Times Square, between 41st and 53rd Streets, are the ones best known to visitors, who will usually not be in New York long enough to discover the 15 repertory theatres, the 15 "off-Broadway" theatres and the large number (approaching 200) "off-off-Broadway" theatres. While the Broadway houses specialise in musicals and light pieces the other theatres largely go in for serious drama, from the Greeks to contemporary playwrights, with particular emphasis on plays by American authors.

Tickets

Tickets should be purchased as soon as possible. The major, new Broadway productions are often sold out well in advance. It is worth enquiring about purchasing tickets for these shows at the travel agents before departure. Many theatres distribute tickets through telephone agencies (Telecharge, tel. 239 6200; Teletron, tel. 246 0102), which are open 24 hours.

Ambassador, 215 West 49th Street, tel. 239 6200
Barrymore, 243 West 47th Street, tel. 239 6200
Belasco, 111 West 44th Street, tel. 239 6200
Booth, 222 West 45th Street, tel. 239 6200
Broadhurst, 235 West 44th Street, tel. 239 6262
Broadway, 1681 Broadway, tel. 239 6262
Brooks Atkinson, 256 West 47th Street, tel. 307 4100
Cort, 138 West 48th Street, tel. 239 6200
Eugene O'Neill, 230 West 49th Street, tel. 246 0220
Gershwin, 1633 Broadway, tel. 586 6510
Golden, 252 West 45th Street, tel. 239 6200
Helen Hayes, 240 West 46th Street, tel. 944 9450
Imperial, 249 West 45th Street, tel. 239 6200
Longacre, 220 West 48th Street, tel. 239 6200
Lunt-Fontanne, 205 West 46th Street, tel. 575 9200
Lyceum, 149 West 45th Street, tel. 239 6200
Majestic, 247 West 44th Street, tel. 239 6200
Marquis, Broadway and 46th Street, tel. 307 4100
Martin Beck, 302 West 45th Street, tel. 246 6363
Minskoff, Broadway and 45th Street, tel. 869 0550
Music Box, 239 West 45th Street, tel. 239 6262
Nederlander, 208 West 41st Street, tel. 944 9300
Niel Simon, 250 West 52nd Street, tel. 581 7907
Palace, Broadway and 47th Street, tel. 307 4100
Plymouth, 236 West 45th Street, tel. 239 6200
Richard Rodgers St. Theater, 226 West 46th Street, tel. 221 1211
Royale, 242 West 45th Street, tel. 239 6200
St James, 246 West 44th Street, tel. 239 6200
Shubert, 225 West 44th Street, tel. 239 6200
Virginia, 245 West 52nd Street, tel. 977 9370
Walter Kerr, 225 West 48th Street, tel. 239 6200
Winter Garden, 1634 Broadway, tel. 239 6200

Repertory theatres

American Place Theater, 111 West 46th Street, tel. 840 2960
Circle in the Square, 1633 Broadway, tel. 239 6200
CSC Repertory Company, 136 East 13th Street, tel. 677 4210

Jean Cocteau Repertory Company, 330 Bowery, tel. 677 0060
LaMama ETC, 74A East 4th Street, tel. 254 6468
Lion Theater Company, 422 West 42nd Street, tel. 736 7930
Manhattan Theater Club, 131 West 55th Street, tel. 645 5590
Negro Ensemble Company, 424 West 55th Street, tel. 246 8545
Playwrights Horizons, 416 West 42nd Street, tel. 564 1235
Public Theater, 425 Lafayette Avenue, tel. 598 7150
Roundabout Theater, 1530 Broadway, tel. 869 8400
Theater for the New City, 155 First Avenue, tel. 254 1109

There are also some 12 to 15 off-Broadway theatres which are rented by | Off-Broadway
different companies from time to time (as is also the practice with the | theatres
Broadway theatres). Like the Broadway theatres, too, they are commercial
enterprises.

Cherry Lane Theater, 38 Commerce Street, tel. 989 2020
Douglas Fairbanks Theater, 432 West 42nd Street, tel. 239 4321
John Houseman Theater, 450 42nd Street, tel. 967 9077
Lucille Lortel Theater, 121 Christopher Street, tel. 924 8782
Minetta Lane Theater, 18 Minetta Lane, tel. 420 8000
Promenade Theater, Broadway and 76th Street, tel. 580 1313
Provincetown Playhouse, 133 MacDougal Street, tel. 477 5048
Theater East, 211 East 60th Street, tel. 838 0177
Variety Arts Theater, Third Avenue and 14th Street, tel. 239 6200
Westside Arts Theater, 407 West 43rd Street, tel. 315 2244
   (Tickets can be booked for those theaters without telephone numbers by
telephoning 564 8038.)

There are about 200 off-off-Broadway theatres, most of them with fewer | Off-off-Broadway
than 100 seats. They usually present their shows over an extended week- | theatres
end, from Thursday to Sunday. The programmes for most of these theatres
can be found in "Village Voice" which appears each Wednesday or by
telephoning "Ticket Central" on tel. 279 4200.

To find out what is on, consult the Friday or Sunday editions of the "New | Programmes
York Times" or the other publications mentioned under Events (see entry).

Tickets can be bought at theatre box offices or, at the cost of an officially | Ticket agencies
regulated additional charge, from one of the licensed ticket agencies.
Among these are:

Edwards and Edwards, One Times Square Plaza, tel. 944 0290
Manhattan Theater Ticket Service, 1501 Broadway, tel. 582 3600
Tyson Original R. and Co., 266 West 44th Street, tel. 247 7600

Times Square Ticket Center, Broadway and West 47th Street. | "tkts"
Open: from 3pm for evening performances and from noon for afternoon
performances.
   Tickets for Broadway and some off-Broadway theatres on the same day
at half price, but there is often a queue.
   Branches in the mezzanine in the 2nd World Trade Center, open: Mon.–
Fri. 11am–5.30pm, Sat. 11am–3.30pm (for evening performances) and in
Court and Montague Street (Brooklyn), open: Tues.–Fri. 11am–5.30pm,
Sat. to 3.30pm.
   Since early in 1992 there has also been an advance ticket office in the
Bloomingdale's Department Store (see Department Stores), where theatre
and concert tickets can be purchased at reduced prices.
   Tickets can also be ordered by credit card, 24 hours a day, by telephoning
Telecharge on 239 6200, or Ticketron on 399 4444.

See Music | Opera, concerts

Time

New York observes Eastern Standard Time, which is five hours behind Greenwich Mean Time.

From the last Sunday in April to the last Sunday in October summer time (Eastern Daylight Saving Time), an hour ahead of Eastern Standard Time, is in force.

Speaking clock tel. 976 1616

Tipping

In the United States tips are never included in the form of a service charge on a hotel or restaurant bill, and must be given separately.

Hotels

If your luggage is taken up to your room or brought down from it by a bell-boy: 50 cents per item.

Chambermaid: after a stay of some days leave $1–$2 in the room. If the hall-porter gets you a taxi: 50 cents or $1.

Restaurants

Usually 15% of the bill (excluding the 8·25% sales tax). The tip is always left on the table. In better-class restaurants the head waiter ("maître de") also expects a tip.

Taxis

15% of the fare shown on the meter. For a short journey rather more than this may be appropriate.

Hairdressers
(men's and
women's)

Here too 15% is usual.

Shoe-shine boys

Usually 25 cents.

Tourist information

In the United
Kingdom

United States Travel Service, 22 Sackville Street (second floor), London W1X 2EA, tel. 0171–495 4466: personal callers Mon.–Fri. 10am–4pm. Postal enquiries to P.O. Box 170, Ashford, Kent TN24 0ZX.

In New York

New York Convention and Visitors Bureau, 2 Columbus Circle (ground floor), tel. 397 8222

Open: Mon.–Fri. 9am–6pm, Sat. and Sun. 10am–6pm.

The Bureau publishes the "Big Apple Guide" annually which contains all important information and "Quarterly Events" with up-to-date information.

Chinatown

Chinese American Arts Council
Chinese Community Cultural Center
(See A to Z, Chinatown)

Telephone
information

The United States Travel Service has a "Visit the USA" Desk which can be called free of charge (800 255 3050, in Kansas 800 322 4350) from anywhere in the United States for information about the country and the people of the United States, travel, dealing with government offices and what to do in case of illness or emergency.

Weather report

Tel. 976 1212

Time

Tel. 976 1616

Transport

Timetables and routes are available from the counters of the New York City   Timetables and
Transit Authority in the subway stations or at the New York Convention &   routes
Visitors Bureau (see Information).

There are 4000 buses in New York operating on 200 routes which cover a   Buses
total length of 1600km (994 miles). They are managed by the New York City
Transit Authority.

  The New York buses – a considerably slower means of getting from place
to place than the subway – run "uptown" and "downtown" services, going
respectively from south to north and from north to south, and "crosstown"
services going from east to west and from west to east. Most services run
round the clock.

The uptown and downtown routes serve almost all the north–south ave-   Routes
nues, but since these are one-way streets the uptown route goes along a
different avenue from the corresponding downtown route. The crosstown
routes follow the principal cross streets, in particular 9th, 14th, 23rd, 34th,
42nd, 50th, 59th, 66th, 72nd, 79th, 86th, 96th, 103rd, 110th, 125th and 135th
Streets.

  See the plans of bus routes on pp. 184–86.

Bus stops are marked by yellow lines on the pavement; in Manhattan there   Bus stops
are plexiglass shelters at many stops.

  Passengers get on at the front of the bus and get off at the rear.

  Smoking is prohibited and dogs (except guide dogs for the blind) are not
allowed. If you want to get off, ring the bell before your stop.

There is a flat-rate fare of $1.25, which is put into a box on entering the bus   Fares
(no change given: have the exact fare ready, in coins or subway tokens).
Children over six pay the full fare. If you want to change from an uptown or
downtown bus to a crosstown bus, or vice versa, ask for a transfer ("Add-a-
Ride") ticket (no additional charge). In 1994 plastic cards valid for one year
were introduced; these are read electronically.

  Information on bus services: tel. 330 1234 (6am–9pm).

The New York subway is one of the world's most complicated underground   **Subway**
systems. It was originally run by three companies, one public and two
private, which were amalgamated in 1940. There are 29 lines and 462
stations, situated in four of the city's five boroughs; the total length of track
is about 350km (220 miles).

Running round the clock, the subway carries 3.4 million passengers every
day; and at the rush hours (7.30–9am and 4.30–7pm) it tends to feel as if
they are all there at the same time.

The New York subways are indicated by a letter or number on a coloured
background. If this is diamond-shaped the train only operates during rush
hours. If it is round then it is a normal line but at certain times (rush hours)
or on certain parts of the route it does not stop at all stations (parallel
routes) or may run less frequently and not stop at some stations after
midnight or at weekends.

Before boarding a train it is necessary to check on the route map whether it
stops at the desired destination. Some time should be allowed to study the
routes carefully.

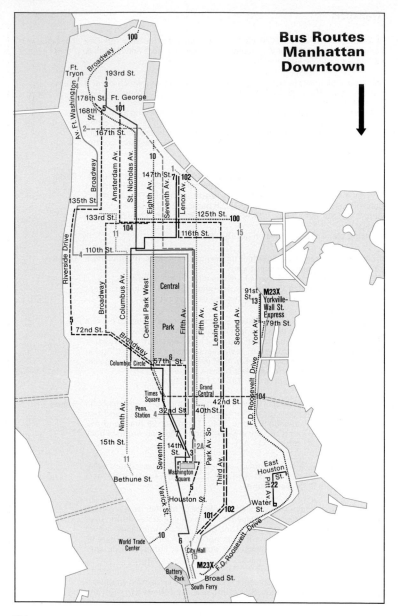

**Bus Routes
Manhattan
Downtown**

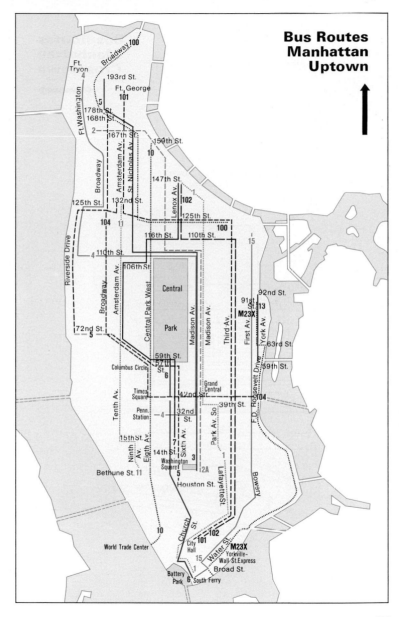

Bus Routes
Manhattan
Uptown

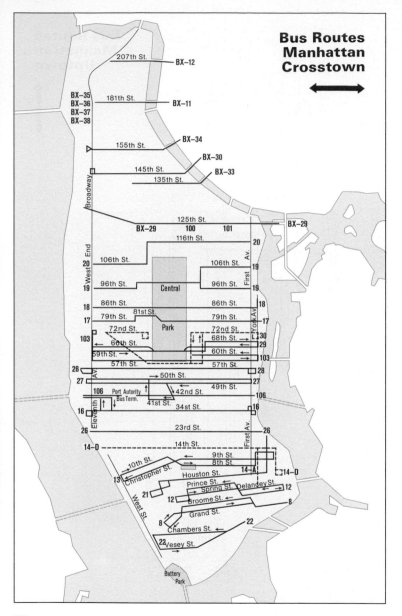

Bus Routes
Manhattan
Crosstown

207th St. — BX–12

BX–35
BX–36
BX–37
BX–38

181st St. — BX–11

155th St. — BX–34

145th St. — BX–30

135th St. — BX–33

Broadway

125th St.

BX–29   100   101   BX–29

West End

116th St.

20   20

106th St.   106th St.   19

96th St.   96th St.   19

19   Central

86th St.   86th St.   18

18   79th St.   81st St.   79th St.   17

17   Park   72nd St.   72nd St.

103   60th St.   68th St.   30   29

59th St.   60th St.   103

57th St.   57th St.

28   28

27   50th St.   49th St.   27

106   Port Autority   42nd St.   106
Bus Term.

16   41st St.   34th St.   16

Eleventh Av   First Av

26   23rd St.   26

14–D   14th St.

9th St.
8th St.
14–A   14–D

10th St.   Houston St.

13   Christopher St.   Prince St.
Spring St.   Delancey St.   12

21   12   Broome St.

West St.   8   8

Grand St.

8   22
Chambers St.

22   Vesey St.

Battery
Park

York Av

186

Smoking is prohibited in the trains and on the platforms, and dogs (except guide dogs for the blind) are not allowed.

There is a flat-rate fare of $1.25. Tokens are sold in subway stations and inserted into a slot in the automatic turnstile: there are no tickets. In many stations Metro Cards (valid for 4 or more journeys) are now issued instead.

Information: tel. 330 1234 (6am–9pm).

The "aerial tramway" is a cableway, opened in 1976, between Second Avenue (corner 58th Street) and Roosevelt Island (15-minute service; fare paid by token). It was only intended as a temporary arrangement pending the construction of a subway station connecting Roosevelt Island (see A to Z, Roosevelt Island) with the main network in 1989. Due to its popularity it has been retained indefinitely.

"Aerial tramway"

Travel documents

Passports are required by all visitors to the United States except Canadian and British subjects resident in either Canada or Bermuda and returning there from a visit to a country in North, Central or South America. British visitors must have a regular 10-year passport: the one-year British visitor's passport is not valid in the United States.

Visitors to the USA must be in possession of a passport which is valid for at least six months beyond the planned departure date. The visa regulations which were in force until July 1989 no longer apply but tourists or visitors on business must complete form I791, obtainable from the airlines, before arriving in the USA. There are over 30 reasons for refusing entry and this is only determined at the airport on arrival. It is not necessary for travellers who already have an unlimited B-1 or B 2 visa in their passports to complete this form.

A visa is necessary for the following categories; visitors planning to stay more than 90 days in the USA; students; journalists; exchange visitors; government officials on business; fiancé(e)s of American citizens; airline crews. Visas, which are valid for more than one visit, can be obtained from US consulates on completion of the appropriate application form. Applications by post should be made at least 3–4 weeks before the expected departure date. In the United Kingdom there are US consulates in:

American Embassy
Visa Branch
24 Grosvenor Street, London W1A 1AE

London

American Consulate General
3 Regent Terrace, Edinburgh EH7 5BW

Edinburgh

American Consulate General
Queen House, 14 Queen Street, Belfast BT1 6EQ

Belfast

Universities and colleges

In Manhattan alone there are more than 30 universities and colleges, and in the whole of New York City there are over 50 higher educational establishments. The largest, with over 40,000 students, is New York University; the most respected is Columbia University. Both of these are privately run. Among leading institutions of higher education in Manhattan are the following (listed in alphabetical order):

Bank Street College of Education, 610 West 112th Street, tel. 222 6700
Barnard College, 606 West 120th Street, tel. 854 5262
Bernard Baruch College, 155 East 24th Street, tel. 725 3000
City College of New York, Convent Avenue and 138th Street, tel. 690 6741
City University, 33 West 42nd Street, tel. 642 1600
College of Physicians and Surgeons, 630 West 168th Street, tel. 305 2500
Columbia University, Broadway and 116th Street, tel. 854 1754
Fashion Institute of Technology, 227 West 27th Street, tel. 760 7700
Hunter College, 695 Park Avenue, tel. 722 4000
Jewish Theological Seminary, Broadway and 122nd Street, tel. 678 8000
Juilliard School of Music, 150 West 65th Street, tel. 799 5000
Mount Sinai School of Medicine, Fifth Avenue and 100th Street,
    tel. 241 6500
New School of Social Research, 66 West 12th Street,tel. 741 5600
New York University, Washington Square, tel. 998 1212
Rockefeller University, York Avenue and 66th Street, tel. 570 8000
School of Visual Arts, 209 East 23rd Street, tel. 679 7350
Teachers' College, 525 West 120th Street, tel. 678 3000
Union Theological Seminary, Broadway and 120th Street, tel. 662 7100
Yeshiva University, Amsterdam Avenue and 185th Street, tel. 960 5400

Weights and measures

Length		
	1 inch=2·54cm	1 mm=0·03937in.
	1 foot=30·48cm	1 cm=0·033ft
	1 yard=91·44cm	1 m=1·09yd
	1 mile=1·61km	1 km=0·62 mile

Area		
	1 sq.in.=6·45 sq.cm	1 sq.cm=0·155 sq.in.
	1 sq.ft=9·288 sq.dm	1 sq.dm=0·108 sq.ft
	1 sq.yd=0·836 sq.m	1 sq.m=1·196 sq.yd
	1 sq. mile=2·589 sq.km	1 sq.km=0·386 sq. mile
	1 acre=0·405 hectare	1 hectare=2·471 acres

Volume		
	1 cu.in.=16·386 cu.cm	1 cu.cm=0·061 cu.in.
	1 cu.ft=28·32 cu.dm	1 cu.dm=0·035 cu.ft
	1 cu.yd=0·765 cu.m	1 cu.m=1·308 cu.yd

Liquid measure   The US gallon and other measures of capacity are smaller than the corresponding British (Imperial) measures, one US gallon equalling 0.83 British gallon. The following metric equivalences are for the US units.

	1 gill=0·118 litre	1 litre=8·474 gills
	1 pint=0·473 litre	1 litre=2·114 pints
	1 quart=0·946 litre	1 litre=1·057 quarts
	1 gallon=3·787 litres	1 litre=0·264 gallon

Weight		
	1 oz=28·35g	100 g=3·527oz
	1 lb=453·59g	1 kg=1·205lb
	1 cwt=45·359kg	100 kg=2·205cwt
	1 ton=0·907 tonne	1 tonne=1·103 tons

The US hundredweight is smaller than the British hundredweight (100lb instead of 112lb), and the US ton is the short ton of 2000lb (compared with the British long ton of 2240lb and the metric tonne of 1000kg – 2204lb). The metric equivalences given above are for the US units.
    The metric system has now been introduced in the USA.

Useful Telephone Numbers at a Glance

Emergency numbers
Fire, police, ambulance	911
Doctor (in Manhattan)	879 1000
Chemist	265 3546

Information
New York Convention and Visitors Bureau	397 8222
US Travel Service "Visit the USA" desk	800 255 3050
Weather Forecast	976 1212
Time	976 1616

City transport
Buses	330 1234
Subway	330 1234

Commuter and long-distance buses
Port Authority Bus Terminal	564 8484
Greyhound	974 6363

Rail services
Grand Central Terminal	736 4545
Pennsylvania Station	736 4545

Airlines
British Airways	247 9297
American Airlines	433 7300
TWA	290 2121

Lost property
Airports
J. F. Kennedy	(1 718) 656 4120
LaGuardia	(1 718) 476 5128
Newark	(1 201) 961 2230
Buses and Subway	(1 718) 625 6200
Commuter and long-distance buses	466 7000 219

Rail services
Grand Central Terminal	340 2571
Pennsylvania Station	869 4513
Subway	(1 718) 625 6200

Hospitals
Lenox Hill Hospital	439 3030
St Clare's Health Center	586 1500
Mount Sinai Medical Center	241 6500

Telegrams
Domestic and international (Western Union)	325 6000

Consulates
United Kingdom	752 8400
Canada	586 2400

Index

Imprint

83 colour photographs, 4 special plans, 3 transport plans, 2 general plans, 2 drawings, 1 large city map

Text: Rainer Eisenschmid, Carin Drechsler-Marx, Henry Marx, Dr Madeleine Reincke
Revision and additional text:
Baedeker-Redaktion (Dr Madeleine Reincke)

General direction:
Dr Peter Baumgarten, Baedeker Stuttgart

English language edition: Alec Court
English translation: James Hogarth, Julie Waller

Cartography: Christoph Gallus, Hohberg-Niederschopfheim
Hallwag AG, Berne (large city map)

3rd edition 1995

©Baedeker Stuttgart
Original German edition 1995

©1995 Jarrold and Sons Limited
English language edition worldwide

©1995 The Automobile Association
United Kingdom and Ireland

Published in the United States by:
Macmillan Travel
A Simon & Schuster Macmillan Company
1633 Broadway
New York, NY 10019–6785

Macmillan is a registered trademark of Macmillan, Inc.

Distributed in the United Kingdom by the Publishing Division of the Automobile Association, Fanum House, Basingstoke, Hampshire RG21 2EA

The name *Baedeker* is a registered trade mark
A CIP catalogue record of this book is available from the British Library

Licensed user:
Mairs Geographischer Verlag GmbH & Co.,
Ostfildern-Kemnat bei Stuttgart

Reproductions:
Filderscan GmbH, Ostfildern (Kemnat)

Printed in Italy by G. Canale & C.S.p.A – Borgaro T.se –Turin

ISBN 0 7495 1254 7 UK
       0–02–860673–6 USA and Canada